GLOBALIZATION AND INDIAN SOCIETY

G.N. Karalay
B.E. (Hons), M.A. Sociology
Former Executive Director, NTPC
Sr. Consultant, Power Finance Corporation,
Chairman, Board of Studies, Rural Services and
Member, Academic Council, R.T.M. Nagpur University

CONCEPT PUBLISHING COMPANY PVT. LTD.
NEW DELHI-110059

ISBN-13: 978-93-5125-186-6 (HB)

First Published 2016

Published and Printed by

Concept Since 1974

Concept Publishing Company Pvt. Ltd.
A/15-16, Commercial Block, Mohan Garden,
New Delhi-110059 (INDIA)
Phones : 25351460, 25351794, *Fax* : 091-11-25357109
Email : publishing@conceptpub.com
Website: www.conceptpub.com

Editorial Office: H-13, Bali Nagar, New Delhi-110 015, India.

Cataloging in Publication Data—DK Courtesy: D.K. Agencies (P) Ltd. <docinfo@dkagencies.com>

Karalay, G. N., 1939, author.
Globalization and Indian society / G.N. Karalay.
pages cm
Includes bibliographical references and index.
ISBN 9789351251866 (HB)
ISBN 9789351251873 (PB)

1. Globalization—Social aspects—India. 2. Globalization—Economic aspects—India. 3. India—Social conditions. 4. India—Economic conditions. 5. India—Rural conditions. I. Title.

HN690.Z9G56 2016 DDC 303.4820954 23

Dedicated to
The Memory of
MAHATMA GANDHI
whose philosophy found universal appeal

Preface

According to 2011 Census of India, rural population constitutes 68.84 per cent of the total population and as such it is the kaleidoscope for the entire country. I had the privilege of being associated with rural society for a long time, which enabled me to write books on the subject of rural development, and one of these titled "Integrated Approach to Rural Development" is a reference book for M.A. Sociology course in R.T.M. Nagpur University.

Indian society has been mostly tradition based. The country took to industrialization only after Independence in 1947. From that time onward, it faced great many challenges in social, economic, cultural and political fields. The greatest challenge, however, has been abject poverty especially in its countryside. All efforts were therefore focused on achieving economic progress with delivery of social justice. While India had in past trade and commerce with other countries, it was in 1991 that India took to the path of liberalization of its economy, paving the way to its integration with the globalization process. Though India made steady economic progress since then, large scale poverty still remains a challenge before it.

The process of globalization has had its impact on every aspect of Indian society namely social, economic, cultural and political. The impact of globalization on the society has always been a subject of intense debate as to whether globalization has benefited the society or not and the kind of socio-economic-cultural transformation that has taken place in the society. As the reader will go through this book, he will find that all aspects concerning globalization are covered in this book.

It took me five years of continuous research work to bring out this book. In this connection, I would like to thank Prof. Dr. B. K. Swain, my Guide for Ph. D. degree in R.T.M. Nagpur University, for enlightening me on the subject. I thank my daughters Meenal and Sonal and son Manoj for encouraging me in this endeavour. My special thanks to my life partner Kunda for inspiring me and bearing with me for years, allowing me to concentrate on writing this book by carrying out the family responsibilities by her single handedly.

G.N. Karalay

Contents

List of Tables

Introduction

What is Globalization and How it Started

Though globalization embraces all aspects of society, it denotes broadly social, economic, political and cultural interaction and integration on global scale. Human being has become part of the society to meet his needs better through interdependency. The process of interaction started right from the time of cave man. People from one place started interacting with the people at another place with the intention of improving their lot. This interaction was taking place, may be on different scale, even thousands of years back. The Silk Road or Silk Route connecting Asia, Africa and Europe and other connecting routes were popular for enabling people to people contact and trading activity between the nations from the olden times. Later, new routes were established *via* land, sea and air and people to people contact and inter-state trade started increasing rapidly. What we see now is the extension of this process.

To start with, the people to people contact between nations was related to economic aspect. Globalization is therefore mainly seen from the perspective of economics. In course of time, globalization took the shape of integrated global economy marked by free trade, free flow of capital and labour and tapping of foreign markets for cheaper products. Later the process included: removing restrictions on private industry and trade and allowing free trade and enterprise; removal of import restrictions and lowering of import duties; removal of controls on capital inflows and outflows; allowing MNCc to establish their business activities in native countries and allow share holding in the native industries and services; gradual restrictions on subsidies in agriculture etc.

However, alongside the economic interaction and integration as part of the process of globalization, the process started extending to all other aspects of the society, to name a few: social, cultural, technology, environment, governance and politics etc. There is now hardly any field which is not touched by globalization. In expanded form, globalization is seen as the process of high interconnectedness and integration of the world. It thus becomes multiple globalizations rather than single one, i.e. globalization of economy.

History of Globalization

The term globalization, though used frequently now-a-days, is an old process. There are, however, different opinions as to when actually the process of globalization started.

In the ancient history there are examples of movement of the people and goods from one place to another *via* land and sea routes. The same process continued up to pre-colonial period. During these times, the movement was slow. There is a perception that globalization started more or less parallel with the birth and the spread of world capitalism, c. 1500. Though globalization and capitalism go hand-in-hand, these terms cannot be interchanged. The essence of the term globalization is free flow of capital, goods, labour, and services. Capitalism is a system in which production and distribution are owned by private entities in order to accumulate profit. Thus globalization has aided capitalism.

Industrial Revolution started first in European countries and availability of raw materials became important to sustain the industrialization in those countries. They looked to other countries for expansion of their power and influence and in the process getting raw materials from them. Global trade started increasing during the colonial period as European nations took away raw materials from their dominions. They utilized these raw materials to make finished products in their countries and in turn sold them back to dominion countries at exorbitant prices. With passage of time, globalized economy started taking conceptual form.

Adam Smith is considered as father of modern economics. Smith first published his pioneering work '*The Wealth of Nations*' in 1776. He held that markets worked most efficiently when there was equality between buyers and sellers. Subsequently, the theory of 'Comparative Advantage' was propounded by the British economist David Recardo. The theory was developed in 1817 by Ricardo in his '*Principles of Political Economy and Taxation.*' Ricardo wrote that nations should specialize in producing goods in which they have a natural advantage. He believed this would benefit both buyer and seller, but only if certain conditions were maintained (Ellwood, 2005: 16-17).

According to the theory of Recardo, it is uneconomical to produce everything in every country. On the other hand, it will be advantageous for each country to produce things in which it is comparatively specialized and export those to another country. Likewise each country can import things from another country which is comparatively specialized to produce those things. Recardo did not presuppose movement of capital in exchange. However, this concept of non-movement of capital under capitalist system underwent a change and now huge capital flows are taking place routinely.

The phase of globalization is an extension of the processes namely industrial, post-industrial and modernity.

Capitalism, Industrialization and Post-industrialization

Capital denotes assets which include property, wealth, funds, money and capitalist means owner of these assets. In capitalism, the ownership of assets is in the private hands and the capitalist uses these assets to make profit. Capital is the prerequisite for industry.

While there has been greater emphasis on establishing and running of factories for manufacturing of products in industrial phase, post-industrial phase saw the rise of services sector particularly as a result of advances in information and communication technology. The rise of services sector is so fast that it has overtaken product manufacturing sector. The services sector now forms larger part of GDP as compared to manufacturing in many countries. The advancement of information and communication technology also led to time and space compression with flows of people, goods or capital taking place at the fastest speed, seen as new socio-economic integration.

Modernity

Sociologists use traditionalism as a reference for modernization. Modernity implies somewhat disillusion from tradition. Whereas by traditionalism, we mean simple, homogeneous and static, by contrast, modernization means complex, heterogeneous and dynamic. Modernization involves increasing use of technology.

The culture of West including Europe and the culture in the East followed the geographical divide. The culture in the East was traditional whereas the culture in the West including Europe was modernity. During colonial period, there had been close interaction between countries in West including Europe and East. This has resulted in greater influence of the Western culture on the societies in the East.

Talcott Parsons, America's leading sociologist of the period has tried to distinguish modernity from the earlier traditional form. He had drawn up a list of traits ostensibly dividing traditional from modern social order: collectivity *versus* self-orientation; ascription *versus* achievement; diffuseness *versus* specificity (Hoogvelt, 1978). Further, modernization thinkers identify a number of logics, tendencies, and institutions that should be encouraged so as to generate development such as urbanization, nuclear families, growth of education and mass media, and the emergence of a system of rational law (el-Ojeili and Hayden, 2006: 41-2)

The process of modernization has led to a shift from the order of traditional social structure to the order of modern social structure which reflects aforesaid characteristics of modernization. Some sociologists believe that modernity ended after Second World War.

Post-modernity, Post-fordism and Globalization

Post modernity signifies the economic or socio-cultural state or condition of society which is said to exist after modernity. It can mean a personal response to a modern society. Modern art is characterized by seriousness of purpose, the idea of progress, whereas post modern art is characterized by stylistic eclecticism, a concern for popular taste, and a move from the serious to the playful (Sim, 2002; Harvey, 1989; Jameson). Post-fordism is a shift from assembly line mass production at one place to establishing multi-stage manufacturing activities at different locations.

All the above processes have become part of globalization. Globalization now pervades every aspect of society including social, economic and cultural aspects. The theme of this book is how the process of globalization is affecting Indian Society. Is globalization improving the living conditions or worsening them? The nature of impact of globalization on society is the most contested subject in the contemporary times.

Globalization and Indian Society

Indian society is broadly divided into urban and rural setting. In earlier times, it was mostly rural and urbanization is a later phenomena. Over a period of time, there has been a steady decline in the rural population and likewise steady increase in the urban population. As per 2011Census, rural-urban distribution is 68.84 per cent and 31.16 per cent. It is noteworthy that although there has been steady decline in rural population, around two third of the total population still live in rural area. Village is basic unit of rural area and it truly represents cultural heritage of the country. Therefore, Gandhiji's statement, "India lives in villages and villages constitute the very heart of India" holds true even today.

Broadly, place with human habitation of below 5000, with agriculture as the main economic activity, with a density of population less than 400 per sq. km., is described as rural area. A village is described as a group of hamlets. Historically village represented entity nearest to the nature, i.e. land, hills, forests, rivers, springs and on the human front, natural (but rich in itself) life, folk and folk-tales. Its richness has inspired great poets and writers. In the hearts of the village people, peace and harmony have been quite apparent. However, beneath this peace and harmony there have also been deeper problems—social as well as economic.

Structure of Indian Society

Social structure of Indian society is based on caste, decided at birth, as a lineage of the four *varnas*. The caste system has perpetuated divisions within the society thus creating unending problems for the rural people. Mahatma Gandhi, Dr. B.R. Ambedkar, Jyotiba Phule and other social reformers have done pioneering work in bringing social change in the society. With the advent of science and technology and movement of people from one place to another for employment etc., social dimension of caste system is losing its strong character in urban area. But in rural area, the social change on this front is quite slow.

Progress after Independence up to 1990

Prior to Independence, the economic condition of rural society was extremely bad. *Panchayati Raj* for self-governance at the village level started in 1950s. India adopted the policy of mixed economy and import substitution industrialization. Industrial Policy Resolution was adopted in 1948 and further amended in 1956 giving major role to the public sector taking into account the scarcity of private capital. Number of development projects were undertaken. On agriculture front, fillip was given to cooperative movement. Good percentage of budget allocation was earmarked for agriculture in five year plans. Agriculture witnessed green revolution in 1970s. Social sector including education and health was fully supported by the state. The aforesaid initiatives started giving results and position by 1990 improved substantially.

Progress after Liberalization of Economy in 1991

Taking a cue from developed nations, India adopted a path of liberalization in 1991 which paved the way for Globalization. Industrial Policy was revised accordingly. There has been steady economic progress since then and presently Indian economy stands eleventh position in the World economy. India has also made good progress in the field of science and technology. China is, however, much ahead of India in economic progress although both countries attained freedom from colonial powers more or less at the same time. As there is always scope for improvement, India could have done better. Some people contend that India cannot be equated with China because there is a big difference in the political systems existing in two countries.

Increasing inequality between rich and the poor in India is one area which raises serious concern. On socio-cultural front, there has been influence of Western socio-cultural ethos. American culture is catching up the imagination of Indian society in the same way as it is happening in rest of the world. Critics of the globalization contend that local cultures are getting wiped out due to the influence of Western culture. The caste system prevalent in India has, however, played a crucial role in determining the outcome of the mingling of different cultures.

The reach of the globalization has not been uniform as its impact has been dependent on several variables, major one being what is the existing stage of development. Therefore, its impact varies from society belonging to one nation to society belonging to another. Further the impact is different on urban and rural society. Effect of globalization has been felt more strongly in services sector which is concentrated in urban area. Gradually, it is diffusing into other sectors of the economy too. Since rural society in India consists of 69 per cent of the total population, the impact on rural society substantially represents impact on the whole Indian society.

As globalization is bringing in its wake systemic changes in the otherwise self-governed society, there is a raging debate about its real impact on the society. There are economic, socio-cultural and political anxieties involved. The most pertinent questions being asked are: whether globalization led to better economic progress and if yes, whether fruits of globalization have reached all sections of society or only to few sections of society, whether development that is taking place is sustainable or focusing on only present generation, whether different cultures are coexisting or some cultures are dominating over others, whether autonomy of nations is being maintained or it is being compromised and so on.

The protagonists and critics of globalization take absolutely divergent views on the above issues. Whereas the former see globalization as a panacea for ushering in the new economic-social-cultural order leading to all round development, the latter see it as emerging new economic-social-cultural order wiping out whatever there is good in the existing order. While both views have been extensively elaborated in the book, taking final view has been substantially left to the reader as his exclusive privilege and prerogative.

It may be noted that in the book at number of places 'state' has been mentioned. Its meaning is in the nature of 'nation-state' and not as 'province' of the nation. Similarly, North and South refer to developed and developing countries respectively.

globalization led to better economic progress and if yes, whether fruits of globalization have reached all sections of society or only to few sections of society, whether development that is taking place is sustainable or focusing on only present generation, whether different cultures are coexisting or some cultures are dominating over others, whether autonomy of nations is being maintained or it is being compromised and so on.

The protagonists and critics of globalization take absolutely divergent views on the above issues. Whereas the former see globalization as a panacea for ushering in the new economic-social-cultural order leading to all round development, the latter see it as emerging new economic-social-cultural order wiping out whatever there is good in the existing order. While both views have been extensively elaborated in the book, taking final view has been substantially left to the reader as his exclusive privilege and prerogative.

It may be noted that in the book at number of places 'state' has been mentioned. Its meaning is in the nature of 'nation-state' and not as 'province' of the nation. Similarly, North and South refer to developed and developing countries respectively.

1
Theoretical Perspectives of Globalization

Definition of Globalization

Before entering into full-fledged discussion on theory of Globalization, it is prudent to define globalization. Globalization embraces all aspects of society such as economic, social, cultural, political etc. This has made all encompassing definition of globalization in few words difficult. This difficulty has been expressed by the authors who have all written on the subject of globalization. There is no consensus on a single comprehensive definition of globalization as it is said that there is not a single globalization, but there exist multiple globalizations. Further, there are so numerous views and perspectives about globalization that consensus about its definition has become elusive. George Ritzer has written most extensively on various aspects of globalization. He has not only written books, but also edited voluminous Encyclopaedia on globalization. Let us have a look at how he has defined the term globalization in his various books.

George Ritzer in a book titled '*The Blackwell Companion to Globalization,*' writes, "Among the terms usually included in the definitions offered were, in order of frequency, speed and time (accelerating, rapidly developing etc.), processes and flows, space (encompassing ever greater amounts of it), and increasing integration and interconnectivity. A composite definition, therefore, might be: Globalization is an accelerating set of processes involving flows that encompass ever-greater numbers of the world's spaces and that lead to increasing integration and interconnectivity among these spaces" (Ritzer, 2007: 1)

In George Ritzer's next book titled '*Globalization: A Basic Text*,' he defines, "Globalization is a transplanetary process or set of processes involving increasing liquidity and the growing multidirectional flows of people, objects, places and information as well as the structures they encounter and create that are barriers to, or expedite, those flows" (Ritzer, 2010: 2).

Paul Dean and George Ritzer in a book, '*The Wiley-Blackwell Encyclopaedia of Globalization,*' write, "Social scientists disagree about definitions of globalization, but they generally define it as a process or condition, or an effect of cultural, political, social, and economic processes, such as imperialism and post-fordism. Whether globalization is defined as a process or condition, the common strand is its connectedness across space and time. In the words of Anthony Giddens, an aspect of "time-space distanciation" under globalization signals that social relations have been disembedded from locales, with processes both shaping and shaped by faraway phenomena" (Ritzer, 2012: 850).

Held and McGrew's (2002: 1) definition of Globalization is, "Globalization denotes the expanding scale, growing magnitude, speeding up and deepening impact of interregional flows and patterns of social interaction" (el-Ojeili and Hayden, 2006: 13).

Webster dictionary's definition of globalization is, "The act or process of globalizing: the state of being globalized, especially: the development of an increasingly integrated global economy marked especially by free trade, free flow of capital, and the tapping of cheaper foreign labour markets."

What Is Theory?

The term theory is a general principle providing an explanation for phenomena. It is a conceptual scheme which provides explanation of the observed phenomena taking into account relationships between two or more variables and also provides a perspective of the unobserved relationships.

el-Ojeili and Hayden writes in their '*Critical Theories of Globalization*,' that while some may argue that the facts speak for themselves, the available data must be reflected upon within a larger frame of concepts, interpretations, and socio-historical events. Ultimately, evidence about globalization is formed, sustained and contested within particular social, political, and economic (and cultural) contexts, and claims about this evidence must be assessed in light of this. Therefore, a new positivity implies the attempt to connect theoretical innovation and elucidation with substantive issues in the public realm—a return, in many ways, to the sorts of theorizing engaged in by the classical social and political theorists of modernity, such as Karl Marx, Max Weber, and Emile Durkheim (el-Ojeili and Hayden, 2006: 2).

Theory of Diffusion—Basic Theory of Globalization

The process of globalization involves a process of diffusion of certain characteristics, systems of knowledge, beliefs, values, technology, methods of production and some distinctive cultural patterns of one society into another. It is implied that the characteristic elements of the developed society which are diffused into another society are gradually percolated to the urban and even rural communities of such societies. The transformation of traditional society into a society of twenty-first century in globalization signifies vast changes. Theorizing these changes is replete with obvious difficulties as these changes are taking place continuously from time to time across multiple aspects of society. These changes which have taken place over time and space include many aspects of society like social, economic, technological, political, environmental, cultural etc.

The diffusion theory helps explaining the phenomenon of globalization *vis-à-vis* the scenario of last mile change that is change in rural society. There is, however, an obvious difficulty in assigning the nature and quantum of change specifically to globalization as this involves an exercise of finding the difference between how the situation exists today and how it would have been had there been no process of globalization. While it may pose less difficulty in ascribing economic development or underdevelopment of a society due to globalization, fathoming the nature and depth of changes that have taken place on the aspects like social, cultural, political and ecological poses extreme difficulty. Then interpretation of any change as to whether it is positive or negative, beneficial or detrimental, also differ from one perspective to another and one interpreter to another. Globalization is thus a most contested concept. Obviously no single theory can explain the changes.

Notwithstanding these difficulties, theorizing changes in society due to globalization has been endeavoured by number of authors.

W.I. Robinson's Discourses on Various Theories of Globalization

W.I. Robinson says, "Recall that there is not a single 'theory of globalization', but many theoretical discourses" (Ritzer, 2007: 128).

The author of the present book admits that in order to enable the reader to benefit from the pioneering article written by W.I. Robinson on *Theories of Globalization* in the *Blackwell Companion to Globalization* edited by Ritzer (2007), some quotes from the article have been incorporated below and the references thereof have been faithfully given herein.

Robinson (Ritzer, 2007: 128-141), among various theories of globalization included the following for discourses:

1. World-system theory
2. Theories of global capitalism
3. The Network Society
4. Theories of Space, Place and Globalization
5. Theories of Transnationality and Transnationalism
6. Modernity, Post-modernity and Globalization
7. Theories of Global Culture

The brief description of the above discourses is given below:

1. World-System Theory

The progress of capitalism has been uneven throughout the world. It started in Europe and then spread to West and Japan. Being early starters and adopting capitalism as an economic policy, the rise of capitalism was very fast in these countries. After colonization of countries in the South, capitalism in these countries in North got a boost as they could obtain raw materials from ruled countries cheaply but the countries in the South remained poor during the colonization period. This led to economic fault line dividing the globe into North and the South.

Arrighi (2005: 33) observes world-system analysis as a distinctive sociological paradigm. The capitalist world economy emerged c. 1500 in Europe and expanded outward over the next several centuries, absorbing in the process all existing mini-systems and world empires, establishing market and production networks that eventually brought all peoples into a single worldwide structure—the capitalist world system. A key structure of the capitalist world-system is the division of the world into three great regions—the first is the core, or the powerful and developed centres of the system including Western Europe, North America and Japan. The second is the periphery, those regions that have been forcibly subordinated to the core through colonialism. Third is the semiperiphery, comprising of those states and regions that were previously in the core and are moving down in this hierarchy, or those that were previously in the periphery and moving up (Ritzer, 2007: 128-29).

According to Immanuel Wallerstein, the principal progenitor of world-system theory, world system is a social system and world-economy is a function of the state of technology. He also states both world system and world economy are changeable in nature.

According to Immanuel Wallerstein, a world-system is a social system, one that has boundaries, structures, member groups, rules of legitimation, and coherence. Its life is made up of the conflicting forces which hold it together by tension, and tear it apart as each group seeks eternally to remold it to its advantage. It has the characteristics of an organism, in that it has a life-span over which its characteristics change in some respects and remain stable in others. One can define its structures as being at different times strong or weak in terms of the internal logic of its functioning (Ritzer, 2010: 205).

2. Theories of Global Capitalism

To start with capitalism in the state was operating within the boundaries of the state but with interaction of people from one country to other country/countries, capitalism became international phenomena making national boundaries largely irrelevant.

According to Immanuel Wallerstein, capitalism is based on the constant absorption of economic loss by political entities, while economic gain is distributed to "private" hands. Capitalism as an economic mode is based on the fact that the economic factors operate within an arena larger than that which any political entity can totally control. This gives capitalists a freedom of maneuver that is structurally based (Ritzer, 2010: 206).

Global capitalism theories focus on a new global production and financial system that is seen to supersede earlier national forms of capitalism, and emphasize the rise of processes that cannot be framed within the nation-state/inter-state system that informs world-system theory (Ritzer, 2007: 130).

Robinson states that Sklair (2000, 2002) has put forward a 'theory of the global system', at the core of which are 'transnational practices' (TNPs) involving three levels: economic, whose agent is transnational capital; political, whose agent is transnational capitalist class (TCC); and cultural-ideological, whose agent is cultural elites (Ritzer, 2007: 130).

3. Network Society

The advancement of information and communication technology made a qualitative as well as quantitative difference in furthering the arena of capitalism. In the process, isolation of one society from another reduced and greater interaction between societies created a new form of society termed as network society.

Manuel Castells (1996) highlights the idea of globalization as representing a new age of information. The latter decades of twentieth century were marked by the development of new information technology with computers and internet and capitalist using the power of this new technology. The networked enterprise makes material the culture of the informational, global economy: it transforms signals into commodities by processing (IT) knowledge (Ritzer, 2007: 132).

Castells (1996) sees 'networked enterprise' as a vanguard of a more general form of social organization, the network society itself. Human society has moved from a verbal order to an alphabetic order and later an audiovisual system. In the globalized age this paves the way to an integration of various modes of communication into an interactive network involving the integration of text, image, and sound, the modes of human communication. The Internet makes virtuality as a reality. As a space of flows substitutes for the space of places, time becomes erased in the new communications systems. The space of flows and timeless time become the material foundations of a new culture (Ritzer, 2007: 132-33).

4. Theories of Space, Place and Globalization

The advancement of communication technology has made interaction between distantly located societies easier and speedier. This process led to space and time compression. The greater connectivity made localities influencing the global events and simultaneously global events influencing the localities.

Anthony Giddens defines time-space distanciation as the intensification of worldwide social relations which link distant localities in such a way that local happenings are shaped by events occurring long distance away and *vice versa*—social relations are picked from local contexts of interactions and restructured across time and space (Giddens, 1990: 64). Harvey (1990) states that the time-space constraint compression is the process whereby time is recognized in such a way as to reduce the constraints of space, and *vice versa* (Ritzer, 2007: 133-34).

Roland Robertson (1995) brings out a new concept of 'glocalization' which suggests that the global is manifest in the local. It means that ideas about home, locality and community have been extensively spread around the world in recent years, so that, the local has been globalized. Similarly, global processes have influenced localities in new ways. For Appadurai (1990: 182) the locality is less a physical than a phenomenological property of social life (Ritzer, 2007: 135).

5. Theories of Transnationality and Transnationalism

In the process of globalization people from one location in one country migrate to another location in another country for the purpose of employment and business. In view of advanced communication facilities being available, the migrated community is still in a position to keep in touch with their native people. Thus, they practically live in two worlds—one is the country in which they have migrated and the other which is their native locality. These societies which belong to different nations are termed as transnational societies.

The transnationality refers to the rise of new communities and the formation of new social identities and relations that cannot be defined through the traditional reference point of nation-states. The transnationalism denotes a range of social, cultural and political practices and states brought about by the sheer increase in social connectivity across borders. Transnational communities among others include new immigrant groups migrating to developed countries. Advanced communication facilities made links between the societies at the place of settlement and the place of migration easier and stronger. Recognizing this new reality, the scholarly literature undertook a paradigm shift from international migration to transnational migration, and began to refer to these communities as transnational communities (Ritzer, 2007: 136).

6. Modernity, Postmodernity and Globalization

Society undergoes changes with time. To start with, human beings were living in caves and were called primitive. Over a period of time certain traditions and customs were developed. They started with hunting for food, then took to agriculture and then to industry. With colonization of South by European and West, the wave of modernity swept across South. The speedy interconnectedness across the globe has set in the process of globalization. Thus, globalization is culmination of the continuum from primitiveness to postmodern society.

Many theorists see continuity in the line of processes viz. modernity, post-modernity and globalization. Some see radicalization of modernity in globalization.

Robertson (1992) defines globalization thus, "Globalization as a concept refers both to the compression of the world and intensification of consciousness of the world as a whole....both concrete global interdependence and consciousness of the global whole in the twentieth century", Robertson (1992), Giddens (1990) and Meyer (1997) view globalization as the universalization of modernity. Globalization is seen as the spread and universalization of sets of modern values, practices and institutions through processes that operate on a global scale (Ritzer, 2007: 138).

7. Theories of Global Culture

In the absence of communication facilities, as happened with primitive societies, the societies remained isolated from each other. However, with the advent of communication, there happened to be close interconnectedness between different societies. The intense interconnectedness happened in the process of globalization has led to social and cultural changes in every society.

A number of theories are focusing on emergence of new cultural form that is called global culture. The rapid advancement of mass media enabled forming the global culture, evoking the popular image of the world put forth by the Canadian philosopher Marshall McLuhan as 'the global village'. The focus of these theories is on such phenomena as globalization and religion, nations and ethnicity, global-consumerism, communications and tourism (Ritzer, 2007: 139).

Robinson states that Appadurai's thesis on the 'global cultural economy' refers to "central problem of today's global interactions, the tension between cultural homogenization and cultural heterogenization" (Appadurai, 1990: 296). Different cultural flows, in Appadurai's view, create transnational cultural spaces and practices not associated to any particular national society and may be novel or combination of different forms of beliefs or pracices (Ritzer, 2007: 141).

In conclusion: There are many theories and the above discourses by Robinson are the sample of the range of theories of globalization. As globalization proceeds, more and more theories would come up. Now, we will discuss discourses of theories narrated by other authors.

Flows Theory

George Ritzer (2010) has used the phrase solid, liquid and gas to the changes over time in the characteristics of people, places and objects. The societies, which were earlier insular from the influences of societies located at a distance, came in contact with other societies by interaction through development of easy and speedy communication. The people, information and things became more and more mobile. The instant communication of massive information approximates the idea of becoming it lighter and gaseous.

Prior to the "*global age,*" people, things, information, places, and objects tended to harden over time. Thus, their common attribute was "solidity," the characteristic of being limited to one place. Solidity also refers to the persistence of barriers that prevented free movement of people, information, and objects in that era (Ritzer, 2010: 28).

Over the last few decades, that which seemed solid has tended to "melt" and become increasingly mobile or 'liquid.' A range of technological developments in transportation and communication have enabled far greater global movement of what was previously solid (Ritzer, 2010: 28).

As the process of increased mobility continues, liquids tend to turn into gases. This implies additional attributes of being light and a capacity to flow even faster and with greater ease. The flow of information in the global age closely approximates the characteristic of gaseousness. The new liquids and gases have both constructive as well as destructive effects (Ritzer, 2010: 28).

Globalization is increasingly characterized by flows of liquid phenomena including people, objects, decisions, information, and places. Many global flows are interconnected—they do not occur in isolation (Ritzer, 2010: 29).

Dependency Theory

Post-Second World War, the focus of development projects started by the Western powers of North was on financial aid to underdeveloped countries in the South. This aid should have been intended to be used for import-substitution. However, the projects led to dependence of South on the

North and could not bring development of substance to countries in the South.

Dependency theory (Cardoso and Faletto 1979) emphasizes the fact that the kinds of development projects led not so much to the development of the nation-states of the South, but more to a decline in their independence and to an increase in their dependence on the countries of the North, especially the US. It also involves the idea that instead of bringing economic improvement, development brings with it greater impoverishment (Ritzer, 2010: 71-2).

A key work in dependency theory is Andre Gunder Frank's (1969) "*The Development of Underdevelopment.*" According to him, the developed countries (DCs) were never in the same position of least developed countries (LDCs) today; the DCs were undeveloped while the LDCs were (and are) underdeveloped. The result is that the path followed by the former is not necessarily the best one for the latter. He also rejects the idea that the underdevelopment of a country is traceable to sources internal to that country. Rather, he argues that it is a product of the capitalist system and of the relationship between developed and underdeveloped countries within this system (Ritzer, 2010: 73).

Edward L. Kick states that dependency theory identifies a global system where economic benefits flow from a poor "periphery" to a wealthy "center" of countries. Dos Santos (1971) says: "Dependency favours some countries to the detriment of others.... a situation in which the economy of a certain group of companies is conditioned by the development and expansion of another economy, to which their own is subjected" (Ritzer, 2012: 400-01).

Core-peripheral Theory

The development had a strong foothold in western and European countries. These countries are called as 'core'. The countries in the South are either developing or underdeveloped. Due to paucity of finance required for development and lack of technology, the South started depending upon North.

The Economic Commission for Latin America established in 1948, as Hume and Turner (1990: 47) note, came to two important (wider) conclusions: (1) the world could be understood in terms of a 'core' of developed industrial nations and a 'periphery' of underdeveloped nations; and (2) that the core and periphery were closely linked, in such a way that these links made the periphery dependent on the core (el-Ojeili and Hayden, 2006: 44).

According to Tom Reifer, World-systems analysis posit that in the period stretching from medieval to early modern times, there developed a new historical system, a capitalist world economy, divided into a tripartite zonal hierarchy of wealth and power, among core, semiperipheral and peripheral zones and regions. ... Core states monopolized high-value production processes, in long distance-trade, high finance and manufacturing and developed relatively strong states (Ritzer, 2012: 295-96).

Theory of Rupture

Arjun Appadurai (2005) in his book '*Modernity at Large: Cultural Dimensions of Globalization*' propounds a theory of rupture that is break from the past as against the transformation of the society over a period of time. According to him an element of imagination associated with the media and migration has brought in radical change in the society.

Implicit in the book '*Modernity at Large*' is a theory of rupture that takes *media and migration* as its two major, and interconnected, diacritics and explores their joint effort on the work of the imagination as a constitutive feature of modern subjectivity. .... The theory of a break—or rupture—with its strong emphasis on electronic mediation and mass migration, is necessarily a theory of the recent past (or the extended present) because it is only in the past two decades or so that media and migration have become so massively globalised, that is to say, active across large and irregular transnational terrains. (Appadurai) considers this theory as ...more than an update of older social theories of the ruptures of modernization. Most important, break caused by the joint force of electronic mediation and mass migration is explicitly transnational—even postnational (Appadurai, 2005: 3,9).

Conclusion

It will be seen that there are number of theories of globalization. This scenario arises as there are number of dimensions of globalization. Some of these are: Geographical: North-South, East-West; Historical: Colonial powers—Countries ruled by colonial powers; Economic: Capitalism-communism; Development: Developed countries-Developing countries; Political orientation: Authoritarian—Democratic; Religious following:

Christian—Islamic—Confucian—Hindu—Buddhism; Cultural: Western-–Oriental; Linguistic: English-other languages. Thus, there existed and still exist unique distinctions as well as sameness between the societies world over. It is therefore well nigh impossible to bring out one single theory that would explain the entire spectrum of changes constantly occurring due to the process of globalization. However, the extent of diffusion of characteristics of two interacting societies will determine the resultant nature of the emerging society and therefore diffusion theory has been suggested as a basic theory of globalization.

2
Global Political Economy

GLOBAL ECONOMIC INSTITUTIONAL FRAMEWORK

Background and Objective of Global Institutional Arrangement

The Second World War devastated the economies of Europe, Japan and underdeveloped countries. USA was the only major western country, economy of which was not severely affected by the war. During those days, the movement of communism was strong and its influence was increasing. With a view that the impoverishment of the people in underdeveloped countries do not lead to anarchy and consequently embrace communism, developed nations thought of the plan of helping these countries to overcome the crisis situation.

That time every country had its own economic policies and systems. The problem was how to bring about systemic changes. The process of globalization involved integration of different economic systems prevailing in the world and consequently economic transformation of the nations involved. Information and communication technology at hand was expected to lead to a greater degree of interconnectedness between the nations, giving support to the process of globalization. In those circumstances, in order to bring out desired economic transformation on a global scale and to continue it on sustained basis, strong need was felt to have the institutional arrangement to support it.

Keeping in view the above objective, the delegates from 44 nations met in a conference at New England village of Bretton Woods in USA in 1944 to set-up a new framework for the postwar global economy—a stable, cooperative international monetary system. The outcome of the conference was formation of three governing institutions namely World

Bank (WB), International Monetary Fund (IMF), and General Agreement on Trade and Tariff (GATT) which was later named as World Trade Organization (WTO).

World Bank (IBRD)

The function of WB (IBRD) was to provide project-specific financial assistance to rebuild the economies of those nations that had been devastated by Second World War. It initially focused on electric power and transportation projects. The World Bank is now concentrating on poverty alleviation programme. It has a capital base of $184 bn. and presently it has a membership of 180 countries.

International Monetary Fund (IMF)

IMF was established to create economic stability for a world which had just been through the trauma of depression (1930) and the devastation of war (1944). Its aim is to oversee the international monetary system and promote exchange stability among its member countries. IMF has been vested with advancing loans to needy countries to boost economic activity. These loans were, however, advanced with certain conditionalities which formed part of Structural Adjustment Programmes (SAPs). These conditionalities at macro-level included supporting privatization, liberalization of economy and reducing trade barriers. At micro level it included reducing public expenditure, reducing subsidies and removing price regulation by the state. The implementation of SAPs in various developing countries, however, created several problems.

IMF has a capital base of $316 bn. and presently it has a membership of 182 countries. Both the financial institutions namely World Bank and the International Monetary Fund are based in Washington D.C.

According to the structure of IMF and WB, developed countries as major donors have more say in the decision making process of the organization. Developing countries contend that for effective functioning and achieving the objectives of the organizations, there is a need to give them larger voice in decision making process.

World Trade Organization (WTO)

In order to bring uniformity in global trade, in 1948, USA and Western Europe set-up the organization named General Agreement on Trade and

Tariff (GATT) which was later renamed at Geneva as World Trade Organization (WTO) in early 1994. The organization came into operation w.e.f. 01.01.1995.

GATT/WTO established a set of rules to govern global trade with the objective of reducing national trade barriers and to stop the unhealthy competitive trade policies. Conceptually, the structure of World Trade Organization was designed to bring all nation-states of the world together to take the process of globalization forward. It was argued that specialization at global level would benefit the countries that establish trade relations with one another. This global economic model comprises four components:

1. Eliminating trade barriers to facilitate free flow of goods
2. Creating conditions conducive to free flow of capital
3. Creating an environment for the free flow of technology
4. Creating an atmosphere for the free flow of labour

The developed countries which are on the forefront of the globalization tend to favour limiting the model to first 3 components, but the developing countries emphasize on the implementation of the 4th one also. There is reluctance on the part of developed countries to implement the 4th component as they feel that it may affect the employment opportunities for labour and wage structure in their countries.

In this highly interconnected world, economic policy pursued by each country has impact on other countries, both favourable as well as adverse. Initially China was out of the world forum. It removed tariff barriers and subsidies to become a member of the WTO. However, later for quite some time, in order to boost exports, China deliberately kept its currency *renminbi* highly depreciated with the result China's exports went up with leaps and bounds and made it a huge trade surplus country. On the other hand increased China's exports posed a balance of payment problem for other countries.

Alongside good work being done, WTO is also perceived to be vulnerable to lobbying by big business organizations. WTO is vested with the power of trade sanctions in case any country violates Intellectual Property Rights (IPR). Occasionally, there are reports of some multinational companies lobbying for declaring their products as patented and gaining in terms of royalties. However, the MNCs contend that they are spending huge sums of money on research and development activities and therefore they are entitled to collect royalties.

Deliberations of WTO

The deliberations of WTO have been polarized and stormy whenever there was conflict of interest between developed and developing countries. Further, the political pressures at home found their reflection in the discussion and this generally acted against arriving at a consensus. This was especially evident in arriving at the Agreement on Agriculture in the Round Doha, Qatar in 2001 and the talks failed over limiting farm subsidies. European Union disagreed with the limits offered by US on farm subsidies. Comparatively poor countries also resisted cuts in subsidies The BRICS countries also took unified stand against reduction of subsidies. If multilateral talks continue to fail, the focus may shift to solve the issues on bilateral basis.

Doha Round (2001) Agreement on Agriculture

As earlier mentioned, while there has been progress on other fronts, the agreement on agriculture always eluded consensus. For the first time, a Doha Round (2001) Agreement on Agriculture proposed ending export subsidies for agricultural products, not sheltering any forms of trade—distorting domestic support, and providing substantially improved access to markets in both developed and developing countries. Though broad agreement was reached, consensus could not be arrived in later meetings about the cap on subsidies that countries should adhere to. The thread was picked up in Bali Ministerial Conference held in 2013.

WTO's Bali Ministerial Declaration December 2013

WTO's 159 member countries attended Bali Ministerial conference held in December 2013. While trade facilitation agreement was more a priority for all countries, what was bothering for developing country like India was adhering to prescribed levels of food subsidy and penalties if the subsidy levels go past the prescribed levels. This acquired crucial importance in the light of ambitious food security programme launched in India.

The background of the issue is that in order to protect the farmers from the fluctuating prices of commodities in the market, Indian government procures foodgrains from the farmers at rates fixed administratively under Minimum Support Price (MSP). At Bali, India took a hard stand on food security as its subsidy for rice was projected to approach the WTO's limit of 10 per cent of the value production in a few years. As a result of protracted deliberations, India was able to negotiate a peace clause, a four-year window under which no country could be penalized for breaching the farm subsidy cap and further talks on finding a permanent solution for public stockholding.

As regards trade facilitation agreement, it is stated to have the potential to bring benefits to the tune of $1 trillion on global scale through reduction in trading costs. The agreement includes framing of easier customs rules, cutting red tape in borders, speeding up clearances at ports, airports, reduce transaction costs etc. The trade facilitation deal is the first major package since WTO was set up in 1995. The Bali declaration is seen as a revival and re-energizing the Doha Round of talks in 2001.

WTO Ministerial Meeting at Geneva, Switzerland in July 2014

As a follow up of Bali Ministerial Declaration in 2013, WTO official agenda at the meet toward end of July, 2014 was to sign and to put in the rule book 'Trade Facilitation Agreement' aiming at easing and standardizing worldwide customs rules. India reiterated that the agreement should be finalized only after WTO members agree to change rules on food subsidies.

According to obligations under WTO, the value of subsidy India provides farmers on any agricultural product must be limited to 10 per cent of the total value of the output of the product at the market price. WTO methodology requires that per unit subsidy be measured by the difference between MSP and the average price of the product that prevailed during 1986-1988. Even though MSP in India now is only marginally above the market price, because the latter is substantially above the average price during 1986-1988, the measured subsidy bill ends up violating the 10 per cent cap.

India felt that a breach of the 10 per cent cap will hurt the ability of developing countries to maintain public stockholding of foodgrains. Meanwhile, a provision of moratorium of four years ending in 2017 to follow the rules, called as 'peace clause', which would allow developing countries like India to run their public food stockholding programmes that result in the breach, was considered by India as inadequate to safeguard the interests of Indian agriculture. The meet, therefore, ended in a stalemate thus failing to maintain the deadline of signing the Trade Facilitation Agreement by all countries by end July, 2014. This development is being interpreted by some WTO members as putting a question mark on the utility of multilateral agency.

However in November 2014, it is reported that India and USA have arrived at the bilateral understanding according to which peace clause will stay till a permanent solution is found for public stockholding of foodgrains required for India's food security programme. The bilateral understanding is expected to bring other WTO members on board.

Organizational Changes in World Trade and Financial Institutions

There is a strong undercurrent in developing countries that the developed countries are using World Trade and Financial Institutions to further their interests. Developing countries feel that there is a need to bring about organizational changes in these institutions to democratize the working of these institutions to usher in sustainable world economy which takes care of developing and least developed countries.

Asian Development Bank (ADB)

ADB was set up in 1966 with 31 members to foster economic growth and cooperation in the Asian region. Its aim is to make Asia and Pacific free from poverty. ADB provides loans to developing member countries in five core areas: infrastructure, environment, regional cooperation and integration, finance sector development and education. It has a capital of \$165 bn. Presently it has a membership of 67 countries. It is located in Manila, Philippines.

BRICS Bank

The 6th summit of the heads of the governments of Brazil, Russia, India, China and South Africa (BRICS), the world's leading emerging economies, was held at Fortaleza, Brazil and launched BRICS Bank in July 2014 with an initial capital of \$50 bn. The bank is aimed at funding infrastructure projects in developing nations. It is envisaged to set up a \$100 bn pool of currency reserves to help the countries overcome short term liquidity pressures. Out of \$100 bn, China will contribute \$41 bn, Brazil, Russia and India \$18 bn each and South Africa \$5 bn. The bank will be located in Shanghai, China.

Asian Infrastructure Investment Bank (AIIB)

Asian Infrastructure Investment Bank backed by China has been launched in October, 2014. The AIIB is in addition to the BRICS Development Bank based in Shanghai formed in July, 2014.

The AIIB will be headquartered in Beijing. India along with 20 other countries has become founding members of the bank. The stated objective of the bank is to aid the infrastructure development in the Asian region.

The authorized capital of the bank is $100 bn. and the initial subscribed capital is expected to be around $50 bn. US is viewing with concern if the bank is being established as a rival to already existing multilateral lenders like World Bank, IMF etc. The aforesaid perspective of US is similar to what earlier countries in the South were holding about West furthering their interests through World Bank, IMF. Whatever it is, there is no doubt that China backed by good reserves is trying to increase its influence in Asia and Africa.

Multinational Corporations (MNCs)

The liberalization of national economies enabled large corporations to spread their business beyond their home countries. Multinational corporations are the enterprises which operate in more than one country. Thus, they differ from the domestic corporations in that the latter operate in one single nation. MNCs operate by way of setting up their branches or creating subsidiaries in various countries. Their presence overseas is either through acquisition of or merger with the domestic company or setting up entirely new facility. MNCs use, for managing purpose, both combinations *viz.* either producing same stage of product in several countries, which is known as horizontal integration, or producing different stages of the product in several countries, which is known as vertical integration. Mixed combinations of these are also used.

MNCs maintain strong relationship with the home country including bringing their profits in the home country. The nomenclature MNCs is interchangeably used for transnational (TNC) or global corporations (GC). But some authors distinguish MNCs from TNC or GCs in that the latter do not identify with the home country and may operate at times disregarding the interests of the home country.

MNCs have their headquarters generally in home country and policies and strategic functions are looked after from the headquarters. The subsidiaries are established in far-flung areas overseas. While subsidiaries are given autonomy in operation, they are fully responsible to the parent organization, i.e. MNC with the headquarters in the home country. Most of MNCs are headquartered in USA, EU and Japan. MNCs have grown very fast in speed and size. They are producing about 20 per cent of the world's total Gross National Product.

There is an element of disjunction of relationship between the nation-state and the MNCs. While MNCs enjoy autonomy in instant movement of capital to and from the host country, the host country is supposed to provide state support to MNCs. The critics of globalization contend that in this way, the principle of interdependency does not work and the position of the nation-state gets compromised.

According to an analysis by McKinsey Global Institute, reported in (ET) October 6, 2013, 158 global large companies have their headquarters in India with combined revenue of $ 898 billion, thus making India the 11th most favoured destination for setting up MNC headquarters. The US topped the chart with 2,123 large firms having their headquarters in the country with a combined revenue of $ 15,221 billion, followed by Japan (1,028 firms, $ 7,347 billion), China (577, $ 5,449 billion), Germany (462, $ 3,788 billion) and United Kingdom (358, $ 2,818 billion), constituting the top five. The next most favoured destinations for setting up headquarters of a global MNC include: France (which hosts 236 firms), Australia (203), Canada (194), Italy (179) and Russia (165).

As per the report on growth of companies in emerging economies, by 2025, nearly half of the Fortune global 500 companies are likely to be based in developing countries including India. As Japanese and South Korean companies became formidable global competitors in the past half century, new players from emerging markets such as Chinese telecom networking giant Huawei, Brazilian aircraft manufacturer Embraer and India's industrial conglomerate Aditya Birla Group are asserting their presence, adding many more are to follow. According to the report, companies from emerging regions are growing faster than their counterparts from the developed world not only on their home turf, but also in overseas markets for example—the aggressive expansion of India's Tata Motors into Europe in the past decade.

Globalization means free market economy. Free market economy leads to free play for the Multi-National Companies and other private players. The positive side of MNCs is that they bring investment and business in the host country. The downside is that they work for profit and are likely to ignore social responsibility. For example, companies will be interested in acquiring land for setting up industries but they may not pay attention to the woes of agriculturists whose land is acquired by the companies. Onetime payment of compensation of meagre amount hardly compensates loss of means of permanent livelihood of agriculturists.

Work Culture of MNCs

MNCs face two-fold challenges while doing their business abroad. MNCs face market competition not only between different MNCs, but also with the indigenous companies in the host countries. Added to this they have to cope with the industrial relation laws of the host country and cultural differences between home country and host country. The culture of home country may be very different from the host country. They have therefore to constantly work for creating a common ground and adopt common values. In the process, host country, particularly developing country, benefits in a big way. For example, punctuality of work timings, efficiency in working, paperless office working, mannerism and etiquette in interaction are some of the qualities which host country like India can imbibe from the working of MNCs.

Conclusion

Hardly any country was left out of the vortex of war effort during WWII. The economies of most of the nations especially underdeveloped countries, Eastern Europe and Japan were in doldrums. It was with a view that these nations should not be in chaos and become pray to communism that the idea of helping these nations financially came into being. It was felt that without appropriate institutional framework this task could not be performed, and therefore World Bank, IMF and GATT/WTO were established.

These institutions advanced financial assistance to needy countries with certain conditions. According to donor institutions, these conditions were designed for long term improvement of the economies of developing countries, but the receiving countries preceived these conditions as strings attached to the financial aid package. Further, Structural Adjustment Programme (SAP) which entailed curbing expenditure on social sector programmes and reducing subsidies in agriculture sector did not go down well with the public at large in developing countries. India's biggest worry is proposed restriction on food subsidy proposed by WTO.

Recently, BRICS Bank and Asian Infrastructure Investment Bank were set-up, in which major shareholding is that of China. West and some other countries see the move of China in setting up parallel banks as aimed at increasing its influence in Asia and Africa.

The process of liberalization of economies gave birth to Multinational Companies, each operating in more than one country and now globally one-fifth of GNP is produced by them. Though MNCs like any other private business organization would work for earning return for their investment, there is no doubt that they have brought with them some very positive work culture aimed at improving efficiency in the working and the host countries are greatly benefiting by the same.

GLOBAL ECONOMIC PROCESS

Prologue

Initially globalization started with trade and commerce between the nations. Thus, very idea of globalization stemmed from the principle that the people will benefit from the specialized mode of production. Though globalization in course of time encompassed all aspects of life, i.e. economic, social, cultural, political etc., in the present times the most discussed and debated aspect of globalization is economic. The advancement in information and communication technology enabled phenomenal increase in the interconnectedness between the nations and people across the world. However, in spite of close interconnectedness, there is a view that globalization has not reached all nations uniformly. Another issue is whether all nations which embraced globalization benefited from it? In order to get the answers to these and many other questions, it is necessary to know how economic aspect of globalization was evolved over a period of time.

Evolution of Economic Globalization

Capitalism

Globalization is closely related to the system of capitalism. The characteristic of capitalism is that each individual has a large measure of freedom in conducting economic activity. West and Europe who were at the forefront of the development were the first to realize that the public ownership of resources like land etc. could not deliver goods as expected.

Therefore, they started adopting private ownership of these resources. With the advent of industrialization, the concept of capitalism came into existence as capital is a basic requirement for the growth of industry. Again the traditional method of production by its very nature is slow and less efficient.

The method of specialized mode of production was first mooted by Adam Smith (1776) who held that one person alone working on making pins may be producing one pin in a day. On the other hand if the method of production is changed to 10 specialized producers, they may deliver 48,000 daily. Karl Marx (1867) too acknowledged exponential increase in production through specialized means under capitalist system. He had, however, highlighted its adverse impact on social relations (Ritzer, 2012: 151).

Accumulation-capital

The production, distribution and associated activities correspond with the quantum of capital available. With certain amount of capital, there would be certain amount of profit. However, the capitalist does not remain satisfied with the constant profit. There is an unceasing urge in him for more and more profit. How this urge for ever increasing profit will be fulfilled? The only way to fulfill it is by way of increasing the investment of capital. But the question is how to generate the additional capital? This is generated through what Karl Marx calls is by increasing surplus value. What is surplus value? It is the difference between the value added by the worker for producing a product and what is actually paid by the capitalist to the worker.

The capitalist is constantly in search of methods to increase this surplus value. The ways adopted by the capitalist are payment of low wages to workers, demanding more efficiency of production from the workers and reduced expenditure on the labour welfare measures. The increased surplus is invested as capital. Thus, privatization works more in favour of capital owners as they can expand their business by way of increasing productivity and spending less on welfare measures. According to Marx, this amounts to exploitation of workers.

In effect, society is getting segmented in two classes namely privileged and underprivileged. The other source of capital is generated through an exchange of commodities, i.e. commodities are constantly bought and sold at the prices capitalist can manage in the market. The additional capital thus generated is put into circulation in the business in the form of reinvestment which fetches more profit. This process leads to what is called accumulation of capital (Ritzer, 2012: 2-3).

Fordism, post-Fordism

With sufficient capital at hand, one of the leading car makers in USA tried innovative method to increase the production. He coined with the idea of centralized mass production from the point of view of cutting down cost per unit. This concept of assembly line was first used on a large scale by Ford in USA for production of cars. Therefore, this process came to be known as Fordism. This phase started in 1918, i.e. at the end of WWI and lasted up to 1978, coinciding with ushering of China's liberalization policies.

The innovations in methods of production and increasing labour productivity continued. In the process, Fordism was succeeded by Post-Fordism. Post-Fordism refers to a period of 1980s and 1990s marked by decentralized production facilities and flexible labour employment. By 1991, India too liberalized its economy. With North already in and now joined by developing countries especially two most populous countries namely India and China, the international trade and commerce took a global shape. During this period a new term 'globalization' the usage of became more and more popular and the usage of the term like post-Fordism started receding (Ritzer, 2012: 681-82).

Globalization Post-World Wars

WWII and its aftershocks shattered the economies of most of the nations except West. They especially affected Eastern Europe, Japan and entire South. There was economic chaos all around. It was feared that this chaotic situation may become breeding ground for communism. IMF, World Bank and World Trade Organization were, therefore, created supposedly to help these devastated countries to tide over the financial difficulties and enhance the international trade by way of removing trade barriers and introducing liberalization policies. These policies coupled with development of advanced Information and Communication Technology resulted in high interconnectedness between nations and peoples globally. This interconnectedness has not remained limited to the field of economics and commerce but it embraced social and cultural fields too. Now, there is no field which has remained untouched by global interconnectedness. The world has thus entered into an era of globalization.

Economic Globalization

While globalization has multiple facets, the economic aspect of globalization has been more dominant. Over a period of time, the process of globalization has touched all nations. However, in spite of greater interconnectedness between nations and peoples, the reach of the globalization process has not been uniform. While some countries are well integrated with the globalization process, some countries are left out and the status of the other countries lies somewhere in between the two categories.

The major contributing factor for early integration has been historical. While due to their early lead in industrialization, the West, Europe and Japan are ahead in reaping advantages of globalization, the South which remained as colonies under subjugation of imperial powers for a long time could not get similarly benefited and stand on a different footing. From 1980s onward, with the liberalization of trade and commerce, developing countries like China, India, Brazil, Russia and some South Asian countries made significant economic progress under globalization.

Keynesian Economy

The noted British economist John Maynard Keynes (5 June, 1883 – 21 April, 1946) argued that both extremes i.e. pure capitalism and pure socialism do not offer solution to overcome the great depression (1929-33). Instead, middle way in the form of mixed, socially regulated market economy offer a solution. This would mean increased expenditure on public projects including expenditure on social services such as health, education etc., if need be, even by borrowing funds from outside the country. According to him, increased spending on public projects would stimulate the economic growth.

Mixed Economy is neither pure capitalism nor pure socialism, but a mixture of the two system. In this system we find characteristics of both capitalism and socialism. Mixed economy is operated by both, private enterprise and public enterprise. Under stewardship of Jawaharlal Nehru as first Prime Minister, India followed the system of mixed economy from the time of independence. Because of the paucity of resources with the private sector, public sector played major role in the economy and the regulatory role of the government in controlling private sector was prominent. This system continued in India till 1990. It was realized that in the face of changing global economic scenario, the existing then system was not conducive to produce the desired economic growth. Therefore, in 1991, with Manmohan Singh as Finance Minister, initiative was taken to liberalize the economy by liberalizing the licensing regime for establishing the private enterprises and reducing the regulatory role of government in controlling the private enterprises.

India's Entry in Post-industrial Economy

India like other countries has been passing through different phases. Till attainment of Independence (1947), Indian economy was dominated by agriculture. After Independence, India started massive industrialization by way of establishing heavy industries under public sector, with the result, the share of manufacturing increased and the share of agriculture reduced. From the beginning of twenty-first century, with globalization in process, services sector which mainly consisted Information and Communication Technology, came to the forefront and the share of both agriculture and manufacturing dwindled. The share of services sector in economy now counts as much as agriculture and manufacturing put together. India is now at the forefront of the Information and Communication Technology in the world. The rise of services sector during this period gave a new dimension to the India's economy. The emergence of services sector as a prominent sector is marked as starting of post-industrial era.

Economic Flows

Opening of Markets

The emphasis of globalization has been for opening of market of host nation to other nations. This applies equally to developed as well as developing countries. While developed countries keep on pressing developing countries for opening of latter's markets, it has to be acknowledged that, on their part, developed countries too simultaneously followed the same course. Thus, opening of the markets was an effort from both sides although the extent of liberalization may vary from country to country.

Ironically of late, developed countries are facing backlash in their own countries over opening of markets. The result of opening of market has been shifting of manufacturing activity to places where the labour is cheap. In the process, much of the manufacturing activity in USA closed down and it shifted to China. This has resulted in loss of jobs in USA. In view of this, internal pressure is now building on US administration to insist on those countries who are supplying products and services to USA to establish production facilities in US itself. This policy is perceived as directed toward India and China, especially toward China because manufacturing is substantially shifted to China.

FDI

In advanced countries, the supply and demand of products and services have stabilized over a period of time. Therefore, the economic growth is in a plateau form and the return on investment in developed countries is much less. On the other hand, because of higher rate of increase in population and less increase in supply position, there have been huge shortages on the supply side in the developing countries. Thus, there is a tremendous expansion of economic activity in developing countries especially BRICS countries. Therefore, a lot of Foreign Direct Investment (FDI) is flowing from developed countries to developing countries to earn more return. For routing FDI, what the entity in the donor country has to do is to establish in receiving country either its wholly-owned affiliate or acquire a local company or form a joint venture.

Since, FDI provides much needed additional capital for investment, there is a general perception that FDI is all good. However, there are serious issues with FDI flows. The advantages associated with FDI are not automatic. For example, mere transfer of capital without transfer of technology does not benefit the recipient country. Moreover, in the long run, this technology has to be indigenized. The advantages of FDI flows thus will depend upon the capacity of the recipient country to derive these advantages. This in turn will depend upon how well the economy of the recipient country is integrated with the global economy. Another disadvantage is that those entities who provide FDI may also withdraw it unilaterally at any time, thus leaving the recipient country in doldrums.

Since, industry requires necessary infrastructure like road communication, power, water etc., investment flows occur in countries where infrastructure is well developed. The development of infrastructure involves huge amount of expenditure. Thus populous countries like China and India are under pressure not only for providing expenditure on development of infrastructure but also for social sector, i.e. education, health etc. China liberalized its economy in 1978. It had been ahead of India regarding development of infrastructure well before embracing globalization. Therefore, China benefited most from globalization. In the case of India, balancing expenditure on development of infrastructure and social sector has become a herculean task. However, in spite of this difficulty, for the last several years, India has been showing economic growth more than 4.5 per cent even during the times of global economic slowdown. During 2005-2008, it was more than 9 per cent.

Special Economic Zone (SEZ)

The export of goods has acquired special significance in globalization. Every country is trying to boost their exports for economic benefit. It is in this context that the term Special Economic Zone has come into being. The term Special Economic Zone is now a days is used as a generic term referring to modern economic zone located within a country's national borders but have different business laws characterized by minimum bureaucracy, special tax incentives and modern infrastructure. The idea of SEZ is to attract investment especially FDI by providing special incentives and governing laws.

Since 1980, China has established SEZs in Shenzhen, Zhuhai, Shantou, Xiamen, and Hainan province. The term became popular thereafter. However, much before China's SEZs, India established conceptually similar but with a different name Free Trade Zone at Kandla in Gujarat in the mid-1960s with special facilities to boost exports. Many countries in Latin America and South Asia have also established SEZs.

In India while two-third of SEZ exports are from IT, manufacturing has not made any headway. The protagonists of SEZ contend that the existing labour laws are not conducive to manufacturing activity. They insist on the state to make the laws business friendly. Thus, while business in SEZs did show growth, but the same has not been spectacular as planned for. Therefore, the basic concept of establishing SEZs is being questioned. The critics of SEZs contend that instead of concentrating on providing valuable resources in developing only selected enclaves, the emphasis of the state should be on improving the general industrial environment across the country.

Economic Growth in India and other Asian Countries

The State of Indian Economy

India started liberalizing its economic policies from 1991. It is worthwhile to look at the results of the changed policies. The state of economy is generally measured by growth rate in Gross Domestic Product. Table 2.1 given below shows year-wise Growth Rate in GDP from 1995-96 to 2014-15.

Table 2.1: Indian Economy: Growth Rate in GDP from 1995-96 to 2014-15

Year	*Growth rate in GDP*	*Year*	*Growth rate in GDP**
	(2004-05 prices)		
1995-96	7.3	2006-07	9.6
1996-97	8.0	2007-08	9.3
1997-98	4.3	2008-09	6.7
1998-99	6.7	2009-10	8.6
1999-2000	8.0	2010-11	8.9
2000-01	4.2	2011-12	6.7
2001-02	5.4	2012-13	5.1
2002-03	3.9	2013-14	6.9
2003-04	8.0	2014-15	7.4
2004-05	7.1		
2005-06	9.5		

Source: Planning Commission: Indian Economy: Some Indicators at a Glance (as on 1st December, 2014)

Website: http://planningcommission.nic.in/data/datatable/data_2312/databookDec2014%2018.pdf

*GOI revised the figures by shifting to the new base of 2011-12 from the earlier base of 2004-05.

Source: http://indiabudget.nic.in/es2014-15/echapvol2-01.pdf.

The above Table 2.1 reveals that the Indian economy did not reach double digit growth rate any time but it did come very close to it during the period 2005-06 to 2007-08. In 2008 there was meltdown in US economy which impacted economies world over including India thereafter.

GDP growth rate comprises mainly Agriculture, Industrial and Services sectors. These have also been named as primary, secondary and tertiary sectors respectively. The growth rate in Agriculture Sector (1995-96 to 2013-14) has been dealt in the topic on Agrarian Position in chapter IV. As a general idea, the growth rate of agriculture has been varying widely on year to year basis because it is heavily dependent on the rain as about 60 per cent of land is cultivated as dry land agriculture. Earlier, India was importing food from outside countries. But after green revolution, India has been able to meet not only its domestic demand of food, but it is also exporting the produce to other countries. However, lately the agriculture sector is facing daunting problems in the context of droughts and fluctuating prices of the commodities in the global market.

Regarding industrial growth, the major Industrial Policy framework was adopted *vide* Industrial Policy Resolutions in 1948 and then 1956. Industrial Policy Resolutions in 1956 identified three categories of industries: those that would be reserved for development in public sector, those that would be permitted for development through private enterprise with or without State participation, and those in which investment initiatives would ordinarily emanate from private entrepreneurs. Keeping in view the scarcity of capital and inadequate entrepreneurial base, the Resolution accorded a predominant role to the State to assume major responsibility for industrial development. With the changing industrial scenario in the country as well as globally, the policy has undergone many changes from time to time.

The major changes were effected in 1991 the year in which the economy was liberalized in a big way. As per Industrial Policy Resolution 1991, industrial licensing has been abolished for all industries irrespective of levels of investment, except those specified for reasons related to security and strategic concerns. There have been many changes even after this resolution and industrial policy has been substantially liberalized.

Table 2.2 given below shows year-wise Industrial GDP Growth Rate from 1995-96 to 2013-14.

Table 2.2: Indian Economy: Industrial GDP Growth Rate from 1995-96 to 2013-14

Year	*Growth Rate*	*Year*	*Growth Rate*
1995-96	11.3	2004-05	9.8
1996-97	6.4	2005-06	9.7
1997-98	4.0	2006-07	12.2
1998-99	4.2	2007-08	9.7
1999-2000	6.0	2008-09	4.4
2000-01	6.0	2009-10	9.2
2001-02	2.6	2010-11	7.6
2002-03	7.2	2011-12	7.8
2003-04	7.3	2012-13	1.0
		2013-14 (Adv. est.)	0.4

Source: Planning Commission: Indian Economy: Some Indicators at a Glance (as on 1st December 2014)

Website: http://planningcommission.nic.in/data/datatable/data_2312/Databok Dec2014%2018.pdf

It will be seen from the above table that there has been decline in the growth rate in Industrial sector especially during two years namely

2012-13 and 2013-14. Manufacturing is the core activity in the Industrial sector. China has almost monopolized the area of product manufacturing and the global market is flooded with its cheap products, even though many of them are not found to be quality products and durable. Even USA is feeling the heat of taking away manufacturing activity from that country to China.

Regarding the growth of services sector in India, it has surpassed the growth of agriculture as well as industry sector. It now accounts for 60 per cent of country's GDP. The services sector in India has been recognized globally for its capability and high growth, and attracts highest foreign direct investment.

Table 2.3 given below shows year-wise growth rate in Services Sector Growth Rate from 1995-96 to 2013-14.

Table 2.3: Indian Economy: Services Sector Growth Rate from 1995-96 to 2013-14

Year	*Growth Rate*	*Year*	*Growth Rate*
1995-96	10.1	2004-05	8.3
1996-97	7.5	2005-06	10.9
1997-98	8.9	2006-07	10.1
1998-99	8.3	2007-08	10.3
1999-2000	12.1	2008-09	10.0
2000-01	5.1	2009-10	10.5
2001-02	6.6	2010-11	9.7
2002-03	6.7	2011-12	6.6
2003-04	7.9	2012-13	7.0
		2013-14 (Adv. est.)	6.8

Source: Planning Commission: Indian Economy: Some Indicators at a Glance (as on 1st December, 2014).

Website: http://planningcommission.nic.in/data/datatable/data_2312/Databok Dec2014%2018.pdf

Information and Communication Technology (ICT) is the main driver of the services sector. India has been quite well in ICT till 2010-11 with near double digit growth rate. India has been front runner with advantage of English language and lower wages. The major part of the services belonged to outsourcing from USA to India. However, in view of the increasing unemployment in USA, of late it started adopting certain policies aimed at reducing its dependence on services from India and instead encouraging ICT in home country. To cope with the reduction of business from USA, India is trying to increase its business in European market, beside domestic market.

Economic Growth of India and China

While comparing economies, Indian economy is generally compared with the economies of BRICS countries and in particular with that of China. Ever since China opened economy in 1978 and India in 1991, the world is watching the growth of economies of these two countries with special interest. This is largely due to the fact that the population of these two countries account for almost half of the population of the globe and these countries are following entirely two different political systems *viz*. China adopting authoritarian and India adopting democratic form of governance. Though presently China is well ahead of India in economic growth, it is predicted that India's growth rate of economy will overtake that of China with both economies leveling at a particular rate of growth. It is said that the major factor for this shift is the build-up of larger youth population in India *vis-à-vis* China. China is saddled with ageing population as it followed 'one child norm' for a long time to restrict the population growth. However, they have recently introduced changes in the norms allowing more than one child in certain cases.

Brazil, Russia, India, China and South Africa have attained so much economic progress that these countries have now attained the level of importance almost next to developed countries (46 Ritzer, 2012: 498). Thus similarly placed, these countries formed a group named BRICS to advance their common interest in the world forum.

Middle Income Trap

The economies of most of the countries are moving up from low income

Table 2.4: World Bank classification of Country Income Groups Country Gross National Income per capita (US $) Standing of BRICS countries

Lower Income	1,045 or less	
Lower Middle Income	1,046 to 4,125	India
Upper Middle Income	4,126 to 12,735	Brazil, China, South Africa
High Income	12,736 or more	Russian Federation

Source: World Bank classification as on 1 July 2015 (WB revises the figures every 1st July).
Website: http://data.worldbank.org/news/new-country-classifications-2015.

to middle income and middle income to high income. Some countries moved up from lower income to middle income group but they are stated to have stuck in the middle income trap.

What is middle Income trap? Each year on July 1, the World Bank revises the classification of the world's economies based on estimates of Gross National Income (GNI) per capita for the previous year. The classification as on 1 July 2013 is given in the Table. According to IMF working paper, "middle-income trap" is the phenomenon of hitherto rapidly growing economies stagnating at middle-income levels and failing to graduate into the ranks of high-income countries. The classification of groups on the basis of GNI per capita is given in the Table 2.4.

According to economists, the host of factors play role in getting over stagnation of economy. The major ones are framework of property rights and sanctity of contract, infrastructure development (road networks, telephone lines etc.), capacity of private sector to increase productivity and innovation, find new markets to maintain export growth, ramping up domestic demand, deregulation of economy, less involvement of government in economic matters etc.

Among various economies, the economies of China and India always attract comparison because both countries became free from the colonial past more or less at the same time and both have large population base. While China is stuck at upper middle Income group, India is still grappling in lower middle Income group. There are different perceptions about the reasons for the gap between the two countries. However, large body of people holds the view that this has something to do with the difference in the political system being followed by these countries. While India has a democratic political system wherein every single decision comes for scrutiny by the public, China has a single party political system wherein decisions do not encounter resistance from the public. In India, every big project encounters not only legitimate, but also many a times illegitimate resistance from local bodies or NGOs.

Unsteady Economic Growth in Asian Countries

WWII affected economies all over the world except American continent adversely. The revival plans were drawn in the Bretton Woods conference in USA in 1944. Afterwards there has been economic growth in the Asian countries but this growth has been unsteady. Japan was the first country to witness high economic growth which happened especially for two reasons. One was that Japan was a developed country even before WWII.

Secondly, USA provided special economic assistance to Japan, in the context of huge devastation caused by atom bombs used by USA against Japan during WWII. The other countries where good economic growth followed were Hong Kong, Singapore, Taiwan, and South Korea. These countries were followed by Thailand, Malaysia, Indonesia and the Philippines. These are now joined by India and China (21 Nissanke, Thorbecke; 2008: 5). However, these countries, leaving India and China, subsequently faced economic crisis in 1997 which has been described in the topic 'downside of globalization.'

Downside of Globalization

Overuse of Natural Resources

Capitalism is an integral part of globalization and capitalism has its own downside. In capitalism stress is laid on maximum usage of natural resources so as to maximize the scale of business and profit thereof. This maximum usage is undertaken in spite of the fact that the natural resources are limited. The capitalists are driven purely by the business growth and they are likely to be least concerned about the exhaustion of natural resources.

Capitalists do not give the same importance to renewable resources as they give to natural resources. For example, capitalists prefer to generate power by using coal rather than generate power by solar or wind resources because the former technology already exists and the latter has to be developed so as to make it commercially viable. This R&D effort requires investment for which capitalists are reluctant. On the other hand, the interest of the local community will be better served by adopting development which is sustainable.

Growing Speculative Business and Illicit Flows of Money

In modern times, information and communication technology has made business transactions across the world easier and speedier. Transactions of millions of dollars can now take place instantly through internet. The technology has facilitated doing business in far off countries and thus is an advantage, but it has also a downside. Greed is dark side of capitalist system. While there are people who do serious businesses, there are also number of entities who do speculative business so as to make money quickly. Thus technology is being used as a tool by the speculative businessmen.

Internet has enabled boom in speculative market with the fluidity of currency exchange rates, interest rates on borrowing, commodity and stock prices. Such speculative businessmen do great harm to fair businessmen who follow norms of business. Speculative business is similar to gambling and represents darker side of globalization. At times this can work adversely against the interests of the nations where such transactions are taking place, as it often bypasses the regulatory mechanism of the concerned states. In these cases, the social and economic costs to the nation-state are very high.

According to the study of Global Financial Integrity (GFI), a Washington DC based research and advisory organization reported in December 2014, nearly money worth $440 billion (Rs. 28 lakh crore) was illegally taken out of India over a period of 10-year period from 2003 to 2012 and that it ranks fourth after China, Russia and Mexico. Obviously taxes were not paid for these enormous sums.

Role of Capital Controls

Prior to 1997, South-east Asian countries namely Thailand, Malaysia, Singapore, Indonesia, and South Korea opted for short term borrowing from developed countries. Things were going well for quite some time. But in 1997 some investors felt that the economy of these countries was overheated they started withdrawing money from these markets. Looking to these withdrawing money, as herd action other investors too followed suit, thus creating panic in the financial circles. This resulted in full blown financial crisis in these countries.

The tremors of crisis in South-east Asian countries were felt in other countries too for example India and China. But, due to capital account controls existing in India and China, these economies withstood the shock. However, there has been a general slowdown of economies in these countries also, which is inevitable because all economies are by and large interrelated. Thus, resistance of India and China to the calls of world financial institutions for removing capital account controls paid rich dividends. This proves that it is dangerous for developing countries to go after liberalizing the economies in literal terms. It is rather necessary to keep these under prudent regulations.

Economic Crises due to External Factors

High volatility in currencies was witnessed from May 20, 2013 onwards and continued through September, 2013. Many countries including China experienced sliding down of their currencies. But rupee was hit most. The value of rupee per dollar was 55.42 on 21.05.2013. This value slided down to 68.83 on 28.08.2013. Besides internal factor of high current account deficit (difference between value of exports and imports) of 4.8 per cent of GDP in India, the major factors which played the part in sliding down the value of currencies were external: Ben Bernanke's statement (22.05.2013) that US Fed (Central bank) may taper off its stimulus—called the 3rd phase of quantitative easing.

The quantitative easing programme is an unusual strategy followed by the US Fed to flood money markets with trillions of dollars of liquidity. This flooding, by way of purchasing government bonds and mortgages, took place in three phases which are termed QE1, QE2 and QE3 and were announced in 2008, 2010 and 2012, respectively to prop up the US economy after the 2008 financial meltdown.

This announcement took the toll on emerging markets, with Indonesian and Indian currencies failing the most. Fears of a spike in crude oil prices after a possible US strike in Syria has pushed the rupee further down.

The above development is reminiscent of the Asian—South-east: Thailand, Malaysia, Singapore, Indonesia, and South Korea—financial crisis in 1997. At that time, economies of both China and India remained unaffected because both countries did not relax capital controls. The occurrence of economic crisis highlights the bitter fact that national economies world over are no more insular from the global developments—economic or political. This is the price involved in the process of globalization. It is alright for the countries if their economies can sustain sudden economic shocks. But in actual practice it is found that unsustainable economic shocks create not only economic instability but also create chaos in the country, which has a potential to take a toll of the democratically elected legitimate governments. Ironically, the rupee stabilized around Rs. 60 per dollar subsequently.

Gold and Globalization

Gold is called a precious metal. Several factors make it most important. It does not wear out as other metals wear and thus acquires permanency of existence. It is malleable and can acquire any shape without much difficulty. Due to anti-corrosive property, it is widely used in electronic products. It is viewed as a measure of prosperity and the quantity of gold possessed by the country is recognized as the economic worth of the country. It is respected and traded globally. In India it is customary to bestow as much as gold in the form of jewellery to a woman getting married mostly by her parents, which practice is called as dowry. It is believed to be helpful in time of crisis.

Earlier it was used as a form of payment but after invention of paper money, it is used as a form of investment. Due to unique features, this metal created fascination among people especially women from ancient times, so much so that people are crazy to acquire the gold.

Though gold has many good properties, it is a great disadvantage to those people or countries who possess little or nothing of it. In India, having Kolar mines exhausted, there are no confirmed gold reserves. Therefore, 100 per cent gold is imported. Together with 90 per cent oil and 100 per cent copper import, India has a large import base. During 2013, due to high inflationary pressure, there was huge demand for gold in India as this is considered as better option to invest money. This resulted in import of large quantity of gold, created serious problem of balance of payment and depreciation of rupee. Ultimately India had to hike import duty steeply to control the demand. However, exercising control over rush for buying gold and thus making it costly can be counterproductive. Global marketing and easy connectivity between countries make gold very prone to smuggling. In view of this, government relaxed the controls. But it is to be seen how the situation develops over a period of time. Thus gold is a unique example of how globalization can affect economy of a country.

Corruption

Corruption is a problem in every country, though it is relatively more in developing countries. The Transparency International Organization headquartered at Berlin in Germany brings out Corruption Perception Index every year. The level of corruption in the Corruption Perception Index ranks countries based on how corrupt their public sector is perceived to be. Corruption Perception Index 2014 includes 174 countries. The CPI for selected 10 countries is given in Table 2.5. The rank 1 means, corruption in that country is least in relation to other countries and higher the rank, more the corruption in that country.

It will be seen from Table 2.5 that India's rank is 85 out of 174 countries. India has improved its rank from 94 in 2013 to 85 in 2014. It is apparent that India has to take more steps to come even on par with Brazil or South Africa. In terms of corruption, China's position is no better. In

Table 2.5: Corruption Perception Index 2014

Country	Rank	Country	Rank
Germany	12	South Africa	67
U.K.	14	Brazil	69
Japan	15	India	85
United States	17	China	100
France	26	Russia	136

Source: Transparency International: Corruption Perception Index 2014: Results. *Website:* htpp//www.transparency.org/cpi2014/results

China, the hold of bureaucracy is much stronger than in India. Further, having one party wielding political power, there is an authoritarian rule. With little freedom of press, most of the corrupt practices go unreported in China. On the other hand, in India, with freedom of press, the cases of corruption are not only reported but many a times highly exaggerated.

The level of corruption in the host country is always taken into consideration as a transaction cost for doing business by the global players. The level of corruption in under developed countries is reported to be relatively high. It is not that there is no corruption in developed countries but it is not there at the level at which a common man has to get his work done. Therefore, a common man is saved from this malady. As against this, in developing countries, it is there at all levels. However, this does not mean, everybody is corrupt. There are people who would do the work without any expectations. Some people attribute the high level of corruption in underdeveloped countries to widespread poverty. There is no reason for the bureaucrats to seek undue favour as they now get handsome salaries. This phenomenon of bribe is related to greed and to no other factor.

Some scholars, as well as international aid organizations, such as the World Bank, tend to downplay the problems created by corruption. Some argue that corruption even fosters economic development, because it enables transactions that remain blocked by bureaucratic red tape to proceed (Ritzer, 2012: 301). While there is some strength in the contention, generally corruption devalues productive investment and therefore is counterproductive. Global players would be too happy if the dealings in the host countries are transparent

Crony Capitalism

Crony means close friend. Crony capitalism is a term used for the economy wherein there is collusion between the businessmen and the politicians and officials in the government who are friendly to businessmen. The term of crony capitalism has come into prominence from the time of Asian Financial Crisis in 1997, which mauled the economy of South Asian countries. Prior to the crisis, these economies were booming limitlessly, but went bust like bubble during the crisis. The impact of crony capitalism is more serious in developing countries.

There are many things in the purview of government like rights of natural resources. If the process of awarding these rights to businessmen is designed to benefit the select few, others are at a disadvantages. This kind of favouritism can take place in the case of grant of contracts, licenses or permits. Many a times, businessmen form a cartel and they try to influence the government policies. It is generally seen that the interested pressure groups become very active at the time of finalization of the annual budget. They try to utilize their influence through politicians also for formulating policies that are favourable to them.

The nexus between businessmen and politicians originate from the time of election process itself. Now-a-days, lot of money is required to be spent on elections and businessmen look to this event as an opportunity to help the politicians financially. Such things happen not only in developing countries but also in a free and democratic country like USA. During presidential elections, the campaign requires several millions of dollars. The funding is done largely by the business community. In this context, the influence of gun lobby in USA is quite talked about.

In order to avoid pitfalls of crony capitalism, state establishes regulatory mechanisms with good intentions. But these intentions are likely to go haywire when the officials of regulatory body, politicians and businessmen get their act together to serve their vested interests.

Table 2.6: Crony Capitalism Index

Country	*Rank in 2014*	*Rank in 2007*	*Country*	*Rank in 2014*	*Rank in 2007*
Russia	2	2	United States	17	12
India	9	6	China	19	19
South Africa	12	11	France	20	20
Brazil	13	14	Japan	21	17
Britain	15	15	Germany	23	21

Source: The Economist March 15, 2014.

Website: http://www.economist.com/news/international/21599041-countries-where-politically-connected-businessmen-are-most-likely-prosper-planet

There are two opposite perspectives held by socialists and capitalists on crony capitalism. Socialists contend that the very basis of capitalism is making profit and for that purpose they are bound to use government machinery for the purpose. Capitalists on the other hand contend that the unfettered power of government itself is a fertile ground for flourishing crony capitalism.

Based on data from Forbes, IMF, World Economic Forum, The Economist brings out Crony Capitalism Index, higher the ranking, the worse the performance. Following Table 2.6 gives the countrywise Crony Capitalism Index rank in 2014 and what was its rank in 2007 of selected 10 countries.

It will be seen from the above Table 2.6 that the extent of crony capitalism in India is more than not only with respect to developed countries but even that in BRICS countries like Brazil, China and South Africa. However, there is some improvement in India's position from 2007 to 2014. The improvement can be attributed to mainly two factors, one is the effect of Right to Information Act 2005 (RTI) and the other is steps taken by the government.

Doing Business 2015 Report of World Bank Group

World Bank Group brings out yearly report on 'Doing Business' in a country. Table 2.7 gives the rankings of selected 10 countries out of 189 countries about which the World Bank Group has brought out the report on 'Doing Business 2015' A high ease of doing business ranking means the regulatory environment is more conducive to the starting and operation of a local firm. The rankings for all economies are benchmarked to June 2014.

It will be seen from the above report that India is low in ease of doing business ranking not only with respect to developed countries but even compared to BRICS countries. This shows India has a long way to go for effecting necessary changes in various economic and bureaucratic systems to catch up with countries having better records.

Potential Transaction Costs

Before making investment, a foreign investor assesses all risks-tangible as well as intangible. They assess whether the environment in the host country is business friendly or not. Factors of particular interests to the foreign investor are clear private property rights, favourable industrial

Table 2.7: World Bank Group: Doing Business 2015: Rankings

Country	*Ease of Doing business Rank*	*Starting a Business*	*Dealing with Construction Permits*	*Getting Electricity*	*Registering Property*	*Getting Credit*	*Protecting Minority Investors*	*Paying Taxes*	*Trading Across Borders*	*Enforcing Contracts*	*Resolving Insovency*
U.S.	7	46	41	61	29	2	25	47	16	41	4
U.K.	8	45	17	70	68	17	4	16	15	36	13
Germany	14	114	8	3	89	23	51	68	18	13	3
Japan	29	83	83	28	73	71	35	122	20	26	2
France	31	28	86	60	126	71	17	95	10	10	22
South Africa	43	61	32	158	97	52	17	19	100	46	39
Russian Fe	62	34	156	143	12	61	100	49	155	14	65
China	90	128	179	124	37	71	132	120	98	35	53
Brazil	120	167	174	19	138	89	35	177	123	118	55
India	142	158	184	137	121	36	7	156	126	186	137

Source: World Bank Group; Doing Business 2015: Rankings.
Website: http://www.doingbusiness.org/rankings.

relations, business friendly economic policies, transparency in statutory approvals, corruption-free business environment, scope for expansion of business, and political stability. Each of the risk factors are assessed as far as possible in tangible terms and marked up as a transaction cost by the foreign investor. Foreign investors naturally prefer to do the business where the transaction cost is less. However, it is not easy to arrive at the correct transaction costs because it is difficult to quantify the impact of political risk etc. In that case, the transaction costs become speculative and may not be representing their real worth.

Social Spending

Social sector comprising education, healthcare etc. require adequate financial resources. The government spends money on social sector through collection of revenue from the public and companies. Tax is a major source of income for the state. However, with a view to earn more profit, globalization favours reduced taxation in the host countries. In the quest for profit, private companies save exceptions do not feel spending part of their earnings on social measures as their responsibility towards the society where they setup their business. In such situations governments in the host countries find it very hard to mobilize the money for social spending. This results in getting education, health and poverty alleviation programmes raw deal (D 08 Went, 2000: 38).

Tariffs and Subsidies

In the initial phase of globalization, respective governments tried to protect their own businesses. Later, globalization has brought down the subsidies and trade barriers and the trade has become considerably free. The need for any further liberalization and reducing subsidies has to be analyzed keeping in view the social impact of such actions. The opinion is growing that the time has now come to adopt growth policies to suit the local conditions and any further lowering the tariffs and subsidies will bc counterproductive. Already the agriculture sector is under strain due to pressure from WTO for lowering of subsidies even as the agriculture in India has generally become unviable.

Currency Valuation

Chinese currency *renmimbi* is not yet freely convertible. So, also India has been slow in removing total capital controls. Unlike South-East Asian and Latin American countries, China and India continue to have considerable control over their domestic economies and this helped them to overcome the economic crises in the past. In the light of quick financial flows and disadvantages of unregulated markets, the role of regulation of the economy becomes important. India has specially been conservative in opening of economy compared to China. China gives priority to manufacturing and export of manufactured products. To support these sectors, in past China allowed the *renminbi* to remain undervalued, the step that caused problem for other countries.

Globalization Prospered in Developed Countries

The process of globalization got fillip after World War II. After about seven decades by now, looking to on one hand the prosperity of developed countries reflected in high level of consumption of resources, and on the other hand poverty in the less developed countries reflected in low level of consumption, one will be inclined to draw the inference that the globalization has worked in favour of developed countries. The argument of some people goes even to the extent that the prosperity of developed countries has been at the expense of less developed countries. However, in this context, we cannot ignore the fact that due to early industrialization, developed countries attained good economic progress even before globalization process got underway. May be, by the process of globalization, they benefited more than the developing countries.

Positive Side of Globalization

Opinions differ as to which one of the two namely liberal or controlled economic policy is more beneficial to the country. Here, liberal economic policy means liberalization of economy by removing trade barriers with bringing tariffs down and controlled economic policy means putting restrictions on trade with other countries by increasing tariffs. The protagonists of globalization contend that while in the former case, achieving the economies of scale is possible, the latter case turns out to be keeping internal market players monopolistic.

The advantage of the specialization of production and competition that exists in the liberalized economy is not there in the controlled economy. It is generally observed that the countries which opened their economies to outside players have gained considerably *vis-à-vis* the nations who have kept restrictions on trade with other nations. However, in the former case too, there is a necessity to put in place well thought out policy to take care of destabilizing effect on the economy when it is exposed to outside economic forces.

There are several advantages to consumers as well as suppliers flowing from the process of globalization. The advantages are: consumer has a wide variety of choice of products; the quality of products is maintained because of competition; and the prices of the products are competitive, The advantage for the supplier of the product is that he has an expanded market in the form of global market involving vast opportunities.

Rural Society

It is generally held that the process of globalization has benefited urban society more than the rural society. However, globalization has an imprint not only on urban economy but also on rural economy. It is observed that a large part of the rural economy which has been, to start with, purely agriculture oriented transformed to include non-farm activities. The labour becoming surplus due to use of more and more machinery in agricultural operations has been partly utilized in non-farm activities. These non-farm activities include development of dairy, cottage industries, small scale industries, food processing, minor repairs of machinery in use in agriculture etc. Gradually, such transformation of rural economy lead to formation of *rurban* area. But along with positive side of globalization, rural people face number of intractable problems under globalization, which have been highlighted elsewhere in this book.

Small Scale Industry is a non-farm activity for the rural people. A small scale unit (industry) is defined as an industry in which the investment on fixed assets in plant and machinery whether held on ownership terms, lease or hire-purchase does not exceed Rs. 100 lakh. In the past, there was a boom in the growth of Small Scale Industry. Under globalization, the future of Small Scale Industries is somewhat uncertain. It is argued that global players with the adoption of techniques of mass production will outplace the small businesses. On the other hand this industry has an advantage of low overheads. With less overheads and personalized supervision, many SSI units are doing well. Further, SSI units are providing substantial employment opportunities to rural people as the skill required to work in SSI units falls in medium category.

Corporate Social Responsibility (CSR)

Under the new Companies Act which came into force in April 2014, certain class of profitable companies in India are required to spend at least two per cent of their three-year average annual net profit for CSR activities. List of permissible areas for CSR funding include such purposes as ending hunger and poverty, promoting public health, supporting education, addressing gender inequality, protecting the environment, helping the aged people, and funding cultural initiatives and the arts. As per the Act the purposes for which the money is to be spent should be outside the part of the normal course of the company's business or on projects for the exclusive benefit of employees or their family members. If implemented in letter and spirit, it will take away part of the grievances harboured by poor people against the big business organizations.

CSR Activities by NTPC

NTPC with which author was associated for 14 years is doing commendable work in the field of corporate social responsibility. It spends substantial amount of financial and human resources for CSR and sustainable development activities. During the year 2014-15, NTPC spent Rs. 205.18 crore on these activities. The CSR projects include activities ranging from infrastructure development to vocational training and women empowerment. The organization plans to give special emphasis on providing girls' toilets and development of model villages.

It also extends support for relief activities concerning natural calamities. For example, it extended support for relief activities during natural calamities in recent past in Uttarakhand, Himachal Pradesh and Odisha.

Conclusion

The method of specialized mode of production was first mooted by Adam Smith (1776). While globalization has multiple facets, the economic aspect of globalization has been more dominant. Over a period of time, the process of globalization has touched all nations. However, in spite of greater interconnectedness between nations and people, the reach of globalization has not been uniform. While some countries are well integrated with the globalization process, some countries are least involved like North Korea.

The major contributing factor for early integration has been historical. While due to their early lead in industrialization, the West, Europe and Japan are reaping greater benefits of globalization, the South which remained as colonies under subjugation of imperial powers for a long time could not get similar benefit and stand on a different footing. For the last three decades, with the liberalization of trade and commerce, developing countries like China, India, Brazil, Russia and some South Asian countries made significant gains from the process of globalization.

The advantages of globalization to the consumers are reflected in the availability of wide variety of choices of products with better quality of the products at competitive prices. It is generally observed that the countries which opened their economies to other countries have gained considerably *vis-à-vis* the countries which kept restrictions on trade with other countries.

In modern times, information and communication technology has made the transaction of business across the world easier and speedier. Financial transactions can now take place instantly through internet. ICT facilitated integration of world economy and economic growth. But it has also given fillip to speculative business. The occurrences of financial crises at different times reflect huge downside of globalization. Countries like China and India survived these crises to a great extent due to currency and capital account controls. This underscores the importance of regulation by the state.

Globalization is an extension of capitalism with some improvements like corporatization. In capitalism stress is laid on maximum usage of natural resources so as to maximize the scale of business and profit thereof. This maximum usage is undertaken in spite of the fact that the natural resources are limited.

It is observed that a large part of the rural economy which has been purely agriculture-oriented earlier shifted to include non-farm activities. The diversification provided employment to the labour which became redundant due to adoption of mechanization in agriculture. It seems that rural economy has not gained significantly by the process of globalization. The protective measures like subsidies and social safety net have been found to be inadequate in meeting the needs of the rural sector. In the light of this, the need for further liberalization and reducing subsidies has to be analyzed keeping in view the socio-economic impact of such actions. In the quest for profit, private companies save exceptions do not feel spending part of their earnings on social measures. The latest provision in India requiring companies to spend at least two per cent of their three-year average annual net profit for CSR activities may benefit the disadvantaged to some extent.

There is general perception that globalization has worked in favour of developed countries. The argument of some people goes even to the extent that the prosperity of developed countries has been at the expense of less developed countries. However, there is no doubt that the benefit of globalization depended upon how early the economy of a country was opened. But the benefit of globalization has not reached equitably within all sections of the society. Rural society in general and urban poor are left behind.

GLOBALIZATION AND EMPLOYMENT

Prologue

Though globalization has several dimensions, economic progress under globalization attracts more attention than any other dimension. This is so because economic progress generates employment which is critical to maintain one's family and material progress. Presently, all nations are facing the problem of unemployment. Globalization is perceived as a process that will bring new economic order. In emerging new economic order, the entrepreneurs look for expansion of their business, increasing productivity and earning more return on investment. On the other hand, the people in general are more interested in economic order that brings sufficient employment opportunities. In this context, the perceptions differ widely about the relationship between market economy under globalization and the generation of employment opportunities. Further, since globalization goes hand-in-hand with advancement of technology, it is important to know the impact of technology on employment.

Youth Employment-Unemployment Scenario 2012-13

After independence, India's Industrial Policy was first formulated in 1948. The Policy underwent number of changes thereafter in consonance with emerging economic and political order in the country. Industrial Policy helped to industrialize the country as well as generate the employment. In this context, the Report on Youth Employment-Unemployment Scenario 2012-13 published by the Labour Bureau, Ministry of Labour and

Box 2.1: Report on Youth Employment-Unemployment Scenario 2012-13

Based on the survey results, Labour Force Participation Rate (LFPR) is estimated to be 31.2, 47.3 and 39.5 per cent respectively among age groups 15-24, 18-29 and 15-29.

Worker Population Ratio (WPR) is estimated to be 25.5, 41.2 and 34.2 per cent respectively among age groups 15-24, 18-29 and 15-29.

Unemployment Rate (UR) is estimated to be 18.1, 13.0 and 13.3 per cent respectively among age groups 15-24, 18-29 and 15-29.

Based on the survey results, majority of the persons employed under the age group 15-29 years are either self employed or casual worker.

For the age group 15-29 years, 41.3 per cent employed persons are self employed followed by 34.7 per cent under casual worker category and remaining 24.0 per cent under wage/salaried employees and contract category worker classification

The survey results show that with increase in education level, the unemployment rate is also increasing for all age groups *viz.* 15-24 years, 18-29 years and 15-29 years.

Every 1 person out of 3 persons who is holding a degree in graduation and above is found to be unemployed for the age group 15-29 years.

In rural areas the unemployment rate among graduates and above for the age group 15-29 years is estimated to be 36.6 per cent whereas in urban areas the same is 26.5 per cent.

Notes:

The above figures are 'under usual principal status-UPS approach', i.e. activity status with reference period of one year-at All India level).

Labour Force Participation Rate (LFPR) signifies labour supply in the country for different age groups.

The Worker Population Ratio signifies the proportion of workers/employed persons in the total population for different age groups.

Labour Bureau, Ministry of Labour and Employment, Government of India Official website: http://www.labourbureau.nic.in/PRESS%20NOTE%20youth.pdf

Employment, Govt. of India brings out certain interesting facts about employment as mentioned in Box 2.1.

The analysis of the above survey results show that—

Majority of the persons employed under the age group 15-29 years are either self-employed or casual worker.

With increase in education level, the unemployment rate is also increasing for all age groups viz. 15-24 years, 18-29 years and 15-29 years. Every 1 person out of 3 persons who is holding a degree in graduation and above is found to be unemployed for the age group 15-29 years.

In rural areas the unemployment rate among graduates and above for the age group 15-29 years is estimated to be 36.6 per cent whereas in urban areas the same is 26.5 per cent. The unemployment rate among the persons who can't read and write any language or are considered as "not literate" as per the survey is lowest with 3.7 per cent for the age group 15-29 years at All India level.

The survey results show that with increase in education level, the unemployment rate is also increasing. These findings are alarming as they show clearly a mismatch between the graduate level educational standard and the skills sought by the employers.

Impact of Relocating Business under Globalization

Skilled/Unskilled Categorization

Globalization rests on the basic principle of free flow of goods, capital and labour across the globe. While developed nations favour free flow of goods and capital, they discourage free flow of labour. They hold the view that their nations would be flooded by the labour from poor nations. Therefore, at best they would like to allow through visa certain number of skilled/unskilled workers on temporary basis so that they can be sent back after a specific period of time and they would allow almost the same number of new workers again, so as to ensure that their country's demography does not undergo any significant change.

Global companies have started differentiating the labour force broadly in two categories namely skilled and unskilled or managers and workers. In this scenario, while companies try to retain the former by redeploying them at various locations across the world as required, the latter are employed locally and their services are dispensed with as and when their local requirement is over. Thus, categorization of labour into skilled and unskilled benefits managers more than the workers. Some would call the skilled labour as core and the unskilled as peripheral workers. This gives the employer functional elasticity. There is substantial difference in the remuneration between the two categories. The former are paid much higher remuneration than the latter.

Relocating Manufacturing

With a view of cutting the cost of labour, the developed countries are establishing their businesses in the countries where the labour is cheap. This is happening especially in the manufacturing sector. For example, the manufacturing facility is created in China to supply the product to

USA for which the design is given by USA. Though on the face of it, the company may be gainer due to cheap labour, the home country loses those many jobs to host country where the manufacturing work is located. In this situation, unskilled labour is affected most. This is what has happened to USA and now USA is trying to woo the home companies to reestablish manufacturing works in their own country.

Impact of Advancement of Technology on Employment

Unemployment of Agricultural Labour

In the process of globalization, big industries and giant projects like special economic zones are coming up in suburban area. In order to locate industries and establishment of special economic zones, big chunk of land is acquired from the agriculturists. For the farmers and labour working on farms, the agriculture is the only source of income. They possess no other skill. Therefore, once their land is taken away, they become unemployed and further marginalized. The compensation in terms of money does not benefit them in the long run as it does not make up the loss of permanent source of income which they were having earlier. Also, most of them being not educated enough, they are unable to find employment in the new situation.

In agriculture, cost of inputs has increased and the income from the produce is not in commensurate with the cost of inputs. Earlier the state strived to provide adequate subsidies to agriculture sector to make the agriculture viable. However, WTO emphasizes liberalization of the agriculture sector by putting a cap on the subsidies by the state. This is making the agriculture non-sustainable more so for the small land holders. This is resulting in reduction of agricultural labour and shift of labour from rural to urban area.

Technology and Labour Reduction

Previously all jobs were done manually, therefore the requirement of labour was high. However, with the advancement of technology and emphasis on increasing productivity, the requirement of labour has drastically come down. Computerization in all walks of life has reduced the worker requirement drastically.

In the competitive market conditions, the concept of getting maximum work out of minimum number of employees is followed. Under globalization this principle is stretched quite far. When the business is down, obviously there is reduction in the employment. but surprisingly even when the business is growing, the growth of employment does not take place in the same proportion because the employers would like to get the things done as far as possible through the same labour instead of engaging additional labour.

Interestingly, some companies reduce labour not only when they do not do well, but reduce labour even when they do well as a regular turnover measure.

Further, globalization is leading to acquisition or merger of companies, which is also causing reduction of manpower as there is always tendency to make the structure of the new organization lean.

Above conditions are leading to a phenomenon which is popularly known as 'jobless growth.' The situation of jobless growth leads to serious discontent in the society as the younger generation obviously looks for more opportunities. Therefore, a way is to be found that under any liberalization measure, there is no loss of jobs on account of introduction of technology and there is creation of more jobs as business increases.

Flexibilization of Employment

Workers in regular employment form labour union and the union takes up the cause of workers with the management through methods like collective bargaining etc. At times management finds it tough to take any disciplinary action against the workers. The unionized labour also insists for proper labour welfare measures at the work place. Managements try to avoid all these obligations by engaging the labour on contract basis or part time basis. Through this system, the management can extract more work from the labour and pay according to the discretion of the management. The engagement of labour on contract, part time or casual basis is now known as the 'flexibilization' of the employment. This type of employment has become much in vogue in globalization process.

Earlier, the progress of business used to be slow but steady, engagement of workforce was completely on regular basis and the situations of retrenchment were as far as possible avoided. In a competitive world under globalization, there is no certainty of business-sometimes business may be poised for expansion and sometimes for contraction. The employers are therefore looking for absolute flexibility for employing as well as retrenching the labour, what is called as numerical flexibility. In such a situation, the concept of flexibilization of employment has been found to be very useful for the employers and they use this method as far as possible (Ritzer, 2012: 667).

Flexi-time and Working from Home

Many of the global top companies have introduced selectively flexi-time working and working from home. The idea is that if the workers are happy and kept motivated, their productivity will increase. In flexi-time working, total working hours may remain the same but timing in and out of the working hours may vary from the normal working hours. The advantage in flexi-time working is that employee can attend to his home task as well as office work. The disadvantage is that all concerned employees may not be available at a time in the office for discussion or taking a decision.

Working from home will cut commuting from home to office and back, and thus will work out to be economic proposition. This will also avoid problems of traffic jams, stress and pollution in urban areas. However, both flexi-time working and working from home propositions suffer from the advantage of personal interaction between employees within and across departments which is possible only within normal office timings and office premises. Dispersion of work to homes will involve more quality checks, close monitoring and come in the way of building team spirit.

Presently the trend of flexi-time working and working from home is limited to multinational IT companies such as Microsoft, IBM, Dell, Cisco, Accenture etc. but the same is picking up. There is also growing trend in smaller companies wherein each employee works as office in itself. U.K.'ş new law empowers employees with a legal right to ask their employers for flexible working hours. The law of course seeks to strike a balance between needs of the families as well as maintaining competitiveness of the business in global context.

Notwithstanding increasing trend of flexi-time working and working from home, Indian managers are reluctant to adopt the system for mainly two reasons. One is that if the work in office acquires sudden urgency, manager may find difficulty to meet the urgency in absence of physical presence of employee(s). The second is that the mangers do not feel sure if the employee will be really putting his worth in the work at home, or, he might be busying himself with attending to personal work as in Indian conditions there is no end to personal works for which his presence may be required to get the work done in government or semi-government offices.

Relationship between Productivity and Employment Growth

Prosperity is created by increasing productivity. Increasing productivity means the same job will be done by less labour. The increase in productivity is achieved by introducing technology. With this background, it is widely believed that technology reduces the employment. The employers contend that this amounts to taking simplistic view. According to them, there is no doubt that the employment does get reduced in the area in which technology is introduced, but the process can also lead to capacity building which increases the employment either in this very area or some other area and thus there is overall increase in employment. Further, they contend that the saving in labour cost due to increase in productivity is useful for increasing the wages in general.

While analyzing the employment opportunities during globalization period, certain trends seem to be emerging. While there seems to be decreasing trend in regular employment, there is slight increase in self employment and much more increase in contract/casual labour. In casual labour, females are outnumbering males. This does not reflect well on globalization.

Mahatma Gandhi National Rural Employment Guarantee Act

Rural labour is mainly dependent on agriculture which is seasonal. The difficulties faced by rural labour under globalization in securing employment have been narrated above. In order to provide succor to the rural labour, Government of India passed National Rural Employment Guarantee Act (MGNREGA) in 2005 with main features mentioned in the Box 2.2.

Box 2.2: National Rural Employment Guarantee Act, 2005

An Act to provide for the enhancement of livelihood security of the households in rural areas of the country by providing at least one hundred days of guaranteed wage employment in every financial year to every household whose adult members volunteer to do unskilled manual work and for matters connected therewith or incidental thereto.

7. (1) If an applicant for employment under the Scheme is not provided such employment within fifteen days of receipt of his application seeking employment or from the date on which the employment has been sought in the case of an advance application, whichever is later, he shall be entitled to a daily unemployment allowance in accordance with this section.

Source: GoI *Website:* http://nrega.nic.in/rajaswa.pdf

The Act was later named after Mahatma Gandhi and the name of the Act became Mahatma Gandhi National Rural Employment Guarantee Act. It is popularly known by the short form MGNREGA. The step has been taken with dual purpose; one is to provide succor to agricultural labour and second, which is implied, is to prevent large scale migration of rural labour in distress. Beside the purpose mentioned, it is also intended to help undertaking development work in rural area. However, the farmers argue that due to the scheme, the availability of labour for agriculture has reduced and the wage level increased. On the whole, the Act has been found to be useful for mitigating the problem of employment, in rural area only criticism being that the muster roll of the labour is not maintained properly.

Conclusion

The statistics of employment-unemployment indicate that the unemployment is increasing in the higher educated class. This shows that there is a mismatch between the graduate level educational standard and the skills sought by the employers. With rush for the higher education likely to remain in future, the problem is likely to continue and aggravate in future. This is a matter of grave concern for the policy makers. Unlike in India, in USA there is no craze for university education and only those who are really interested in higher studies opt for joining university. The rest of the students learn skills that help them to make livelihood. In India too, a time may come when students would prefer to choose vocational courses instead of university education. Further over a period of time, there may be saturation in the jobs that require soft skill like working on computers and demand may increase for the persons having hard skill like working on shop floor of the factory.

With a view to cut the cost of production of the product, manufacturing is being located at the places where labour is cheap. Likewise, products are being produced at places where related resources like raw materials are available. There is a trend to employ only skilled or managerial positions on regular basis and the most of the unskilled labour are engaged through contract, part time or on casual basis. This process has increased the labour force working as casual workers. The engagement of on contract, part time or casual basis is now known as the 'flexibilization' of the employment

Advancement in technology like computerization etc. is reducing the labour requirement. Further, there is so much competitiveness in the product cost that greater emphasis is being placed on increasing productivity and getting the job done through the same number of workers who are already in place. Thus while there is growth in business, the employment is not increasing to that extent. This tends to result in 'jobless growth.'

The protagonists of globalization contend that if the business profit is increased by way of reduced labour cost in one area and the same is utilized for expansion or diversification of business, the net result will be overall increase in the business and consequently in employment. Thus while the critics say that globalization is leading to jobless growth, the protagonists contend that though there may be reduction of labour in one area, the globalization is leading to business expansion of scale and consequently overall increase in the employment.

The effect of globalization has been in the weakening of labour unions and their bargaining power due to hire and fire policy. Multi-national companies expect host nations to adopt industrial relations policy to allow hire and fire policy. According to them, this policy aids in increasing the productivity, expansion and diversification of the business, and consequently increases the overall employment. Thus, while this is an economic proposition, it has a social cost.

GLOBALIZATION AND POVERTY

Prologue

The discussion on the subject of poverty always begs the question as to what is the real measure of poverty. There is a raging debate on this issue. Is economic progress the real measure of poverty or there are other dimensions too which are important for measuring poverty? Another issue is spread of poverty across society, especially rural society. The remoteness of villages and their thin population have turned out to be great disadvantages for the rural society. The rural population is mainly depending upon agriculture and 80 per cent of the land holdings fall into the category of small holdings. The cultivation of these small holdings is becoming now unviable and there is widespread poverty in villages. However, protagonists of globalization contend that under globalization the overall poverty has declined, which contention is contested by the critics.

Measuring Poverty: Different Approaches

Capability Poverty Measure

The impact of globalization on poverty reduction is a subject of great interest. But measuring poverty is itself a subject of different approaches. UN Human Development Report 1996 proposes the Capability Poverty Measure (CPM) to assess the poverty comprehensively. It considers the lack of three basic capabilities. The first is the lack of being well nourished and healthy, represented in this case by the proportion of children under five years who are underweight. The second is the lack of capability for healthy reproduction, shown by the proportion of births unattended by trained personnel. The third is the lack of capability to be educated and knowledgeable, represented by female illiteracy. The composite index emphasizes deprivation of women because, says the report, "It is now well known that the deprivation of women adversely affects the human development of families and of society" (Reddy and Bhaskar, 2005: 68).

World Bank and UNDP on Poverty

The formulations of World Bank on poverty are falling broadly in two categories. One is to measure poverty on the basis of income alone. In this context, World Bank has brought out a measure of poverty as income of $2 a day and extreme poverty $1 a day or less. The other is to measure poverty on multidimensional scale which includes parameters like education, health and income. This is similar to Human Development Index which has been brought out by UNDP. While the first measure indicates simply the economic status, the second measure indicates the socio-economic status. Thus, while for simple count, the first method can be applied, for better appreciation of status in a holistic manner, socio-economic measure is preferred.

Tendulkar and Rangarajan Poverty Line

(Late) Suresh Tendulkar and Chakravarthi, Rangarajan headed committees, at different times, to arrive at the poverty line. Tendulkar was India's economist, former Chairman of the Prime Minister's Economic Advisory Council and the National Statistical Commission. Chakravarthi. Rangarajan is economist and former Governor of Reserve Bank of India.

World Bank brought out a measure of extreme poverty as income of $1 a day or less. Government of India appointed a committee headed by Tendulkar, and the poverty line adopted by Tendulkar is close to the UN and World Bank's poverty line. Applying the concept of Purchasing Power Parity (PPP), Tendulkar computed poverty line for 2004-05 as equivalent to Rs. 16 per day in India. PPP refers to a method used to work out the money that would be needed to purchase the same goods and services in two places. Across countries, this is used to calculate an implicit foreign exchange rate, the PPP rate, at which a given amount of money has the same purchasing power in different countries.

As per the Tendulkar methodology for 2011-12, the poverty line was Rs. 816 in rural areas and Rs. 1,000 in urban areas, which if calculated on a daily basis come out at Rs. 27 per day in rural areas and Rs. 33 in urban areas. Since there was lot of furor hinting obliquely that the figures of Tendulkar line are too low, Rangarajan panel was formed to review the poverty line. Rangarajan panel has suggested a poverty line as Rs. 972 a month in rural areas and Rs. 1,407 a month in urban areas in 2011-12. Calculated on a daily basis, this translates into a per capita expenditure of Rs. 32 per day in rural areas and Rs. 47 per day in urban areas in 2011-12.

The Rangarajan panel's recommendation results in an increase in the below poverty line population, which is estimated at 363 million in 2011-12, compared to the 270 million estimate based on the Tendulkar formula—an increase of almost 35 per cent.

Hunger and Malnourishment: Major Problems in India

According to the UN Millennium Development Goals report 2014, India is home to the largest number of poor with one-third of the world's 1.2 billion extreme poor living here. As regards malnourishment, there are an estimated 160 million children of ages up to 6 years in the country as per 2011 Census. Of these, about half, i.e. 80 million are attending *anganwadis* (day care centers). According to the status report on the *anganwadi* programme under ICDS, about 23 million or 28 per cent of the children who attend *anganwadis* are suffering from malnutrition and are underweight.

Against the backdrop of development being in focus under globalization, the contrasting issues namely. hunger and malnourishment have acquired special importance. While hunger refers to non-availability of quantity of food required, malnourishment refers to non-availability of type of food required for keeping oneself healthy. With the improved seeds, fertilizers etc. the quantum of food production is steadily increasing except during the years of drought. It is contented that the food produced world over is sufficient for mankind. If there is hunger, the problem is that of its proper distribution. There are occasions when the food gets rotten in warehouses or hoarded for the sake of jacking up prices.

Hunger and malnourishment are not the problems with rich, but the same are serious problems specific to poor. Further, since most of the poor live in rural area and their main occupation-agriculture becoming unviable, hunger and malnourishment are the problems more prevalent in rural area. It is an irony that on one side there is affluence and on the other side some people remain hungry either because of non-availability of food or their inability to afford buying food. There is a strong opinion that the aforementioned problems of distribution and un-affordability of poor are mainly administrative and political problems and the same are resolvable in democratic set up if there is a political will.

The hunger is also related to type of produce that is cultivated in agriculture. If agricultural production is increased with non-food items, it will not help to reduce the hunger. Due to high labour cost in developed North, it is concentrating on production of staple food in their countries and it imports non-staple food from developing South. For money sake, developing South is changing its crop pattern to suit export demand. However, this is leading to reduction of staple food in the developing South and many developing countries at times are required to import staple food from developed countries. Logically, people should be producing the food that meets the local needs and suits local environment.

Widespread Poverty in Rural Population

Though globalization has brought number of benefits to some class of people, it has not changed the lot of poor. The Socio-Economic and Caste Census (SECC) pertaining to rural India released by the Union Government on July 03, 2015 brings out that the monthly income of highest earning household member is less than Rs. 5000/- and such households constitute 74.5 per cent of the total household. Poverty brings in its wake number of social problems. Rural population suffers from many disadvantages including some natural ones. Among these are: Villages are situated in remote locations. They are not only away from towns but they are also away from one another. Isolation is their biggest problem. They are thinly populated as a result of which they do not possess organized power to influence the state to provide necessary infrastructure like proper roads, schools, electricity, drinking water etc.

Rural people lack access to basic facilities like sanitation. Most of the households do not have toilets at home and the people just defecate in the open. On the eve of the first ever UN World Toilet Day on 18th November, 2013, the World Bank reported that currently more than 2.5 billion people worldwide lack access to toilets, one billion people practice open defecation. In India alone, over 600 million people or 53 per cent of Indian households defecate in the open.

Rural people have largely agriculture as the mainstay for livelihood. Their main occupation—agriculture is vulnerable to the vagaries of nature such as draught, floods etc. The only plus point acknowledged as favourable to rural people is their proximity to nature, which gives them pollution free environment as against high degree of environmental pollution in urban area.

Agriculture being major occupation of rural people, they do more physical work compared to people in urban area where most of the people are engaged in white collar or sedentary occupations. Therefore, nutritional requirement of rural people is more compared to urban people. However, due to poverty, rural people suffer severely from malnutrition as a result of which they are more prone to all kinds of diseases.

Lack of education, health and income form a vicious circle, i.e. not only each deficiency generates ill effects of its own but also one deficiency leads to another. Deficiencies are thus compounded. It is evident that due to absence of social safety, rural people have no choices of life and they are just left to the mercy of nature.

Market Access—Problem for Rural Poor

Globalization means market economy. Market access is therefore crucial for the agriculturalists. But market places are situated in towns and road connectivity from villages is not good because roads are generally in poor condition. Therefore, access to market is extremely difficult for the villages. Most of the villages have no internet facilities as a result, agriculturists are not aware of the trend of prices of their produce. Obviously uninformed price fluctuations put agriculturists in great difficulty.

Price Fluctuations

As mentioned, the main feature of globalization is market economy in which prices of commodities depend upon their supply and demand. Since demand and supply of commodities are always fluctuating, the prices of commodities are also always fluctuating. The impact of price fluctuations in the market is more severe for the poor as they do not possess assets large enough to absorb the shocks of price fluctuations as rich can manage them. They are also not having individual storage facilities, so that, they can wait for better price. Further the impact of price fluctuations depends upon whether the commodity is of daily need of the local population. In this context farmers should be free to choose that commodity for production. Thus, if poor farmers are producing staple food, they are less likely to subjugate themselves to price fluctuations as they will purchase these items less from the market. However, in the market economy, the demand may be for some other commodity and in that case the farmer is more likely to choose that crop for the sake of money. Thus farmers are always subjected to uncertainty of market conditions.

Export of Produce

Globalization has created more demand of certain types of produce such as fruits and flowers. The farmers have to switch over to cultivate these produce to obtain market benefits. In rural area, labour is abundantly available and they can benefit by way of getting engaged in agribusiness which is expected to grow with globalized market.

In spite of availability of labour, rural people are unable to derive benefits from globalization as the benefits can be derived only when rural people are able to sell their produce to supermarkets or export to developed countries. However, supermarkets or exports require exacting standard of the produce which small farmers find it difficult to meet. Meeting such standards require more expenditure which small farmers ill afford.

Through Information Technology, information can be obtained about how to improve quality as well as productivity of the produce. But presently internet facility is scarcely available in rural area. Ways and means have therefore to be found to provide internet facility in rural area so that poor are not left behind in reaping the benefits of globalization. Unless these facilities are created in rural area, only rich people will reap the benefits.

Impact of Globalization on Poverty—Different Perceptions

There are differing claims about reduction of poverty due to globalization. Report of World Bank titled *Globalization, Growth and Poverty* states that the policies of globalization have led to poverty reduction. This is based on the premise that the trade liberalization due to globalization leads to demand for unskilled labour and the increased employment spurs economic growth. India and China are stated as examples regarding reduction of poverty. However, this contention is contested by the critics of globalization. They argue that many of the countries which have reduced tariff more than India and China found little evidence of poverty reduction (Ritzer, 2012: 425).

Some protagonists of globalization hold the most optimistic view that with globalization, not only poverty will be reduced, but even inequality between the countries as well as within the countries will also be reduced. In this context they cite the example of India and China. The critics of globalization contend that though it is correct that these countries experienced good growth in certain years, but the same has not been steady. Further, it is not certain that the growth of economy experienced by these countries is going to be sustainable in future. As regards inequality, it is generally held that the inequality is increasing and not reducing.

Fall in Poverty as per Tendulkar Poverty Line

As per Tendulkar poverty line, the economic growth in India led to poverty rate down from 37.2 per cent in 2004-05 to 21.5 per cent in 2011-12, i.e. net 15.7 per cent fall in 7 years. This is faster than the decline of 10.5 per cent that happened during the earlier decade, i.e. between 1993-94 and 2004-05. Since, rural poor accounts for major portion in the poverty of total population, Mahatma Gandhi National Rural Employment Guarantee Act 2005 (MGNREGA) and increased agricultural production seem to have contributed to faster reduction in the poverty during last 7 years.

The report of UN throws light on how India and China stand on the subject of extreme poverty. UN measures extreme poverty on the basis that those who lived on income less than $1 a day come in the category of extreme poor. According to the UN Millennium Development Goals report 2014, in India extreme poverty came down from 49.4 per cent in 1994 to 42 per cent in 2005 and 32.7 per cent in 2010. On the other hand, extreme poverty in China came down from 60 per cent in 1990 to 16 per cent in 2005 and 12 per cent in 2010.

It will be seen from the above statistics that the figures vary widely as the same depend on the income base on which the poverty or extreme poverty is measured. It will be suffice to deduce from the above that the poverty has come down in both countries and that China has done much better in the matter of poverty alleviation. In this context it is to be noted that Mahatma Gandhi National Rural Employment Guarantee Act 2005 (MGNREGA) also played crucial role in reducing poverty in rural India.

According to poverty estimates, rural India is going through faster improvement than its urban counterpart. The decline in poverty was steeper in rural area as BPL population came down to 25.8 per cent (2011-2012) from 42 per cent (2004-05), a drop of around 17 per cent, as against a drop of around 12 per cent in urban areas. The probable cause could be because there has been extreme poverty in rural area in the past and therefore any step toward improvement produces relatively better outcomes.

Homeless is another characteristic of poverty. According to Census of India, the population of India's homeless has fallen both as a proportion of the total population and in absolute terms between 2001 and 2011. Census defines homeless households as those which do not live in buildings or census houses but live in the open or roadside, on pavements, in Hume-pipes, under flyovers and staircases, or in places of worship, *mandaps*, railway platforms, etc. The fall in homelessness in urban areas recorded a growth rate of 20.5 per cent as against a decline of 28.4 per cent in rural areas. The factors which are contributing to the fall in homeless population in rural area are government support for housing to SC/ST community through various schemes and migration of homeless from rural to urban area.

Economic Growth not Always Pro-poor

The liberalization of economy has generally led to overall economic growth. But economic growth or the growth of production in quantitative terms by themselves cannot reduce poverty unless they are coupled with proper distribution of the benefits flowing from them. The distribution of growth is not an easy process because firstly beneficiaries of growth would not like to part with the wealth voluntarily and secondly they would always resist enactment of state policies that will lead to parting of their wealth.

Thus, there is no direct relationship between the growth and reduction of poverty. Though it is contended that the poor will benefit from the 'trickle down effect,' poverty reduction depends upon many factors. First and foremost is the availability of natural resources in the country and the second is how these resources are utilized and then how benefits thereof are distributed. Thus, poverty reduction requires a multidirectional approach. Establishment of institutional framework for regulating market economy and political will to ensure balanced economic growth are the most crucial factors. In this context, state can play an crucial role by way of formulating suitable policies.

The effective way to alleviate poverty is through empowerment of people, so that, they can participate in policy making. It is observed such a process helps the state in creating policies that enables the poor to have better access to basic facilities like education, healthcare etc. This shows that the poor should have a say in community and national policy making process.

Food Security for Fighting Hunger and Malnourishment

Hunger and malnourishment are the biggest problems in developing countries. As a remedy to mitigate these problems, India has embarked on ensuring food to to seventy-five per cent. of the rural population and up to fifty per cent of the urban population of the country through Food Security Act passed by the Parliament in 2013 (Box: 2.3). To implement this scheme, the total estimated annual foodgrains requirements will be 61.23 million tones and is likely to cost Rs. 1,24,724 crore. This is the largest ever food security programme undertaken by any country in the world.

Poverty does not Allow Option to Choose Life Paths

Normally poverty is related to economic deficiency because due to lack of money poor are not able to fulfill even basic necessities of life such as shelter, education, health etc. However, according to Amatya Sen, Nobel laureate, poverty denotes much more than this. According to him, poverty is unavailability of freedom to choose one or the other life paths. In order to attain such a freedom, one's capability will have to be raised. For example, illiteracy is a great impediment in making progress in life. Thus, educating people is expansion of their capability. Educated person can have many career options in life. Such a choice is not available to illiterate or less educated person. Similarly by providing basic health and sanitation facilities, one will be able to avoid illness, premature death and live normal life span. If skill of the people is upgraded, they can opt for many jobs which call for skill. This is also known as 'capability approach' to globalization enunciated by Sen. It is argued that more benefits can be achieved out of globalization process by increasing first the capability of the people before they are exposed to globalization process (Dreze and Sen, 2002: 35-36).

Box 2.3: The National Food Security Act, 2013

10th September, 2013

An Act to provide for food and nutritional security in human life cycle approach, by ensuring access to adequate quantity of quality food at affordable prices to people to live a life with dignity and for matters connected therewith or incidental thereto.

CHAPTER II

PROVISIONS FOR FOOD SECURITY

3. (1) Every person belonging to priority households shall be entitled to receive five kilograms of foodgrains per person per month at subsidised prices specified in Schedule I from the State Government under the Targeted Public Distribution System:
Provided that the households covered under Antyodaya Anna Yojana shall be entitled to thirty-five kilograms of foodgrains per household per month at the prices specified.
(2) The entitlements of the persons belonging to the eligible households at subsidised prices shall extend up to seventy-five per cent. of the rural population and up to fifty per cent. of the urban population.
4. Every pregnant woman and lactating mother shall be entitled to—
(a) meal, free of charge, during pregnancy and six months after the child birth, through the local anganwadi, so as to meet the nutritional standards specified.
(b) maternity benefit of not less than rupees six thousand.
5. (1) Every child up to the age of fourteen years shall have the following entitlements for his nutritional needs, namely:—
(a) in the case of children in the age group of six months to six years, age appropriate meal, free of charge, through the local anganwadi so as to meet the nutritional standards specified.
(b) in the case of children, up to class VIII or within the age group of six to fourteen years, whichever is applicable, one mid-day meal, free of charge, everyday, except on school holidays, in all schools run by local bodies, Government and Government aided schools, so as to meet the nutritional standards specified.
(2) Every school and anganwadi shall have facilities for cooking meals, drinking water and sanitation:
Provided that in urban areas facilities of centralised kitchens for cooking meals may be used.
6. The State Government shall, through the local anganwadi, identify and provide meals, free of charge, to children who suffer from malnutrition, so as to meet the nutritional standards specified.

CHAPTER III

FOOD SECURITY ALLOWANCE

8. In case of non-supply of the entitled quantities of foodgrains or meals to entitled persons, such persons shall be entitled to receive such food security allowance from the concerned State Government to be paid to each person.

Source: Govt. of India Website: http://indiacode.nic.in/acts-in-pdf/202013.pdf

Conclusion

There has been increase in wages and the consumption expenditure of labour and part of population has crossed over poverty line. In this context MGNREGA has played an important role. However, even according to Ragarajan (former economic advisor to Prime Minister) panel, nearly quarter of the total population is still below poverty line. In this respect, the condition of rural population is bad. Rural population suffers from many disadvantages. Among these are remoteness of villages and their thin population. These disadvantages make it difficult for them to get organized and make their voice heard at the higher levels of the state.

There is a wide difference of opinion as regards what should be the ideal measure of poverty. In this context, deprivation of the poor should not be seen only from the point of view of economic perspective but it should be seen from socio-economic point of view. Social capabilities such as education, health etc. makes tremendous difference in getting benefits of globalization.

In globalization, it is a competitive market. Only those products can be sold which are of good quality and are cost competitive. The overwhelming majority of poor depend upon agriculture. The benefits can be accrued if agriculturists are able to sell their produce to supermarkets or export to developed countries. However, supermarkets or exports require good quality of produce which small farmers are unable to meet. Meeting standards require more investment which small farmers are unable to afford. Therefore, a way has to be found to help the agriculturists to compete in the global market.

Many a times, we take a simplistic view that every problem including poverty can be alleviated by providing resources. But it is not so. Many oil rich countries which have a lot of money have not been able to make all round socio-economic progress. In many countries, a lot of money is spent on big schemes only to find at the end that the schemes are ill founded (D 10 Friedman, 2005: 564L).

The crux is that in order to eradicate poverty, capabilities of the poor are to be improved. This can be done by making available to them easy access to information and communication technology. Their empowerment through participation in the policy formulation at the national level is important. There is a general consensus that the process of globalization has reduced poverty. However, there is also a strong opinion that the inequality between nations as well as within the nations has increased due to globalization.

3
Globalization and Society/Social Organization/Rural Society

SOCIAL CHANGE

Prologue

The objective of globalization is perceived as directed more toward economic progress. The critics of globalization point out that emphasis on economic progress is resulting in ignoring the importance of the overall welfare of the society. There are contesting views about the impact of globalization on the social aspect of the society, which is broadly categorized as rural and urban.

Rural-Urban Population Distribution

Population-wise India ranks second highest in the world, just next to China. With one child policy followed by China so far, it is predicted that India will overtake China in population by 2030. Since socio-economic aspects of the society are closely related to rural-urban differentiation, it is worth-while to note the status of population statistics given in the following Table 3.1 as per the latest 2011 Census Data.

It is interesting to note from the above data that as per the latest 2011 Census Data, Rural-Urban distribution of population is 68.84 per cent and 31.16 per cent. This means still more than two-third population resides in rural area and less than one-third population resides in urban area. Therefore, as mentioned earlier, Gandhiji's statement, "India lives in villages and villages constitute the very heart of India" holds true even today. Further it can be said that the rural society largely represents Indian society.

Table 3.1: Population Data Highlights—Census 2011

(Population in crore)

	2001	*2011*	*Difference*
India	102.9	121.0	18.1
Rural	74.3	83.3	9.0
Urban	28.6	37.7	9.1

- For the first time since Independence, the absolute increase in population is more in urban areas that in rural areas.
- Rural-Urban distribution: 68.84 per cent and 31.16 per cent.
- Level of urbanization increased from 27.81 per cent in 2001 Census to 31.16 per cent in 2011 Census.
- The proportion of rural population declined from 72.19 per cent to 68.84 per cent or say 69 per cent of the total population.

Source: Census of India 2011.

Social Change under Globalization

There is good amount of literature dealing with various facets of Indian society. Many sociologists in their interactive sessions, articles, research papers, books have discussed the subject of social change in India. The peculiarity of India is its diversity in terms of language, religion and geographical location, i.e. urban and rural. This diversity together with down the line caste and creed has resulted in stratification of Indian society. The process of change in the society has therefore been very slow.

When society strives for development, new challenges are faced by the society. In the process, structural changes take place in order to deal with systemic challenges. Occurrence of social change along with forming new structure is thus a normal feature of the society. As economic aspect has definite impact on social aspects, the process of globalization has impacted Indian society greatly. The process of globalization in India started with the policy of liberalization adopted by the state in 1991. It is seen that the rate of change in the social aspect taking place since then is much more than it used to be in the past. It has to be acknowledged that the impact of growing interconnectedness and interdependence under globalization is leading to profound changes in the social aspect of the society. While the pre-modern societies had natural feelings toward each other, in modern societies it is rationality that matters.

Caste System in India

Caste system existing in India has distinction of being unique in India. How did it come into being? As societies evolved, their social structure was also evolved in response to the requirements of their times for survival as well as development. Since survival and development are intimately connected with the occupations, the social structure has intimate relationship with the occupations. It is in response to this relationship that social structure of Hindu society has been based on caste system as a lineage of the four *varnas* namely *Brahmin, Kshatriya, Vaishya* and *Shudra.* The four *varnas* as described in the *Vedas* represent division of labour at macro level. The castes and sub-castes represent divisions related to occupations at micro level. It is said that in India about 3,000 castes and 25,000 sub-castes exist. Every person becomes a member of the caste by birth and thus caste, marriage and other customs are highly interrelated.

Some people believe that originally the concept was that there was nothing like upper caste or lower caste and it denoted only division of work. This means everybody will have the same social standing. If it was so, such a concept could have worked well. However, from the time unknown, people with vested interests started differentiating social standing on the basis of caste. Obviously, such a system was bound to become repugnant to the common sense.

There are different opinions as regards utility of the caste system. Some people contend that Indian culture withstood undue influence of other cultures only because there was rigid social structure in the form of castes in place. Also any number of invasions could not break the wall of castes. However, vast majority of people contend that caste system came in the way of nation's progress and India could have developed better had there been no caste system.

Caste system is deeply ingrained in Indian Society. In rural India where vast majority of people live, the practice of untouchability has gone, but otherwise there is a marginal change in the caste system. The natural tendency of the local people is to continue and promote the social order they are used to, the reason being they are familiar with it for a long time. They feel the process of globalization is trying to change that social order and therefore, for those who are privileged, the globalization is not a welcome process. However, over a period of time there has been attempt in one caste to adopt some good features of the other caste, which has been referred as a process of *Sanskritisation.*

The process of globalization is bringing in high degree of interconnectedness between people all over the globe. With the migration of large number of people from rural to urban area for employment, wherein caste distinctions do not matter, the hold of caste is weakening. Therefore, though caste system may have a sway in rural population, it has much less significance in urban population. Rather with the quickening of the pace of globalization, there is likely to be steady dilution of the caste system even in rural population.

As globalization is leading to dilution of caste system, reciprocally caste system has also effect on the process of globalization. The development of agriculture even during the worst times has been due to the contribution of a class of labour who were actually doing the physical and strenuous work. They were mostly drawn from the castes that did not have any financial assets or social standing. Today, India is not only self sufficient in food but it is also exporting food, the credit for which should go to the agricultural labour. However, this should not be interpreted as justifying the caste system because the agricultural labour has always got the raw deal compared to the privileges enjoyed by other classes without doing strenuous physical work.

Joint Family System

Just as Hindu society is synonymous with caste system, joint family system is another peculiarity of Indian society. Its origin and strength could be attributed to agriculture as the predominant occupation so far. Joint family system provided much needed continuity of managing the agriculture as a profession. However, as industrialization started, the youth in rural area saw it as an opportunity for improving their living conditions. This has translated into migration of youth in steady and large number to urban area, resulting in weakening of the joint family system. In rural area, the joint family system is still there but in urban area, there is increase in nuclear family system. Thus, joint family system which was peculiarity of Indian society so far has weakened.

The change in the family system has impacted the living of old people badly. They were feeling quite comfortable in the joint family system. In a way, Indian society is now slowly moving to the system prevalent in developed countries. The dilution of caste system and joint family system are major changes in the Indian society under globalization.

Influence of Media

Media has become part of social system. Though use of TV and cell phone is common in urban area, it is increasing in rural area also. Through media, rural people are exposed to social system outside their familiarity. This has potential to create new attitude. Women's participation in the spheres of activity which were being done earlier exclusively by men, is bound to change the attitude of men toward females. Girls education which was neglected area earlier is getting due attention now.

Social Impact of Panchayati Raj

Gram Sabha and Gram Panchayat at village level have brought in certain social change in rural society. There is a provision of reservation in these institutions for women as well as Scheduled Castes and Scheduled Tribes. The empowerment of women and marginalized sections of the society have brought a sense of their participation in the governance as well as improved their social standing.

Perceived Downside of Globalization

Rural population suffers from some distinct disadvantages. Firstly, they are thinly populated. Secondly, they are remotely located. Because of these reasons, they are not organized and thus they have no bargaining power in securing development priority from the state. In these circumstances, development in rural area suffers. The rural area lacks basic infrastructure like proper roads, access to markets, regular availability of water, electricity, proper education and health services. The sanitation facilities are extremely poor.

Occupation-wise there is no diversity, agriculture being the only mainstay. In agriculture, only a small percentage of villagers is having irrigation facility. Due to ever increasing costs of inputs and inadequate prices for the produce, cultivation of agriculture is becoming unviable. Because of financial constraints, there is no range of choices available for the rural people in matters of lifestyle as they are available for the urban population under globalization.

World Bank's Structural Adjustment Programme

The structural adjustment programme created by the International

Monetary Fund and World Bank for advancing loans to developing countries consisted of conditions which exerted pressure on the economies of the developing countries to become more market oriented. The emphasis has been on growth of economy and less spending on social sector that includes education, health, rural development etc. In propping up exports and repayment of loan with interest on borrowing from World Bank/IMF, financial constraints further reduce the state's capacity to spend on social sector. Thus, rural poor are the worst hit. Stung by the criticism, IMF and WB have started insisting the borrowing countries to submit specific plan for reduction of poverty when they apply for the loans.

Uncertainty of Market Condition

Rural people face major problem due to uncertainty of market condition. Market economy under globalization brings in its wake wide fluctuations in the prices of commodities, which depend upon demand and supply position. To some extent the poor may get reconciled to live on meager income. But, they suffer more from the vulnerability to wide fluctuations in commodity prices because they have no capacity to cope with them.

Shifting of Rural Population

Globalization is bringing qualitative change in the rural societies. Shifting of rural population to cities is not only leading to urbanization on a big scale, but in the process it tends to disturb the family ties in the rural societies.

It is generally observed that whenever new industry is set up, villages only get uprooted, never towns or cities. Establishment of industries results in displacement of large number of people, who are mostly poor and belonging to backward classes, and their plight after displacement becomes worse. The compensation paid for acquisition of their houses and land is always paltry taking into account high cost of livelihood, and once the land is gone they lose the only traditional occupation inherited from generations past. However, lately the state has increased the compensation for acquisition of land. But even then, it does not fully compensate for loss of asset which has been a permanent source of income.

Diet Changes

The large scale diet changes are discernible under globalization and its influence is found in Indian society too. In US, faster way of life has influenced the type of diet which is called fast food. It contains more fat and less fiber. It is also called junk food as it is generally prepared in advance and stored for some time. This type of food either does not have nutrients or if it has any, its nutritional value is destroyed by the way it is processed. Due to additives, it tends to taste well but it is not found to be good for the health.

Due to adoption of diet with high content of fat and no physical work, people are suffering from obesity, diabetes, heart problems and several other diseases. Unfortunately, this type of diet is caught up with popularity not only in developed countries but also catching up in developing country like India. This type of diet has become more popular especially with younger generation and office going people.

Another feature of diet change is that vegetables and fruits are steadily becoming part of the diet which earlier used to be wholly staple.

Child Labour

Child labour is quite rampant especially in rural area as parents seek their help in their occupations particularly in agriculture. Thus, instead of learning education in school and enjoying childhood, many children have to do jobs meant for adults. Critics of globalization contend that globalization which seeks cheap labour works as an incentive to enlargement of child labour. However, proponents of globalization contend that abject poverty is actually breeding child labour and improvement in economic condition, as an outcome of globalization, will wean away children from working as labour and promote them to take to education (D 19 Bhagwati, 2004: 90).

Globalization's Reach not Uniform

By the word globalization, one may assume that it would cover the entire world. However, it is seen that globalized business activities are confined to certain areas only and others are left behind. For example, there is much less penetration of globalization in rural area.

The critics of the globalization argue that globalization stands for big businesses and these are swallowing the small businesses. In the process, communities undertaking small businesses are getting affected adversely. Under globalization, there is more emphasis on facilitating manufacturing and services sectors as against agriculture. Developing countries are asked to reduce the subsidies in agriculture, thus affecting rural occupation adversely.

Disparity causing Resentment

Due to long sufferance and finding little change in their condition of life, poor people tend to carry resentment against those who are in power as well as who are rich. It is difficult to make a distinction between the two. It is quite possible that their resentment against those in power may be a manifestation of their resentment against the rich or *vice-versa*. Further, rich people get their place easily in state power and similarly many of those who are in state power get rich quickly. Against this background, poor are always skeptic about the state policies which are framed by those who are generally rich and in power.

Economists in general would like the participation of all people in the economic growth. Hardliner economists, however, argue that primacy should be given to economic progress and spending more on the social sector affects the economic progress of the country negatively. However, anthropologists have a different view about the progress. According to them, importance of social sector which include education, health, rural development etc. cannot be ignored. They are not so much enamored by sheer economic progress advocated by the protagonists of globalization. In this situation, what seems to be rational is adopting balanced approach toward both, minimizing the economic costs of meeting the social objectives.

Besides above mentioned points of downside of globalization, the critics of globalization highlight that globalization is leading to levelling down labour wages, jobless growth, lower priority to social welfare measures, encouraging consumerism, disturbing ecological balance and weakening of the authority of nation-state.

Perceived Positive Impact of Globalization on Society

Indian society has been recognized as typically tradition based. It is only after liberalization policy adopted in 1991 that it has been exposed to globalization in a large measure. The protagonists of globalization contend that the globalization plays greater role than generally perceived. According to them it is a necessity to integrate the local economy with national economy and national economy with the global economy; the consequences of the left out societies could be disastrous; the fully protected economy means closed society and such a society could become a place of extreme poverty. According to them, extreme poverty would generate animosity and therefore a secluded society poses a liability to other societies as many of their members will be prone to developing hatred toward other societies resulting at times in violence.

Globalization through the process of interconnectedness brings about integration of diverse societies together and thus it is supposed to reduce the enmity between the nations. Globalization prospers better in functional democracies and no two functional democracies are expected to go to war with each other. In the case of China, though it is not a democracy, it is still wedded to globalization.

Division of Labour

Division of labour is being interpreted in two different ways. While economic activities based on the principle of division of labour as expounded initially by Adam Smith increases productivity, according to Marx, it does not go down well with the interests of the workers. According to Adam Smith, if manufacturing of a product is broken down to number of specialized activities and these are carried out by workers each one separately dedicated to each of the activities, the product will be manufactured efficiently. The car manufacturing is one such example. On the other hand, if all activities are carried out by a single worker, manufacturing the product will take a long time. While Karl Marx admitted that the division of labour increases productivity, workers in the capitalist system become machine minders and get alienated from the satisfaction that they should get for accomplishing the job. In short, workers become robots (Ritzer, 2012: 453-54).

Some sociologists contend that in the division of labour under globalization, matters like whether the job is skilled or unskilled or the level of skill is determined subjectively. This can become discriminatory and work with gender or racial bias. For example, companies make out that women are better at doing secretariat jobs and men are better at doing managerial jobs. This distinction works against women and in favour of men. It follows that females are paid less than their male counterparts even though both may be doing the same job. Thus, in the division of labour, persons are segregated not on the basis of their actual abilities, but on the basis of their perceived abilities. Such segregation leads to one set of people being at advantage and the other set of people being at disadvantage (Ritzer, 2012: 454-55).

Industrialization started first in the North America, Europe and Japan in the nineteenth century and the countries in the South provided raw materials to them. However, the advancement of information and communication technology has changed from the earlier division of labour based on locating industrial production in developed countries and supply of raw material from underdeveloped countries to a new division of labour that allows locating manufacturing activity anywhere in the world where the labour is available cheaply. With the help of information technology, multinational companies with their headquarters located at any place can now manage their operations which may be spread anywhere in the world.

Rise of Middle Class

Earlier there were few who were economically well off and most of the people were in poor condition. During last two decades, there has been reduction in poverty and rise in middle class. The rise of middle class is corroborated by the increasing consumption of consumer goods like automobiles, TVs, cell phones etc. Along with economic progress, there has been progress on the social front too such as improvement in literacy, health services etc. More and more people are now participating in the political process. The protagonists of globalization attribute this rise to the process of globalization.

Middle class denotes not only enhancement of economic progress but also a mindset that they can attain better standard of living and enhancement in social status. Thus, the protagonists of globalization attribute the entry of large population of Brazil, Russia, India, and China in middle class to the process of globalization.

It is interesting to analyze the rise of middle class and its impact on the rural poor. The middle class is a class of people who fall socio-economically in the middle of a societal hierarchy, i.e. between upper class and the labour (working) class. Historically, this class was seen as positioned between nobility and peasantry. Economically, as against the labour class who earn wages just enough to sustain living, the income of a middle class person has about quarter of his income which he can use for discretionary purpose also. The middle class consists of people who are educated, academicians; professionals like engineers, doctors, chartered accountants, lawyers; managers, white collar civil servants etc. Rather than spending time only on life subsisting activities, they generally participate in socio-cultural activities of the society. The upsurge of middle class has been a driving factor in French Revolution.

People are constantly migrating from rural area abandoning marginal farming and taking up remunerative jobs in factories or services sector and earn good amount of money. The globalization has given fillip to this process. Thus, middle class is growing now faster than ever and it is estimated that they constitute about 40 to 50 per cent of the global population.

Among the developing countries, China is leading in the growth of middle class followed by India. The criteria for a person to fall in this class depend upon the income and the purchasing power of the people, which vary widely from one country to another. However, in India, assuming that a person falls in middle class if his earning is between say Rs. 2 lakh to Rs. 10 lakh a year, it is estimated that, presently middle class constitutes about 25 to 30 per cent of the total population.

Though earlier middle class did not seem to look beyond the job and family concerns, of late it is showing lot more expectations from the government and gradually it is shaping as a pressure group having greater influence in electing the ruling political formation and formulation of state policy matters. Since the middle class is largely situated in towns and cities, the state is always under pressure to spend more on providing amenities in towns and cities, resulting in less attention to problems of rural population. The rise of assertive middle class is therefore likely to affect the lives of rural poor adversely.

Conclusion

It will be simplistic to assume that globalization comprises only economic aspect. Due to close interconnectivity, globalization touches every aspect of life including socio-cultural aspect of the society.

The reach of the globalization is not uniform. From economic perspective, it has bypassed rural area and the extreme poor in the sense that they have benefited only marginally from the process of globalization. It is having impact on traditional values at the local level, diluting to some extent caste and joint family systems.

The critics of globalization contend that it is leading to levelling down of labour wages, jobless growth, lower priority to social welfare measures, encouraging consumerism, disturbing ecological balance and weakening of the authority of the nation-state. Big businesses are displacing community (small) businesses. In the process of development, many people got displaced and their life has become miserable because their only age-old livelihood has been snatched. The vulnerability of the poor to economic slowdown has increased.

There is a definite increase in the middle class which suggests that some of the lower income group people have benefited from globalization enabling them to move up the economic ladder. The advancement in information and communication technology has brought in definite change in the concept of division of labour. Manufacturing and IT services which were largely concentrated earlier in developed countries shifted to developing countries where labour is cheap.

Concluding, social and economic aspects of society are intertwined and globalization is influencing both. Though, condition of the poor has improved to some extent, those who are left behind especially unemployed or underemployed feel the pinch of globalization severely on account of steep rise in the cost of living. One of the positive impacts of globalization is that through the process of interconnectedness it has brought about integration of diverse societies and this process is expected to reduce the chances of serous conflicts between different societies.

AGRARIAN POSITION: LARGEST LIVELIHOOD PROVIDER IN INDIA

Prologue

In India, agriculture has acquired unique position as even now it is livelihood of about 60 per cent of India's population. Agriculture is production of food and fiber, and management of land resource. The socio-historians put agriculture on the high pedestal stating that the quality of land determined the strength of civilizations.

Historians held that especially river adjoining land laid the foundations for major civilizations. The examples are Indus or Nile rivers. The analysis is based on the premise that the major civilizations were originated from the places of agricultural fertile land along the river bed. Here, the constant renewal of the nutrients of soil along the rivers provided special advantage in terms of production of food which acted as a basic and important resource for livelihood and rise of the civilizations. This brings into focus the social importance accorded to agriculture from the immemorial times (Solbrig, Paarlberg, and Castri, 2001: 302).

Broadly economy is divided into three sectors namely agriculture, industry, and services. Earlier agriculture was overwhelmingly dominating the economy. Subsequently with industrialization, industry occupied major share of the economy and agriculture lost its position. Under globalization, services sector occupied the centre stage with first position, shifting industry and agriculture to second and third places respectively. These shifts are reflected in Table 3.2 below.

Table 3.2: Per cent share of each sector in Labour/GDP in 1970, 2000 and 2013
Year-wise per cent share of Labour/GDP

Sector Year % share of	*1970 Labour/GDP*	*2000 Labour/GDP*	*2013 Labour/GDP*
Agriculture	*74 / 48	60 / 28	47 / 14
Industry	11 / 20	16 / 25	22 / 26
Services	15 / 32	24 / 47	31 / 60
Total	100 / 100	100 / 100	100 / 100

* *Explanation*: 74/48 indicate labour in agriculture sector is 74 per cent of the total labour in all the three sectors and the share of agriculture in GDP is 48 per cent. Similarly read other figures.

Source: Karalay, 2005: 210; *ToI* 11.07.2014; World Bank Report.

It will be seen from Table 3.2 that while the share of agriculture in GDP has gone down abruptly, that of industry remained almost constant and that of services has gone up by leaps and bounds. However, the wok-force engaged in agriculture is still much more than industry and services. This indicates that the work-force engaged in industry and services which are much smaller than agriculture are associated with huge amount of product value and in turn reaping high benefits. This does not augur well from the view point of overall perspective as it has increased income disparities between the sectors to a high level. In this context, the role of government for improving infrastructure in rural area, offering more subsidies to farming and increasing the Minimum Support Prices of the agricultural produce becomes important.

Since agriculture produces basic necessities of life such as food and fibre, there is a strong opinion that the agriculture which occupied priority at one point of time deserves better attention in terms of policy formulation as well as budget outlay. The second aspect is that under globalization, though agriculture has been insulated from WTO's uniform policies so far, there is a tremendous pressure from developed nations to make agriculture to fall in line as is happening to industrial sector. The third aspect is shift of agriculture from producing staple food to agribusiness which includes fruits, horticulture etc. The fourth factor is shift from using conventional seeds to genetically modified seeds for enhancing production. We will discuss here how these changes under globalization are affecting agriculture which is the mainstay of two-third of Indian population.

Impact of Changing Food Habits/Agribusiness/Monoculture

In past, there was little awareness about the influence of food especially nutrition on health. However, now people are generally very conscious of their health. In this context, both factors, i.e. type of food as well as quality of food have become important. In the age of internet, people seek full information about the product before they choose it, especially about the product related to health. Therefore, agriculturists will have to adopt methods of production in commensurate with latest requirements of the consumers and they will also have to convince the consumers about the process adopted and quality of products they produce. This is a new dimension for the agriculture and challenge before the farmers in modern times.

Atkinson's Diet: Revolution in Diet

Robert Coleman Atkins (October 17, 1930—April 17, 2003) was an American physician and cardiologist, best known for the "Atkins Nutritional Approach", or "Atkins Diet." The Atkins diet caught attention of the people around the globe and many people started changing their traditional food habits to suggested diet regime. The Atkins diet, officially called the Atkins Nutritional Approach, is a low-carbohydrate diet advocated by Atkins in his research paper in 1972. This diet among other low-carbohydrate food items includes salad, fruits and vegetables. Atkins stated that he used the study to resolve his overweight condition. Though many differ with the contention of Atkins, the popularity of Atkins diet can be gauged from the fact that it has greatly impacted the type of food demand globally and consequently also impacted food producing agriculture sector. Atkinson diet is one example which shows how under globalization research in the subject by one individual can effect far reaching changes in the traditional consumption and production of food globally.

Outsourcing Agriculture by North to South

During colonial period, colonial powers outsourced some of the food commodities to the colonies. History is replete with examples of imports of food even from those countries which faced food famine conditions. When India was under British rule, India was exporting foodgrains to Britain in nineteenth century even as India was facing famine. These situations cannot be termed as normal. The compelling factors for such a situation seem to be clearly extraneous as the issue of firstly sustaining the country's population is definitely ignored over in the process.

Developed countries are trying to maintain intensive cultivation of traditional food crops in their countries, and they are outsourcing non-traditional items from developing countries. With increasing cost of producing agricultural produce in developed countries, the process of outsourcing agriculture to developing countries is gaining more momentum. In order to obviate the adverse effect of outsourcing commodities, developed countries are providing suitable compensation to agriculturists in their home countries. Developing countries are accepting the move in order to get the price and the foreign exchange.

Rise of Global Agribusiness

Just as Marx saw new relations of production in industry between capitalists and labour, new relations of production is emerging in agriculture under globalization. Due to global interconnectedness, there is impact of global market on the agriculture. At some places, local and more traditional farms are giving way to factory farms; local and more traditional agricultural products are giving way to agribusiness which is promoted by global North. Global corporations are entering into the agricultural field and there is a trend to establish factory farms. Also new relations are emerging between corporations and local farms, i.e. corporations are promoting local farms to be dedicated to cultivation of particular products as required by the corporations. In such cases local farms are working as captive farms for corporations, though ownership lies solely with the local farmer. In this arrangement, farmers are required to produce particular product only.

The fostering of agribusiness by global North to South is projected as working with comparative advantage to global South as labour is cheap. In this case global North can concentrate on doing capital-intensive agriculture of staple products. In this scenario, global South is expected to export agri-products to global North and the demand of global South of staple products is supposed to be met, if need be, by way of import from the global North. In this case, the import is supposed to be at cheaper price. However, the import of staples by South faces two difficulties. One is availability of staple products in the global market and the other is the price. The fluctuations in the availability and pricing in the global market are fraught with uncertainty and involve a factor of dependency on the North. Further, due to requirement of capital, the replacement of traditional farming of staple products by agribusiness is leading to forcing out farmers from their own farms to work as agricultural labour on some others' farms.

Agribusiness/Moving Toward Monoculture

Under globalization, new terms are coming in vogue in respect of agriculture. Traditional mode of agriculture refers to cultivation of products, i.e. though mainly local staples, but also includes other products. This represents genetic diversity. Agribusiness refers to products such as horticultural produce like special fruits, vegetables, flowers, or ornamental plants; food/fruit processing; aquaculture, i.e. cultivation of fishes; production of special commodities such as livestock and feedstuff.

The traditional mode of agriculture in global South has been production of staple food and mixed variety. As against this, the global North fosters agribusiness in global South, thus loosing genetic diversity in the global South. Fostering agribusiness in global South leads to changeover to items oriented toward export of non-traditional agriculture related products. The critics of globalization contend that agribusiness leads to adopting monoculture in the global South. The monoculture is meant as growth of a single variety of crop, as against the mix of local staples and other traditional products leading to genetic diversity.

Global North is working on the model according to which their own farm sector will be left undisturbed of any change from the traditional products. On the other hand the global South will have to shift from agriculture of traditional products to agribusiness of non-traditional exports. Agribusiness products require costly inputs which are beyond the reach of small landholders.

The change from traditional products to agribusiness is viewed as bad as well as good in the sense that this offers option to agriculturists in global South (D 02 Ritzer, 2007: 216-17). The argument in favour of good is that the traditional agriculture involves producing mostly staple food crops. By increasing the productivity which is presently low, the production will increase. Once the need for certain level of production of staple food is met, whatever surplus area becomes available on account of increase in productivity, it can be used for undertaking agricultural diversification or agribusiness rather than overproducing traditional staple food crops.

Land and Water as Resource

Land Holdings

India has a large land mass, though not as large as of China or USA, but surely more than that of most of the European countries. Prior to Independence of India, there were large land holdings, but British rulers did not venture to bring in land reforms because they did not want to displease big landlords. It is only after Independence that the land ceiling act was brought, which put limits to the land holdings. Further to these limits, land holdings are getting fragmented due to divisions in the family from generation to generation. In the process small holdings have become 80 per cent of the total holdings. Fragmentation of land is resulting in low use of mechanization in agriculture leading to operations in agriculture such as tilling, sowing, harvesting etc. still being done, at least partially, manually with bullocks and labour. In developed countries as the farms are large, most of the agricultural operations are done mechanically.

Though land reforms were intended to benefit the poor, in actual practice this did not happen in all cases. The land declared by the rich as extra to the ceiling has always been observed to be barren or low grade. When the poor people started tilling this land, they found that the cultivation of this land is cumbersome. Only consolation for the poor seems to be that the land gave them a feeling of belongingness.

It is generally believed that bigger farms are better because they would help in reaping maximum benefits from mechanization and that the smaller farms are unviable. This is based on the premise that higher the size of the farm, more mechanization is possible. However, this cannot be generalized because it is also observed that smallholders of land use whatever resources they have (land, labour, money or other inputs) more efficiently, as they ill afford to squander their limited resources.

Land Acquisition for Industries

For setting up their industries, industrialists prefer land near cities/towns from the point of view of availability of infrastructure and easiness in marketing their products. This land is invariably agricultural and often fertile. There is irresistible pressure to give away such agricultural land to industries. The land which is away from cities/towns is not preferred because conditions there are in hospitable. Agriculturists thus lose their precious permanent source of livelihood. Moreover, the compensation paid for the land acquisition is quite meagre. It is only in 2014 that the problem of agriculturists for fair compensation was addressed through enactment of a law.

The salient features of new Land Acquisition Law (2014) are given in the Box. 3.1

Commenting on the new Land Acquisition Law, the industry has expressed serious concern that all economic development will come to a standstill. However, the protagonists of the law say that this view is unsubstantiated. On the project cost front, the protagonists of the law say

Box 3.1: Land Acquisition Law (2014)

The new law enacting 'The Right to Fair Compensation and Transparency in Land Acquisition, Rehabilitation and Resettlement Act' comes into force on January 1, 2014 replacing a 120-year-old British-era Act of 1894. The law provides for fair compensation to owners whose land is taken over, brings transparency to the process and lays down measures for rehabilitation of those displaced.

The law is brought as the archaic Act of 1894 suffered from various shortcomings. It is meant to bring transparency to the process of acquisition of land, generous compensation and resettlement and rehabilitation of those displaced by acquisition of land.

It will apply to all special economic zones to be set up from now.

It stipulates mandatory consent of at least 70 per cent of landowners for acquiring land for public private partnership (PPP) projects and 80 per cent for private firms.

It provides for compensation of up to four times the market value of land in rural and two times the value in urban areas.

It envisages compensation also to those who will lose their livelihoods from any land acquisition,

It provides for 20 per cent of developed land in a project to be returned to land owners.

The process of obtaining consent shall be carried out along with the Social Impact Assessment (SIA) study.

R&R is mandatory even for privately negotiated land purchases exceeding 50 acres in urban and 100 acres in rural areas. It has the provision that the companies can lease the land instead of purchasing it.

The law has a retrospective clause which will apply in three circumstances under the old Act: (i) where land acquisition proceedings has started and the award has not been announced; (ii) The award has been announced for the acquired land 5 years ago but its physical possession has not taken place; (iii) land acquisition proceedings have started 5 years ago but a majority of the farmers have not been paid the compensation.

To implement the law, states have to set up at least six bodies, including the R&R authority to hear disputes arising out of projects where land acquisition is initiated, social impact assessment unit, the office of the commissioner R&R, and monitoring committee.

that the land cost is not more than 5 per cent of the total cost of the project, and while the financial cost will go up, the social cost will come down.

Subsequently ordinance amending the above law has been issued which seeks to waive the "consent clause"—the requirement to secure specific consent of 70 per cent–80 per cent of land owners—if acquisitions are meant for defence and defence production, rural infrastructure including electrification, housing for poor, industrial corridors and infrastructure projects including projects under PPP mode where ownership of land continues to be vested with the government. Multi-crop land can also be acquired for such purposes. Such acquisitions will also be exempt from social impact assessment and application of the Food Security Act (*ToI* 30.12.2014). However, this as well as subsequent Ordinances on the subject lapsed as no parliamentary consensus could be reached on the changes proposed and as such Land Acquisition Law (2014) as already passed remains in force.

There is no doubt that the compensation for the land acquisition so far has been pathetic. History is replete with numerous farmers' movements against the acquisition of the land, which has been the only source of their income for generations. The worst effect has been the birth and rise of Naxalite movement in India, which entailed violence in many cases.

As regards difficulties involved during the land acquisition, only time will tell the actual impact of the provisions of the law on the delay in the execution of the projects particularly in the context of uncertain role of civil society in democratic country like India. In authoritarian country like China, the project development goes unhindered. However, bulldozing land acquisition just for the sake of setting up industries should not happen at the cost of land owners as land is the only permanent resource for their livelihood.

Water Use Efficiency (WUE)

On one hand, as the population is increasing, the requirement of food is increasing, but on the other hand, the area of agriculture is reducing. The problem arising from the requirement of increased production and availability of reduced area for agriculture can be solved only by increasing productivity.

Since 60 per cent of all foodgrains and oil seeds are being grown in the Kharif season (June-September) in the country where only 40 per cent of arable area is irrigated, Indian agriculture continues to depend on good monsoon. The agricultural output thus varies directly as per the optimality of monsoon. In 2014 there was a deficiency of around 12 per cent rain which reduced agricultural production substantially. It is believed that the monsoon is affected by the presence of El Nino effect in the region. El Nino is a weather phenomenon that occurs when the Pacific Ocean heats up abnormally and is usually associated with deficient rainfall in India.

While water is essential for crops, flooding or excessive pumping also creates problems like erosion of soil and increased salinity. Similarly, wind also causes erosion of soil. These cause reduction in nutrients and fertility, and consequently reduction in productivity.

Depletion of groundwater takes place due to intensive cultivation and reaping multiple crops. Poor quality land also increases requirement of groundwater. Due to depletion of water table below ground, the availability of water for irrigation is a major problem. This underscores the importance of water use efficiency (WUE). Use of irrigation sources during nights reduces evaporation losses because of less exposure of water to temperature which is high during the day time. Similarly use of piped water, sprinklers and drip irrigation reduce wastage of water and erosion of soil.

Use of Technology in Agriculture

Biotechnology/GM Seeds

Sometimes agriculturists claim that their traditional knowledge of agriculture is good enough to do agriculture. However, there is no point in sticking to old ways of doing agriculture when it is known that it is not helping to get good productivity. There is a need to take advantage of the knowledge from agriculture extension services, media, and knowledge coming from new researches in the field.

Japan is one of the most developed countries. With scarcity of land and more population to feed, this country has been in the forefront in using genetic engineering to improve its agricultural production.

After fertility of land, quality of seed plays important role in productivity. Earlier farmers were meeting seed requirement by way reproduction by themselves. With the advent of globalization/WTO, a change is taking place in the ownership of seeds. Multinational companies who can genetically modify the seeds and patent them claim Intellectual Property Rights and thus they are becoming monopolies. GM seeds no doubt increase productivity but GM seeds are pretty costly. Further, GM seeds once used cannot be reproduced by farmers for use next time. Farmers have to purchase new seeds every year.

Genetically Modified Food

Genetically modified food crop involves a process of transfer of genes from an organism belonging to one species of a taxonomic group to the food crop that belongs to a species of another taxonomic group. GM food is a food which contains ingredients made from GM plants, animals or micro-organisms, or food produced from GM seeds. Plant species, animal species or a bacterium can be the source of genes. It is scientifically held that foreign genes implanted into crop plant develops a property of enhancing yield, produces toxins that enable the plant to resist the diseases and pest attacks (Ritzer, 2012: 766).

Roundup Ready Soybeans (RRS) are being used in Argentina. But in India, only non-food crops such as cotton are allowed to use GM seed such as Bt cotton, a transgenic crop. So far, Food crop is not allowed to be grown from GM seed in India as it is adopting cautious approach toward adopting GM technology as far as food items are concerned.

In India, GM seed is coming for criticism on two major counts. One is that the seed is much costlier than the conventional and the other is that the farmer is unable to harvest the seed for the next crop. He has to perforce purchase new seed. As regards use of GM technology for food crops, though Bt corn (crop in which a gene from a bacterium called Bacillus thureingensis Bt is implanted) is being produced in some parts of the world and China developed transgenic rice, in India even the trial of GM technology for food crop has not been allowed so far. In this regard, reservations in India are on the same lines as those of European countries. (46 Ritzer, 2012: 768). Earlier, the technical expert committee (TEC) set up by the Apex Court suggested an indefinite moratorium on field trials unless strict regulatory mechanism is put in place.

It is argued that since there is little scope of area expansion for agriculture and on the other hand the burden on land is bound to increase, the use of GM crops is essential to meet the growing demand of food-grains, fruits and vegetables in the country at the time. The government therefore contends that the field trials be allowed in the first place. Finally after protracted debate, on 27.02.2014 the Union Environment Ministry has given a go ahead to the field trials of Genetically Modified (GM) food crops including wheat, maize and rice. The field trials will however be done only after the concerned state agrees for the same. Earlier around half of the Indian states have rejected the GM companies' bid to get field trials done. The field trial will be conducted in the earmarked field ensuring that the GM crop is not mixed with non-GM crops.

Later on, field trials of contentious mustard and brinjal have also been allowed. The critics of the field trials of Bt brinjal are opposing the decision of the government to allow field trials. They point out that earlier the process of allowing Bt brinjal was halted because the scientific community held that our biosafety (prevention of risks associated with biotechnology processes) competence has not improved. They argue that the field trials are being allowed in spite of the fact that there is no change in the biosafety competence since then.

Further to research in genetic engineering, there is also a move to adopt a process of transfer of genes from one variety to another within a specie or within a primary gene pool of a crop. Before resorting to genetic engineering, genes in the primary gene pool of a crop have to be explored fully to improve crops and specific traits within a crop (Ritzer, 2012: 768).

Technology in Agriculture

It is well known that irrigation used for crops gives rise to faster growth of weeds. On the other hand, regular weed removal substantially economizes the use of water. Manual weed removal is a laborious and costly process. Presently various types of herbicides have come up to remove the weeds. However, herbicides which help to remove weeds are potentially harmful to humans as well.

There is always apprehension that increased productivity will result in less requirement of labour. Though increase in productivity leads to reduction in requirement of labour, increasing demand of agricultural produce on account of ever increasing population increases the labour requirement. However, use of machines like tractor-trailers, machine-tillers, threshers etc. has definitely affected the requirement of labour in a big way. This factor together with increased opportunities in industries resulted in migration of labour from agriculture to urban area.

As regards wages, it is basically governed by supply and demand of labour. Due to general increase of requirement of labour in industry and services sector, the wages of labour have increasing trend. However, the labour especially agricultural labour contend that the wages they get do not fully compensate the increased cost of living.

Capitalization of Agriculture

The development model that we adopt affects the society. We have, therefore, to take this into account while choosing the model. For example, capitalization of agriculture and use of technology in agriculture which brought green revolution reduced the requirement of labour. This has had tremendous effect on rural society, resulting in large migration of rural labour to urban area. Another effect of capitalization of agriculture and use of technology in agriculture is seen that small farmers are unable to afford to adopt this high investment mode. Unable to compete with the rich, they are opting out of the cultivation of agriculture altogether. Technology is, thus, leading to increasing inequality in the rural society.

Green Revolution

Green Revolution means significant increase in agricultural production. This has happened because of introduction of High Yielding Variety (HYV) seeds, increased use of irrigation, chemical fertilizers and pesticides. Norman Borlaug, American agronomist (Nobel laureate in 1970) is known as the father of green revolution. He worked with Rockefeller Foundation and started his pioneering work in Mexico in increasing the yield by developing HYV (high yield variety) of seeds. His methods were then replicated in India, Pakistan, and other developing countries with great benefits. He is credited with increasing food production by leaps and bounds, thus saving lives of millions of poor in developing countries who would have otherwise died due to hunger.

High-yielding variety of wheat was first introduced by Borlaug in 1968, which proved to be a boon for increasing the production of wheat, much needed for India to be self sufficient in food production.

It is to be noted that in order to obtain significant benefits from HYV seeds, inputs like irrigation facilities, high level of chemical fertilizers and pesticides are required. As of now, India is set to surpass the agricultural growth target of 4 per cent during the 12th Five Year Plan (2012-17). The critics contend that the above method of obtaining high yield through increased use of chemical fertilizers and pesticides has negative impact on the soil and it leads to soil degradation. According to them this is clearly downside of globalization.

As mentioned, green revolution in India meant increase in productivity of agricultural crops through increased area of irrigation, use of high yielding variety of seeds, chemical fertilizers and pesticides. These inputs have increased the cost of production steeply. On the other hand, the prices of produce in the market have not increased proportionately. This has led to such a situation for the farmers that the cultivation of agriculture is becoming increasingly unviable and causing loss to the farmers. It is for this reason that government introduced Minimum Support Price (MSP) for the produce to the farmers. WTO does not support MSP as it contends that the very concept of MSP goes against the free market conditions. WTO, therefore, wants to put certain limitation to MSP.

Green Revolution Proved Malthus Wrong

Malthus, influential in eighteenth century in the fields of political economy and demography, observed that sooner or later growth of population will be checked by famine and disease. He predicted that while growth of food production will be linear, the growth of population will be exponential. According to him, such a condition of shortages will lead to famine and disease which in turn will try to control the population. However, in the present scenario, his predictions have been proved to be wrong. With the increase in cultivable land and improvement in seeds, fertilizers, pesticides and increased irrigation, the production of agricultural produce has increased at a faster rate. On the other hand, in developing countries, there has been slow down in birth rate because of awareness in the people about advantages of small family. In the context of green revolution, suffering from want of food is only on account of faulty food distribution system or because of extreme poverty which prohibits poor from affording to buy food.

Growth Rate of Agriculture

Table 3.3 gives Plan-wise Growth Rate of Agriculture.

Table 3.3: Plan-wise Growth Rate of Agriculture

Five Year Plan	*Growth Rate of Agriculture*
9th Plan (1997-98 to 2001-2002)	2.5
10th Plan (2002-03 to 2006-07)	2.4
11th Plan (2007-08 to 2011-12)	3.7
12th Plan (2012-13 to 2016-17)	4.0 (target)

The average of annual growth in agriculture during the Eleventh Five Year Plan is now placed at 3.7 per cent as against the target of 4 per cent. The target for the 12th plan is again 4 per cent.

Table 3.4 below shows in Indian economy year-wise growth rate in Agricultural Sector from 1995-96 to 2013-14.

Table 3.4: Indian Economy: Agricultural Sector Growth Rate from 1995-96 to 2013-14

Year	*Growth Rate*	*Year*	*Growth Rate*
1995-96	–1.0	2004-05	0.1
1996-97	10.4	2005-06	5.5
1997-98	–3.0	2006-07	4.1
1998-99	7.1	2007-08	6.3
1999-2000	2.4	2008-09	–0.3
2000-01	–0.6	2009-10	0.4
2001-02	6.5	2010-11	9.5
2002-03	–8.1	2011-12	5.3
2003-04	10.8	2012-13	0.9
		2013-14 (Adv. est.)	4.9

Source: Planning Commission: Indian Economy: Some Indicators at a Glance (as on 1st December 2014).

Website: http://planningcommission.nic.in/data/datatable/data_2312/DatabookDec2014%2018.pdf

It will be seen that the growth of agricultural sector on year to year basis is uneven and shows large swings. This is mainly because Indian agriculture is heavily dependent on the rain as about 60 per cent of land is cultivated as dry land agriculture. Ever since green revolution has set in, India has been able to meet not only its domestic demand of food, but it is also exporting the produce to other countries. However, the agricultural sector is now facing daunting problems in the context of global market, as mentioned in this chapter.

Critics of green revolution argue that though quantum of agricultural food production has increased, it lead to downward trend of traditional mixed variety of crops and in their place led to those variety of crops for which HYV seeds are available.

Market

Market access is one of the most important factors for the farmers who are normally situated far away from the markets. Market access has several dimensions. First is physical. The physical distance between the farm and the market has bearing on the transportation cost which is quite substantial. This puts farmers who are situated in remote areas at a disadvantage. Second is personal presence of the farmer in the market.

The personal presence in the market matters in deciding about its correct grade and weighing of product at which it is entitled to. Many a times, the products are downgraded/under-weighed unilaterally by the buyers. Further, farmer can negotiate the price better if he is personally present. However, if the market is situated at a distance from the market, he is unable to know the market trend and manage both: grade, weight or price of the product. Third is structural. The price of the product will depend upon how much market is fair to the seller. Fourth factor is intermediary. If there is intermediary or number of intermediaries, part of the profit will be appropriated by the intermediaries.

Marketing Boards

Many developing countries have formed marketing boards to help farmers to sell their produce at fair price. Initially Agricultural Produce Marketing Committee (APMC) helped the farmers in a big way. However, over a period of time the functioning of these boards has deteriorated and the experience is not very encouraging for the farmers especially to small land holders. It is contended that APMCs are plagued with politics, inefficiency and corruption, which result in farmers not getting fair price. However, disbanding state institution does not automatically mean private entity will do any better. In fact, state institution is expected to do better because it is a cooperative institution run by the farmers as members.

Retailing-Supermarkets and Farmers

The growth of supermarkets has been favourable as well as unfavourable to the farmers. The favourable factor is that the middlemen are excluded from the relationship between the farmers and the supermarket, and the farmers get better price. The unfavourable factor is that supermarkets insist on quality standards to be followed by the supplier-farmers and farmers are paid less price for any deficiency (as determined by the supermarkets) in the standard. Since the supermarkets have upper hand in determining the standard, there is no question of appeal and thus farmers are at the receiving end.

Meeting Export Quality

Globalization involves export. With regard to export, North sets the standard to be followed by the South. Incidentally, Global markets insist on better quality of produce from the farmers. On the other hand, due to cost involved, small landholders find it difficult to meet the quality requirement of products for export. The quality of produce to be exported is required to be always better than that is sold in home market. The production of quality produce requires more investment in terms of better seeds, fertilizers, pesticides, land preparation and harvesting methods, the cost of which the small farmers are unable to afford. The small farmers thus get excluded from reaping the benefit of exporting the produce.

Removing Trade Barriers in Agriculture

There are conflicting views on opening agricultural sector to global market. The proponents of liberalization contend that trade barriers and subsidies in agriculture harm both consumers as well as producers because they unnaturally increase the costs. According to them, freeing market in agricultural sector will bring down prices of commodities and help the poor.

On the other hand, critics of liberalization in agriculture contend that further opening up agricultural markets is likely to increase volatility of agricultural prices and this would put farming community to hardship. According to them, some big transnational players create monopoly in the global market and appropriate benefits to themselves. These companies foster agribusiness in developing countries, promote factory farms and drive out small and diversified agriculturists out of their traditional business.

The state has an important role to regulate the market conditions especially futures contracts because farmers and small players can hardly manage price fluctuations, which is a characteristic of futures contracts.

The choice of crops to be sown is driven by the price that farmers happened to get for the crops on previous occasion. For example, if the price of cotton in the previous year was more remunerative than soybean, the farmers choose cotton for the current year. However, when farmers sow more cotton and market is flooded with more cotton, the prices of cotton come down. This discourages the farmers to sow cotton next year. But due to scarcity of cotton in the market next year, the prices go high. This cycle goes on. Under globalization there is likelihood of getting this 'endemic cycle' more pronounced, hurting farmers most.

WTO: Cap on Subsidy

The farmers are provided at subsidized rates some water conservation systems (like pipes for piped water, drip, sprinklers etc.) to reduce wastage of water in conventional irrigation and depletion of water table. They are also provided power and fertilizers at subsidized rates to overcome the high input costs. Economists contend that the major beneficiaries of subsidy on fertilizer are the fertilizer industry and farmers having large land holdings. They contend that the national economy suffers due to heavy expenditure on direct or indirect subsidy to the agricultural sector. However, the farming community holds just the opposite view. In spite of subsidies, due to ever increasing cost of inputs like electricity, seeds, fertilizers, pesticides, and labour, the agriculture is steadily becoming unviable.

North wants to outsource agribusiness products to South. Agribusiness involves skill and higher investment which are beyond the reach of farmers in general and small farmers in particular. Borrowing investment leads to increase in the cost of production. After doing all this, the farmers have to depend upon the pricing in the global market which is always unpredictable. Further, a lot of margins are eaten away by the intermediaries. Agricultural occupation has thus become a costly occupation for the farmers. Unable to face such a situation, small farmers turn to taking up labourers' jobs in agribusiness to subsist their livelihood. Thus, small landowners become labourers working for non-traditional jobs.

As per WTO obligations, the value of subsidy India provides to farmers on any agricultural product must be limited to 10 per cent of the total value of the output of the product at the market price. WTO methodology requires that per unit subsidy be measured by the difference between MSP and the average price of the product that prevailed during 1986-1988. This methodology does not provide leeway to India about continuing to provide the existing level of subsidy and subsidy is must to subsist the Food Security Programme. India, therefore, tried to resist the cap on subsidy.

Further to WTO's Doha Round, issues of Trade Facilitation Agreement and Food Subsidies were discussed in Ministerial Meet at Bali (Indonesia) in 2013 and Geneva (Switzerland) in July, 2014. India reiterated that the Trade Facilitation Agreement should be finalized only after WTO members agree to change rules on food subsidies that caps to 10 per cent of value of production, value based on 1986-88 prices. The meet at Geneva, therefore, ended in a stalemate.

However, in a new development, on November 27, 2014, WTO member countries agreed to give flexibility to developing countries such as India in pursuing public stockholding programmes without fearing about breaching the prescribed 10 per cent cap. The member countries also agreed to decide on a new formula for calculating the level of food subsidies by 31 December, 2015 on a best endeavour basis. Although India is still away from breaching the subsidy ceiling of 10 per cent of value of production, it is possible that, in future, the rise in global prices in commodities especially rice and higher procurement may result in breaching the cap. However, now with this agreement, going past subsidy ceiling will not result in penal action under WTO till new subsidy formula is evolved and agreed.

With agreement on food subsidy, way is expected to be cleared for endorsing Trade Facilitation Agreement. However, it is contended that India may not gain significantly from this agreement because volume of trade export is not large. But China is likely to gain much from their large exports.

It is to be noted that MSP is provided to select crops like rice, wheat and sugarcane. In view of the protection from the government about the minimum prices for these crops, farmers tend to grow these crops more. However, it is seen that there is more demand for the commodities like flowers, fruits, vegetables, and organic food in the global market. These commodities are not covered under MSP programme and therefore farmers are not enthusiastic about growing these commodities. Indian farmers are therefore not in a position to take advantage of the global market. A way has to be found to give minimum support prices for the commodities for which there is more demand in the global market.

Though developed countries appear to push through WTO subsidy-free regime for agriculture, in practice they are providing heavy subsidies to agriculture in their own countries to protect their farming community. Instead of direct subsidies, they are providing monetary support under the Blue Box and Green Box arrangements, such as deficiency make up payments in the US and compensations for losses to farmers in European Union *via* acreage and head age premiums. Thus, the form of providing subsidy is different which appear to be on the surface not attracting reduction commitments (Reddy and Bhaskar, 2005: 317).

Post-Doha/NGO Movements

Proponents of globalization and WTO contend that the countries in the global South will benefit by increased access to global markets and improvements in the WTO Agreement on Agriculture (AoA) offering option of protecting their farm sector and production of staple crops to make certain their food security. According to them international trade governed by rules of fairness in trade practices will benefit farmers. On the other hand, La Via Compesina and other critical social movements contend that food sovereignty and not the food security is the answer for alleviating hunger and poverty. According to them food sovereignty model based on local and regional approach alone, i.e. without involvement of outside agency like WTO, can only be beneficial to farmers (Desmarais, 2007: 130).

La Via Campensina (Desmarais, 2007) is NGO which espouses, at the international level, the cause of agriculture in developing countries. It is a social movement claiming to work for protecting the interests of agricultural community in the South. According to La Via Campensina, food sovereignty and not food security is the answer for alleviating hunger and poverty. It contends that while food security deals with production, food sovereignty deals with not only production but also method of production. It argues that global institutions like WTO looks after interests of global North especially MNCs and overlooks the interests of global South. La Via Campensina advocates a system of diversified farmer-based production-guaranteeing the independence and the food sovereignty of population, providing remunerative prices for farmers and protecting internal markets against imports at low prices.

The traditional agriculture involves producing food to meet basically local needs and the cash crops for earning cash by way of marketing products in the open market. However, under globalization, the farmers are influenced to shift to agribusiness relating to products that are required by developed countries. This amounts to a shift from subsistence farming for meeting the local and regional needs to commercial agriculture for meeting the global demand.

In the production cycle of agriculture, seeds play the most vital role. The quality and output of crops depend more on the quality of seeds than any other factor. In traditional farming, local farmers were the sole producers and owners of the seeds. With the dawn of the regime of patenting, farmers have started using patented seeds as they promise to increase the yield. The promise of course is real and productivity has definitely increased from the previous times. The advantage of increased output of course comes with tags. Great majority of agricultural patents are owned by a few MNCs like Monsanto, DuPont, Syngenta, Dow, and Bayer. MNCs are the ones who can utilize and are utilizing the advances in genetic engineering and biotechnology to control the food system and gain huge profits.

These seeds are costly. These are not regenerative and the farmers have to purchase every year new seeds. Patented seeds, for more output, require irrigation facilities which small land holders are unable to provide.

The modernists view peasantries following traditional agriculture as resistance to the change which is actually intended to favour the latter's interest. The traditionalists counters this contention by an argument that while modernists see local use of agricultural resources to meet local needs as leading to poverty, actually so called development under globalization has led to poverty (Desmarais, 2007: 67). NGOs like La Via Campesina, Karnataka Rajya Raitha Sangha-Karnataka State Farmers Association, Bharatiya Kisan Union who are critical about globalization contend that WTO agreements greatly benefit the MNCs dealing with agri-food and seed, and destroy the livelihoods and displace small farm holders.

Depeasantization Leading to Peasant Movements

The term peasant refers to small land holder who does farming to produce mainly for his family and rest for the market to earn income for survival (D 46 Ritzer, 2012: 1651). Historically peasants are considered as a peaceful lot. "Marx famously likened the French peasantry to a sack of potatoes—great in number but irrelevant to the course of history" (Ritzer, 2012: 1651). However, Mahatma Gandhi mobilized Indian peasantry into a mass struggle for their welfare as well as for attaining freedom for the nation.

It is generally observed that small holdings are no more viable in view of increasing cost of inputs and fluctuating prices of agricultural produce in the market, which depend upon global conditions of supply and demand. Therefore, many small landholders are dispensing their land and opting for working as labour in the agricultural sector or migrate to urban area to work as labour in the industry. In this context, the critics of globalization contend that depeasantization is a logical outcome of the process of globalization, capitalism, and liberalism. All the aforesaid processes lead to urbanization, displacement of peasants from rural area and conversion of peasantry into urban proletariat (Ritzer, 2012: 399-400).

There is a rapid shift of population from rural to urban area. The main causes are that the conditions of farming and farm work are now no more encouraging monetarily as well as from the point of view of availability of basic facilities like education, health, sanitation etc. in rural area. Further, the opportunities in farm and farm work are shrinking due to increasing use of mechanization. On the other hand, the opportunities in urban area are increasing. Farm and farm work which were at one time considered as honourable, in modern times and in times of market economy under globalization, they stand now considerably devalued.

Small land holders in India constitute more than 80 per cent of land holders. With capitalization of agriculture and increasing use of technology in agriculture, these land holders find their traditional occupation of agriculture no more economically viable. Many of the farmers particularly older ones are depending upon remittances from their family members who migrated outside their village.

While there is a continuous migration of rural people to urban area, the development of infrastructure in urban area is not keeping pace with the number of incoming people. This is resulting in mushroom growth of slums in towns and cities. The industrialization is turning these slum dwellers easily exploitable as cheap labour. The condition of slums is also becoming conducive to rise in crimes. It is social responsibility of the state to provide necessary facilities to these people.

Employment

Rural Concern about Capitalization

Agriculture had a dominant position in the economy earlier. But with the advent of industries, it is no more dominant. It is, however, even now important occupation in the rural area and about 60 per cent of the total population of the country still depends on agriculture. The capitalization in terms of use of machines (tractors, threshers, etc.) in agriculture has substantially reduced the requirement of labour. But it is contended that the introduction of machines, besides increasing the cost of production, also led to unemployment in rural area.

While costs of input for agriculture are increasing, there is overall external pressure to reduce the subsidies being given to agriculture. In globalized market conditions, the prices of agriculture are steeply fluctuating from time to time. All these factors are alienating farming community from doing agriculture and shifting to non-farming activity.

Traditional agriculture of cultivating food crops keep the agricultural labour engaged mostly during the period September-November and April-June. Agricultural diversification in the form of agribusiness can keep the labour engaged for a longer time. Thus agricultural diversification besides earning can also help to generate employment in the agriculture sector.

Mahatma Gandhi National Rural Employment Guarantee Scheme (MGNREGS)

As mentioned, the agricultural work is seasonal and therefore for rest of the period of the year, rural people remain idle. Unemployment is the main cause of poverty in rural area. The objective of Mahatma Gandhi National Rural Employment Guarantee Scheme is to provide yearly at least one hundred days of employment to rural person. The minimum wages for the worker are fixed by the government from time to time. Thus, the scheme has been quite beneficial to the labour.

However, the farmers look at the scheme differently. According to them the scheme has resulted in reduction in availability of labour for agricultural work. Further, the agricultural labour demands wages on par with the scheme, which are unaffordable for the farmers. The scheme has thus increased the labour cost for agriculture which is already tottering due to increased cost of other inputs like seeds, fertilizers, pesticides etc. But on the whole the scheme has been found to be beneficial to rural population as a whole as it has given an option to work.

Continuing Farmers' Suicides

There have been quite a number of farmers' suicide cases in various states in India every year. The following Box 3.2 gives the position as latest as in the year 2014 on the subject.

Government of India now revised the methodology to categorise the data regarding farmers' suicides. According to new methodology, farm labourers who used to be treated as part of the farmers' suicides have now been taken out of the ambit of the definition of farmers' suicides, thus bringing down the number of suicides by half. According to data released by National Crime Records Bureau, on July 17, 2015, the number of farmers' suicides in 2014 in the country is 5,650 which otherwise would have been 12,360 including farm labourers. (*ToI*: 20-7-2015).

While reasons vary from case to case, analysis of the cases point out that the major reason for the suicides has been loss of income on account of higher input cost and low price for the produce, mounting debt and pressure from private money lenders for repayment. Over the past, the agriculture has never been economically viable occupation. Prior to green

Box 3.2: Farmer Suicides

Supreme Court while hearing PIL about farmer suicides said on 18.12.2014 that it was intending to take *suo motu* cognizance of the incident when a 75 year old farmer ended his life by lighting his own funeral pyre. Supreme Court was referring to the following news item.

***Quote*: Distressed over crop failure, farmer lights own funeral pyre**

PTI | December 01, 2014

Kashiram Bhagwan Indare, who had one acre of land at Manarkhed village in Balapur taluka, Akola district, was depressed over the failure of cotton and soyabean crops due to inadequate rains in the drought-prone district of Vidarbha, which has gained infamy for farmer suicides. On Friday 28.11.2014, Indare built a pyre in his field and set it afire, Investigating Officer Mohan Khandare told PTI over the phone. Unquote

Government of India informed Parliament on 19.12.2014 that more than 800 farmers have committed suicides this year due to agrarian distress, with maximum cases reported from Maharashtra. Maharashtra government reported 724 suicides by farmers up to October, 2014 due to agrarian reasons. Among other States, Telangana reported 84 suicides by farmers, Karnataka (19), Gujarat (3), Kerala (3), and Andhra Pradesh (3). Government said centre has taken several steps to revitalize the agriculture sector and improve the condition of farming community on sustainable basis by increasing public investment, improve farm practices, rural infrastructure, extension and marketing, among others.

revolution, it has always been subsistence occupation. In the past, it was sustainable to only big landlords who could hire labour cheaply or to those who could afford to undertake non-farm business besides agriculture. But to those who were small and medium land holders, it has never been a sustainable occupation.

With green revolution, while the production improved substantially, the cost of inputs including labour cost too increased substantially. In the process, the life of small landholders became miserable. Even medium landholders find things difficult. They tried to manage time somehow by borrowing money from money lenders which were called *Sahukars* earlier. The interest rate of borrowing was always heftily unreasonable. The market has been very inefficient and unfriendly. Unable to repay the loan through income from agriculture, many landholders had to sell their part or whole land. They started working as labour on somebody else's land, i.e. big landlord. Many landholders found difficulty in marrying off their daughters due to poverty. Not everybody was able to sustain the socio-psychological shock of such changed pathetic situation and it led to suicide by many landholders.

The situation of coercion by private money lenders has to some extent improved as government started extending credit to farmers at low rates and does not use coercion to repay the loan. However, farmers do not get the loan unless they clear the previous dues. If the previous year has been a failure and farmer is unable to pay the loan, he cannot get the fresh loan. Farmers are provided subsidies in various ways such as subsidized power, fertilizer, fixing MSP for specific items of produce etc. But on the whole, the condition of agriculturists in general is bad and suicides of farmers continue unabated. It is a matter of serious concern that even six decades after independence, the country is witnessing large scale suicides by the farmers.

Funding Agriculture

While in absolute terms the investment in agriculture is increasing, the investment in agriculture as a percentage of total public outlay is decreasing year by year. Table 3.5 gives from independence plan-wise percentage of agriculture expenditure in total public outlay.

Table 3.5: Plan-wise Percentage of Agriculture Expenditure in Total Public Outlay

Five Year Plan	*I*	*II*	*III*	*IV*	*V*	*VI*	*VII*	*VIII*	*IX*	*X*	*XI 2007-12*	*XII 2012-17 (Plan outlay)*
% of agriculture expenditure in total public outlay	32	21	20	22	21	18	15	13	11.4	10.6	7.2	7.1

Source: Five Year Plan Reports of Planning Commission/Statistical Abstract-India.

Website: http://planningcommission.nic.in/plans/planrel/fiveyr/12th/pdf/12fyp_vol2.pdf

With 60 per cent of India's population living on agriculture, the decline in investment is disturbing. There is no doubt that the agricultural production is increasing but the rate at which it is increasing is not encouraging. While many put blame on erratic monsoon for less production, the inadequate public investment is also a major handicap.

Another area of concern is the inadequate public funding for Research and Development in agriculture. While there has been increase in the yield per acre with improved seeds, fertilizers and pesticides, further improvement is possible only if R&D activities in agriculture are supported with commensurate investment in line with the level recommended by the Consultative Group on International Agricultural Research (CGIAR).

Agricultural Sensitivity

In an article on vulnerability to globalization in India, based on empirical studies, Ravikumar and Vishwanathan state: "Agricultural Sensitivity: Sensitivity of agriculture is considered to be important, given its role as the livelihood provider for a large section of the population. The extent of agricultural sensitivity is measured through the dependency of a region on agriculture (share of agricultural GDP of the region) and access to agricultural markets and public food distribution mechanisms (with the per capita calorie consumption of a region acting as a proxy). Both of these indicators cannot be changed in the short to medium term by the entity. Per capita calorie consumption is determined among other things, by the infrastructure and institutions in a region, and these cannot be modified by the individual in the short run. Applying Fuzzy methodology, it is inferred that the overall vulnerability of agriculture sector increases with an increase in the share of agricultural GDP, but decreases with an increase in per capita calorie consumption." (Nissanke, Thorbecke; 2008: 181).

Explanation about first part of the statement: As agricultural GDP increases, agriculture becoming increased or larger part of economy, state's exposure to globalization on economic front is increased and therefore state's vulnerability to globalization increases. The second part about calorie consumption is self-explanatory.

New Trends and Sustainability

Productivity

Crop yield per unit area of all crops have grown since 1950, due to the special emphasis placed on agriculture in the five-year plans and steady improvements in irrigation, technology, use of high yielding variety of seeds, application of modern agricultural practices and provision of agricultural credit and subsidies. The position has considerably improved since the Green Revolution in India. However, international comparisons reveal that the average yield in India is much lower than many countries in the world, including China.

China and India became self-governing more or less at the same time and they inherited similar problems like huge population to feed, low productivity in agriculture etc. However, over a period of time, China's development in various fields including agriculture production has been faster than India. This fact was acknowledged by no less a person than Jawaharlal Nehru when he visited China. Faster development in China could be partly attributed to the (authoritarian) political system in China which is different from that of India meaning that in democracy development has also to be followed by consensus.

Organic Farming

Presently farmers are using chemical fertilizers and pesticides. Due to increasing health awareness, people world over are looking forward to chemical free food. People especially in developed countries are trying to switch over to organic food. Since prevention of disease is better than cure, they are ready to pay extra money for the organic food. Developing countries can take advantage of this trend by way of switching over to organic farming and exporting the products. The greatest benefit of organic farming is that the process allows soil to retain the quality of its fertility and regeneration, as against GM crops which, as critics claim, only temporarily increase yield and call for extensive use of chemicals endangering the fertility of the soil. Further it is said that the productivity of even adjoining non-GM crops gets adversely affected. The potential of organic farming in India is huge because of its immense bio-diversity and natural resources in the country.

Notwithstanding several advantages, farmers are not enthusiastic about organic farming. They see the production of organic manure as a tedious process. Similarly, getting *neem* extracts considered as alternative to chemical pesticides is also a cumbersome process. Both these processes of organic production require labour which farmers find difficulty in getting and involve more cost.

In spite of difficulties, as the severity of diseases will increase, people in the future are bound to change from the present chemical based produced food to organic food and thus there will be huge demand for the organic food. Therefore, there is an urgent need of formulating policies to encourage organic farming by way of more research in finding further organic alternatives and providing incentives for undertaking organic farming. This would also give boost to installing *gobar* gas plants in rural area thus saving firewood and green space.

Sustainability in Agriculture

Any method, which disturbs the natural and ecological system least, will help sustainability. It is contended that one of the measures to bring sustainability in agriculture is to take recourse to no-till farming. Edward Falkner is noted as the first one who mooted the idea in 1940s. No-till or zero tillage farming is growing crops without disturbing the soil by tilling. This mode of agriculture enables increased retention of water and organic matter in the soil which would otherwise be lost if the soil is inversed with plough. It only involves increased use of chemicals for destroying weeds. Notwithstanding overall economy involved, no-till farming has not become popular so far, perhaps due to low productivity. We can only draw inspiration from this for doing agriculture as much in natural form as possible.

The relationship between sustainability and type of agriculture, i.e. intensive or extensive is a debatable point. Here, intensive agriculture means maximizing the output or production from the same area of land. Use of intensive irrigation and multi-cropping comes under intensive agriculture. Extensive agriculture means to obtain more output or production by enlarging the area of agriculture. The negative aspect of intensive agriculture is erosion of soil and decreasing the nutrients in the soil. The negative aspect of extended area of agriculture is loss of organic matter in agriculture and change that happens in ecology on account of taking up the very activity of agriculture like cutting of trees, bushes and damage to flora and fauna etc. With pros and cons, it is difficult to say which of one the two, i.e. intensive or extensive agriculture is more or less sustainable. This would depend upon the environment in which the site is located, condition of the soil and type of technology being adopted.

Traditional plant breeding is considered as moving toward sustainability. Similarly, use of bio-technology so long as it conserves land and increases the yield is also considered as moving toward sustainability.

In view of the growing awareness about the importance of ecology, the sustainability in agriculture is going to acquire increasing attention in future.

Conclusion

The socio-historians put agriculture on the high pedestal stating that the quality of topsoil determined the strength of civilizations Historians held that the topsoil, especially river-based systems, laid the foundations for major civilizations. The examples are civilizations developed around Indus or Nile rivers.

Agriculture being labour intensive and requiring physical hard work, historically European nations outsourced agriculture to their colonies in a large measure and concentrated on industries and automation. In course of time, the advancement of technology particularly in developing high yielding variety of seeds, genetically modified seeds, irrigation, improved fertilizers, pesticides etc. has considerably improved the yield and developing countries like India ushered in Green Revolution.

There has been popularity of Atkinson diet which among other low-carbohydrate food items includes salad, fruits and vegetables. Over a period of time, North started concentrating on production of staples in their countries, which is lesser labour intensive and outsourcing agri-products like more exotic fruits, vegetables, flowers, or ornamental plants; food/fruit processing; aquaculture, i.e. cultivation of fishes; production of special commodities such as livestock and feedstuff, production of which is tedious and labour intensive. This is leading to weaning away South from their traditional agriculture of mixed crops including staples. Agribusiness has now become a buzzword in the South. Global corporations are entering into the agricultural field and there is a trend to establish factory farms in the South.

There has however been downside of capitalization and increasing use of machineries in agriculture because these are beyond the capacity of small land holders who constituted and still constitute bulk of the farming class. As agriculture is becoming economically increasingly unviable, most of these farmers are dispossessing the land and started working as a labour on big farms. Another factor for dispossession of land from farmers is the land taken away from them for establishing industries. These dispossessed farmers either work as labour on others' farms or migrate to urban area and seek employment there. Many of them have to live in subhuman conditions in slum area. It will not be exaggeration to say that these people pay the price for the nation's development.

Globalization of course has opened up export market and multi-national companies are trying to tie up food supplies from farmers directly thus breaking the chain of middlemen who appropriate bulk of the profit. The farmers are of course required to maintain quality of their products.

Presently, farmers are using chemical fertilizers and pesticides. Due to increasing health awareness, people world over are looking forward to chemical free food. People especially in developed countries are trying to switch over to organic food. This area is going to be very promising. However, the farming of organic food is a tedious process as well as costly and it will take some time for organic food to become commercialized on a big scale.

Though government is providing direct or indirect subsidy to agriculture, but the same is inadequate. Public outlay on agriculture has reduced drastically as a result there is practically no infrastructure development in agriculture. It is, therefore, increasingly becoming unviable on account of higher cost of inputs and low price of the produce. This condition has led to occurrence of large number of cases of farmer suicides especially in Maharashtra, Telangana, Karnataka and Andhra Pradesh. Looking to the overall situation it is evident that the support being given to agriculture by the government is far too inadequate.

RURAL EDUCATION

Prologue

Literacy is one of the most important indicators of Social development. In Census terminology, a person aged 7 years and above, who can both read and write with understanding in any language is treated as literate and the percentage of literates in the age group seven years and above is called literacy rate. The following Table 3.6 gives literacy rate in India from 1991 to 2011, i.e. up to last census.

Table 3.6: Literacy rate in India 1991-2011

	1991			*2001*			*2011*		
	Total	*Rural*	*Urban*	*Total*	*Rural*	*Urban*	*Total*	*Rural*	*Urban*
Persons	52.21	44.69	73.08	64.84	58.75	79.92	74.04	68.91	84.98
Males	64.13	57.87	81.09	75.26	70.70	86.27	82.14	78.57	89.67
Females	39.29	30.62	64.05	53.68	46.14	72.86	65.46	58.75	79.92

Source: Census of India website http://www.censusindia.gov.in/2011-prov-results/paper2-vol2/data_files/Mizoram/Chapter_6.pdf

The above Table 3.6 reveals that at national level during 1991-2011, the increase of 24.22 (68.91-44.69) per cent in rural literacy rate is more than double that of increase in urban literacy rate of 11.90

(84.98-73.08) per cent. In gender distribution, the female literacy has recorded higher increase than that of the males in both rural and urban areas. However, the most worrying point is that even in 2011, females' rural literacy rate is 58.75 and total literacy rate is 65.46 which are abysmally low.

Education lays the foundation for the development of human beings and the society. With all round economic disparity, education can act as a great leveller. However, to have equal opportunities of education for all, its reach should be available across the country. While better educational facilities are available in urban area, similar facilities are not available in rural area. This is clear discrimination against rural society.

There is a general perception that the standard of education of a student passing from rural school is inferior to his counterpart in urban area. This is a result of the difference in the quality of education imparted in urban and rural area for which the student is not at fault.

In the era of globalization, there are more opportunities for the students who possess higher education. Many students from rural area are not able to prosecute higher education. If the percentage of rural students passing higher education is less, is globalization encouraging or discouraging providing level playing field to both rural and urban students? Is this not leading to increasing inequality between rural and urban students?

E-learning was thought to be useful to get over the problem of absentee teacher in remote locations. Why E-learning is not being implemented in rural area effectively? The process of globalization has shifted the emphasis from the subjects of humanities to mathematics, science, and information and communication technology. How are rural students placed to cope with the changed pattern?

These are some of the most critical issues which require through discussion.

Role of Education

Though education plays multidimensional role, two of its dimensions are most prominent. One is reforming the human behaviour and the other is to prepare the person for taking up the responsibility of occupation to satisfy his material needs. It appears education has not been able to fulfill the first role. At the time of Independence, literacy rate in India was just 12 per cent. After the 2011 census, literacy rate increased to 74.04 per cent. Earlier, though literacy level was low, general perception is that there used to be respect for the human values in the society such as respect for teachers and elders. Although, there is now much improvement in the literacy rate but this has not resulted in creating respect for human values. It has to be seen as to whether the process of globalization has changed the emphasis from values to mostly satisfying material needs.

The other role of education as mentioned above is to equip the learners with the skill necessary for taking up the responsibility of the occupation so as to satisfy his material needs. In the context of globalization, since economy plays vital part in globalization, the role of education has to be structured around producing the worker who is capable of working efficiently in any field, i.e. agriculture, factory, business office or any other field. Further, the occupational needs go on changing. Accordingly, education has always to take care of the changing needs of the occupation.

Education as an Identity

The book titled '*Rural Education for the Twenty-First Century: Identity, Place, and Community in a Globalizing World*,' edited by Schafft and Jackson deals vividly about how, in the context of education, identity of rural and poor is perceived by the society.

The message about the term 'rural' is perceived as backward. The backwardness is referenced to perception of education in rural area more than any other aspect of rural society. It is taken for granted that the rural schools mean they are inferior to urban schools. Such perception is gathered due to unavailability of proper infrastructure as well as quality of education in rural schools. It is also taken for granted that after passing from rural schools, students will have to study extra hard in colleges to catch up with the urban students. They are thus stamped as backward right from their entry in the rural school.

If identity is contextualized and generally it is so, rural and poor always take poverty as a marker of the identity. The identity of the rural and poor seen as belonging to local community gets differentiated from the perceived identities of the members of the globalized society, who are economically better off.

Poverty is rendered as deficiency—deficiency not only in terms of income, but also socially, of which education is one of the major components. Thus poor will always carry a stigma of deficiency. Though these are wrong notions, the terms 'rural or poor' do carry a notion of backwardness, inferiority and deficiency.

Rural identity of the students of rural schools inhibits them from getting higher education. When they migrate to urban area they find difficulty in getting the employment. Social and family endowment also matter in this respect. When they get the jobs, these are mostly low paid jobs and that too in unorganized sector. Many of them live in urban slums. The condition of employment and consequently their welfare becomes still more difficult in hard times of economy.

Reach of Education

Villages are remotely located and the rural area is thinly populated. Therefore, it is a great challenge to provide education for all. Non-enrollment of students of poor families is still a grave problem. In this context, number of initiatives were taken by the state from the time of independence such as District Primary Education Programme (DEEP) etc. The Government of India project Sarva Shiksha Abhiyan (SSA) pioneered by Prime Minister Atal Bihari Vajpayee in 2001 gave further push to the enrollment process. Mid-day Meal Scheme has also helped to boost the enrollment. However, school drop-outs is still a serious problem. Abject poverty is at the root of this problem. Parents of poor families, rather than allowing their children to pursue education want them, especially girls, to help in their occupation. The problem that India is facing is being faced by other developing countries too. Related point to be noted is that there is a big gap in the education level between the countries in the North and the South.

Inequality in Education

Rich and Poor

Education includes learning skills. Skills give poor people more opportunities of jobs. It is generally held that with education, the inequality between the poor and the rich will reduce. Thus, education is said to be a great leveller. However, it is also observed that income of the people who get higher education rise faster than the less educated. Thus, while spread of education tries to bridge the gap between the poor and the rich, the difference in the level of education increases the inequality. The protagonists of globalization, however, contend that globalization is helping even poor and less educated people to earn better and thus improve their wellbeing.

When we view capital as a requirement of economic progress, the poor are not only devoid of capital but they have also no means to access the capital. However, education can become capital for the poor otherwise. Education serves as a foundation for one's progress in life in future. Therefore, if everybody gets more or less same level of education, they will have equality of opportunity in coming up in life. It is observed that many students hailing from poor families, by studying hard, rise in various fields in life. However, if there is a marked difference between two persons in attainment of the level of education, say one is just 12th pass and the other is graduate, the inequality gets manifested right from starting of the service career.

Rural and Urban

Rural schools lack basic infrastructure like enough class rooms, toilet facilities, drinking water facility, sports ground etc. As an example, report (19.12.2014) tabled in Indian Parliament states that only 68.9 per cent elementary schools have girl toilets of which 74.59 per cent are functional. Qualified teachers are reluctant to serve in rural schools as they are in remote locations where they feel families cannot be shifted. Rural schools also lack latest teaching aids. Thus, whole environment in rural school is such that there is a great difficulty for the students to improve their personal ability. The lower level of educational achievement results in the lower level of occupational status that these students attain after their education.

The problem of rural-urban gap in regard to provisions, access and quality of education is not specific to India alone but it is there across the world. The process of globalization has accentuated inequality between the rural and urban population. Globalization is more beneficial to those who have higher education. Very few from rural population are lucky to go in for higher education because low standard of primary and secondary education works as a great handicap for these students in general. Thus, while education is supposed to be great leveler in lessening the hierarchies, the position is emerging otherwise.

The criticism of globalization comes more from the developing countries. But the protagonists of globalization contend that for this, the developing countries are themselves to be blamed for not being able to derive the benefit of globalization. According to them state should be able to provide education to all in the first place. Inaccessibility to even primary education for most of the poor can be cited as a prime reason as to why developing countries are not able to reap the benefit of globalization. If primary education becomes inaccessible to poor who count as a major population in the developing countries, the accessibility to higher education is a distant dream for them. Thus, in the long run, major population is left out of benefiting from advancement of technology say information and communication technology which is a major component of globalization. The greater investment in enhancement of human capital in terms of creating greater access to education for the poor could help the situation.

Globalization is based upon market economy or economic liberalization. Since, market economy is driven by private players who fiercely compete with each other, the spirit of competition is manifested in every activity of life down the line. The theory of 'survival of fittest' enunciated by Darwin is equally applicable to the present mankind who are directly or indirectly participating in the process of globalization. In this world of' survival of fittest', rural population lags much behind urban population. Rural population has none of power, wealth or level of education to compete with urban population. The public policies too are not fashioned to achieve a fair balance between the depraved rural population and privileged urban population. For example, even developed country like USA, though pursuing 'No Child Left Behind (NCLB)' programme, could not achieve fair balance in the field of education between rural and urban population.

> "Rural communities have always been peripheral to the centers of power and privilege in the US (Howley 2004; Theobald 1997). Consequently, public policies have rarely been kind to the social, cultural, and economic 'inefficiencies' of rural life. With sink-or-swim economic policies and economic reforms, too often rural people, and institutions have been left to sink."

The rural schools are often directly or indirectly controlled by the local community. So long as this control is positive, it is good for the school. However, often the control of the local community over the school and autonomy of the school itself can work against the interest of the school as they can create stiff resistance to change in the functioning of the school that may be necessary to bring it in line with the global trend.

Rural population is not well organized to demand even basic infrastructure from the state. Thus, though in developing countries like India, rural population is much more than urban counterpart, it has little

Box 3.3: Right of Children to Free and Compulsory Education Act, 2009

Background of the Act

Education is a fundamental right of every human being. It lays the foundation for the development of society. The Indian Parliament enacted the Right to Education Act in 2009, to provide free and compulsory education to all children in the age group of six to fourteen years. The Act notifies that it is a legally enforceable duty of the Centre and the States to provide free and compulsory education.

Major Provisions of the Act

- Every child of the age of six to fourteen years shall have a right to free and compulsory education in neighbourhood school till completion of elementary (class first to eighth) education.
- No child shall be liable to pay any kind of fee or charges or expenses which may prevent him or her from pursuing and completing elementary education.
- Where a child above six years of age has not been admitted to any school or though admitted, could not complete his or her elementary education, then, he or she shall be admitted in a class appropriate to his or her age.
- The appropriate government and local authority shall establish a school, if it is not established, within the given area in a period of three years from the commencement of this Act.
- The Central and the State Governments shall have concurrent responsibility for providing funds for carrying out the provisions of this Act.

The Right of Children to Free and Compulsory Education Act finally came into force on 1st April, 2010.

As per the provision of the Act, the Central Government has authorized the National Council of Educational Research and Training (NCERT) as the academic authority to lay down the curriculum and evaluation procedure for elementary education and develop a framework of national curriculum.

This Act is an essential step towards improving each child's accessibility to secondary and higher education. The Act also contains specific provisions for disadvantaged groups, such as child labourers, migrant children, children with special needs, or those who have a disadvantage owing to social, cultural, economical, geographical, linguistic, gender or any such factor.

Private schools are also bound to admit certain percentage of children belonging to weaker section and disadvantaged group. According to Act, a school shall admit in class I, to the extent of at least 25 per cent of the strength of the class, children belonging to weaker section and disadvantaged group in the neighbourhood and provide free and compulsory elementary education till its completion. A school shall be reimbursed expenditure subject to limits mentioned.

The Act has provisions like:

Per teacher 30 no. of children

School building: one classroom for every teacher

Separate toilets for girls and boys

Source: http://mhrd.gov.in/sites/upload_files/mhrd/files/RTEAct.pdf.

voice in governance and by all standards they lag much behind urban population with regard to proper educational facilities.

Millennium Development Goal and Right to Education

Among the Millennium Development Goals set by the United Nations in 2002, the goal for education is: Ensure that by 2015, children everywhere, boys and girls alike, will be able to complete a full course of primary schooling.

The levels of education vary from country to country. In India, the levels of education are: Elementary education which starts from the age of six consists of class one to eight (primary from class one to five and upper primary from class six to eight), secondary education consists of class nine and ten, higher secondary education consists of class eleven and twelve and finally higher education or university education, i.e. graduation starts after class twelve.

Though literacy level in India has increased from 12 per cent at the time of independence in 1947 to 74.04 per cent as per census 2011, it is a matter of concern that still so many people in India cannot even read and write. Poor and rural population are the worst affected. To improve the situation, major initiative was taken by the Central Government in the year 1998 by starting Sarva Shiksha Abhiyan. Further, Mid-Day Meal Programme to cover primary classes was started from health point of view as well as to attract children who otherwise would be used for working in the field due to poverty.

Poverty still remained a major bottleneck to achieve the universal elementary education. In view of this, another major initiative was taken by the Central Government by promulgating the Right of Children to Free and Compulsory Education Act, 2009

Quality of Education

Quality of education is a subject matter of intense discussion particularly quality of education being imparted in rural schools. According to ASER reports, millions of schoolchildren are growing up "functional illiterate" unable to divide, subtract or construct proper sentences even in secondary school.

Wikipedia states: "A useful distinction can be made between pure illiteracy and functional illiteracy. Purely illiterate persons cannot read or write in any capacity, for all practical purposes. In contrast, functionally illiterate persons can read and possibly write simple sentences with a limited vocabulary, but cannot read or write well enough to deal with the everyday requirements of life in their own society."

Teaching aids can improve quality of education. 3-D diagrams can explain certain things better than drawing the sketches/figures on blackboard.

The globalization has opened several opportunities, but all these opportunities are available mostly for skilled persons meaning thereby that the level of education has acquired importance now more than ever. While Right to Education Act has widened the reach of the education to children, there is a vast difference of the quality of education being imparted in urban and rural area. Learning outcomes in reading and writing and especially in mathematics have been a matter of great concern. If the present trend continues, especially the rural students will be condemned to remain inferior in education to urban students for ever.

Training of Teachers

There are serious problems with the quality of education rendered in government schools or the government aided schools: The quality of education depends upon quality of teachers. Due to remoteness in rural area and lack of facilities and infrastructure like proper roads etc., qualified teachers are less motivated to serve in rural schools.

Aware of the lack of quality of education in schools, special efforts are being made by both state and Central Government. In order to improve the quality of education, Maharashtra State Council of Education Research and Training (MSCERT) has started evaluating and monitoring the teachers on a trial basis in a few talukas. The evaluation is based on several parameters, including innovative methods of teaching, application of training in teaching, progress of students etc. This brings to the fore the importance of training of teachers.

There is institutional structure for training of teachers in the form of District Institutes of Education and Training (DIET) at the district level and National Council for Teacher Education (NCTE) at the Central level. However, the main problem is the content and the process of the teacher training. Although the number of teachers trained is high, the problems are non-observance of standards and norms with respect to entry-level qualifications, certification requirement for recruitment of teachers, duration of training, institutional infrastructure and profile of training staff. The greatest challenge in the training process is sensitizing the teachers about the holistic approach to child's development including its mind and health.

The Central Board of Secondary Education (CBSE) is urging schools to train their teachers for conducting Assessment of Speaking and Learning (ASL) skills. The board is collaborating for the technical knowledge part with Trinity College (UK). However, for this, firstly teachers have to be trained for the purpose.

Design of Curriculum

Right of Children to Free and Compulsory Education Act, 2009 provides for certain guidelines regarding design of curriculum like:

- All round development of child
- Building up child's knowledge, potentiality and talent
- Development of physical and mental abilities to the fullest extent
- Learning through activities, discovery and exploration

However, designing a curriculum is one thing and implementation at the ground level is another thing. There are serious problems with the quality of education rendered in government schools or the government aided schools: The main problems are:

- The quality of education depends upon quality of teachers. The villages are situated in remote areas they lack proper infrastructure such as roads, health services etc. No well qualified teacher save exceptions likes to serve wholeheartedly in these remote locations. Most of the teachers are residing in nearby towns or cities and make up and down trips between schools and their places of residence. The journey itself exhausts them and it is humanly impossible to give their best for the teaching.
- Teachers point out that they are unable to concentrate on teaching in the school because they are also assigned non-teaching duties which take away their time and energy. These include election duties, *aadhar* card registration, pulse polio vaccination and arrangements for serving mid-day meals to the students. They say that the present system lays stress on extra-curricular activities. While these are good for overall development of students, these take away time from the teachers. They say that the system of evaluating students through new assessment methods has increased

accountability of the teachers and this involves more of record keeping. They say that the teacher who is under stress with the above assignments can't give the quality education.

- The learning methods in the rural area are age-old because funds necessary for upgrading them are just not available for rural schools.

School curriculum (course of study) is very important part of education and it should be based upon facts. However, it is observed that many times text is changed based on political considerations, i.e. say philosophies of political parties in power. These changes bring in utter confusion in the minds of the young students in knowing correct position. These difficulties are especially encountered in the history texts. The inclination of each political party is to rewrite history in a way it suits to further its interest without regard to facts.

The design of teaching is the convergence of ideas of academicians, education department, public, media and political class. Since, the process of globalization is embracing in many ways every facet of life, it is important to design the curriculum in such a way that the student after completing his education is able to cope up in the global scenario.

E-learning

Now-a-days the concept of E-learning is being discussed widely particularly in the context of education in rural area. It is contended that there is no substitute for face to face teaching by the teacher. Teacher is more than knowledge provider. During his time with the students, he plays the role of guide, friend and parent. E-learning option can only be considered either in the context of the absentee teacher or as additional aid.

However, because of the remoteness, there is a preponderance of the idea of introducing e-learning in rural area. The idea becomes stronger in the context of difficulty in finding qualified teachers to teach in the rural area. The distance e-learning project envisages satellite supported two-way broadband Internet protocol to support interactive teaching and learning for distance education students. Australia as a continent is facing the problem of remoteness of location similar to India. The experience of E-learning practiced even in Australia is that the system does not seem to grasp the context in which the rural students live. But then some form of value addition in education through e-learning is better than no other thing to cope with the absentee teacher.

E-learning would obviously require availability of reliable internet service in rural area. The new infrastructure in terms of equipment is required to deliver primary, secondary and vocational courses in the rural area. India faces a special problem of the availability of electric power in remote area. If e-learning is to be adopted there, the difficulty can only be solved by providing a back-up power through diesel generators. Further, there is little knowledge of communication technology in rural area. There has to be at least some skeleton assistance for managing operation and maintenance problems of the equipment.

Thus, though online learning will always remain an inferior substitute to the conventional method, such courses can reinforce the conventional education method. These can add to their learning and skills. The real problem is providing necessary infrastructure facilities required for e-learning in rural area. Internet Service providers and state agencies are skeptic about providing broadband connectivity in rural area because it requires high investment and gives low returns at least during initial period of installation. It is estimated that presently digital penetration in rural area is less than 6-7 per cent. However, it is to be acknowledged that several initiatives by the state as well as Internet Service providers in regard to providing connectivity are visible and these are expected to make progress as time passes. If inequality in educational facilities between urban and rural area is to be reduced, there is no way, but to concentrate on providing online education facilities in rural area.

Inadequate Allocation of Funds for Basic Education

The non-availability of requisite funds is by far the greatest obstacle in maintaining as well as spreading the basic education. On the recommendations of the Education Commission, the Government of India quantitatively accepted to target the investment of 6 per cent of national income in education. Although yearly allocation for education is increasing in absolute term, the same is around half of the promised 6 per cent of GDP. The inadequate funding is coming in the way of building basic infrastructure for education in rural area. This includes construction of required classrooms, toilets, providing drinking water facility, teaching aids, sports facilities etc.

Global Trend

In US, the quality of rural education is not as good as in cities, but it is much better than in India. There, willing students go from villages to live in Dorm (shared accommodation) in cities and take education. Those who pass high school, there is no difficulty to get admission in city colleges. Everybody has a car and there is no problem about travelling a distance of 15 miles for education. If the standard in rural area is not very good, even then it is generally better than in the area where black people live in cities. As regards healthcare, since everybody has a car, they go to the nearest city.

Australia is a large continent, but sparsely populated. The problems there are similar to India. However, their economic position being better, they are trying to overcome the problem of remotely located areas through extensive e-learning mode.

Earlier, the subjects of humanities were all important. With the advent of industrialization, there has been increase in the importance of subjects of science and mathematics. With globalization the importance of these subjects has phenomenally increased. So also the subject of information and communication technology acquired special importance. With this development, the subjects of humanities do not carry the same kind of attraction as it used to have in earlier times. Thus, world is moving away from investing in human and social capital to mathematics, science, economics, information and communication technology etc. Industries and Multinational companies are now influencing the type of education that is to be delivered by the schools and universities. The educational change of this nature is bound to have serious repercussion on the future of the global society.

The big problem in India is that the standard of education in rural area is too low. The situation is different as regards students coming out of institutions of higher learning such as IITs, which are dominated by urban better offs. In respect of higher education, the fact that India stands very well among the comity of nations is recognized by no less a person than Barak Obama, President of USA when he said in his remarks to students at the Pathways in Technology Early College High School in Brooklyn on 25.10.2013:

> "Billions of people from countries like India and China are striving hard to "out-educate" Americans in mathematics and technology. In previous generations, America's standing economically was so much higher than everybody else that we did not have a lot of competition. Every year they are pulling ahead in, especially in math, science and technology. So, we

have a choice to make. If the workforce is not educated enough, it will be left behind and find it hard to get a job that pays a living wage. In a global economy, jobs can go anywhere. Companies are looking for the best educated people, wherever they live, and they will reward them with good jobs and good pay."

Thus, while there is a great deal of opinion in India that the process of globalization has not worked in favour of India, the above quote from the President of USA confirms that Indians in the higher learning group especially from IIMs and IITs are standing very well in the global competition. In this respect, India has added advantage of having better knowledge of English language as compared to China. But as far as education in the rural area is concerned, the position is just dismal as narrated above.

Conclusion

After attaining Independence, India began its journey towards providing universal and free education for all children until they complete the age of fourteen years. Education lays the foundation for the development of society. With all round economic disparity, education can act as a great leveller. But there are inherent problems that rural area is facing in terms of education. The major problem is remoteness of villages from the cities which are development centers. Another factor is that the rural area is very thinly populated.

The messages about the term 'rural' are perceived as rural means 'backward'. Because of lack of quality education in rural area, the term backward is more implied in the matter of education in rural area than about any other aspect of rural society. It is taken for granted that the rural schools mean they are inferior to urban schools. Rural population is not well organized to demand even basic infrastructure from the state. Therefore, though in developing countries, rural people are in majority, by all standards they lag much behind urban population.

The process of globalization has accentuated further inequality between the rural and urban population. Globalization is more beneficial to those who are having higher education. Very few from rural population are lucky to go for higher education, because, low standard of primary and secondary education works as a great handicap for students in general from rural area. Thus, while education is supposed to be great leveler in lessening the hierarchies, the position is emerging just the other way round.

In the above context, Right of Children to Free and Compulsory Education Act, 2009 Act is an important step towards improving each child's accessibility to secondary and higher education. The Act also contains specific provisions for disadvantaged groups, such as child labourers, migrant children, children with special needs, or those who have a disadvantage owing to social, cultural, economical, geographical, linguistic, gender or any such factor.

The curriculum of education needs change to include some part of vocational courses as it is observed that the unemployment in graduates is increasing, which means industry is looking for persons who are having knowledge of application instead of only theory.

There are serious problems with the quality of education rendered in government schools or the government aided schools: The quality of education depends upon quality of teachers. Due to remoteness in rural area and lack of infrastructure like roads etc., qualified teachers are less motivated to serve in rural area or put in their whole hearted attention in teaching in rural schools.

E-learning was thought to be useful to ease the problem of absentee teacher in remote locations. But presently infrastructure required for e-learning is poor in rural area and the same has to be improved if e-learning is to be adopted as a regular mode of education.

As mentioned in the beginning, education has two main objectives. One is reforming the human behaviour and the other is to prepare the person for taking up the responsibility of occupation to satisfy his material needs. The spirit of utter competitiveness forming integral part of globalization hardly gives any space to the first objective, i.e. reforming the human behaviour. The whole education system is now oriented toward how one can succeed in one's occupation.

The process of globalization has shifted the emphasis from the subjects of humanities to mathematics, science, and information and communication technology. The long-term impact of this shift is bound to be there in the future.

RURAL AND URBAN HEALTHCARE

Prologue

World Health Organization (WHO) in 1948 made a comprehensive definition of health as, "Health is a state of complete physical, mental and social wellbeing and not merely an absence of disease or infirmity." The definition has since been enlarged to include "ability to lead a socially and economically productive life."

The importance of health as an indicator of socio-economic progress can be gauged by having 'longevity' or 'life expectancy at birth' as one of the three components of Human Development Index developed by UNDP for measuring the country's progress. Life expectancy largely depends upon healthcare services available to the society.

The process of globalization affects healthcare services in developing countries in two ways. Firstly, globalization puts more emphasis on economic progress and in this context, the public spending on education and health services under social sector is considered as frugal, i.e. expenditure that can be economized. Secondly, globalization puts more emphasis on controlling life-style diseases like heart disease *vis-à-vis* eradication of communicable diseases like tuberculosis etc. which is a matter of concern for the developing countries.

Provision of Healthcare in Rural Area

When India attained Independence there were no healthcare facilities in rural area. The people were left to their fate. After Independence, the goal was set to provide 'Health for All' through providing primary healthcare which can cover entire rural population. The healthcare setup covers:

(i) ***Primary Health Centres (PHC) and Sub-Centres (SC)***: The basic or essential healthcare is provided at this level. Each PHC covers 30,000 population and SC covers 5000 population. One *Dai* is provided in each village to assist in deliveries, initial mother and childcare.

(ii) ***Secondary level***: District Hospitals (DH) and Community (rural) Health Centres (CHC) form the secondary level at which better medical facilities are available. These also serve as the first referral hospitals. DH and CHC covers population of about 80,000-1, 20,000.

(iii) ***Tertiary level***: Medical college hospitals and specialized hospitals come under this level. At this level, highly sophisticated diagnostic equipments as well as more experienced specialists are available. These hospitals are expected to deal with more complex medical cases.

Present Status of Important Health Indicators

Infant Mortality Rate

Of all the health related factors, two factors namely Infant Mortality Rate (Table 3.7 and 3.8) and Life Expectancy at Birth seem to have relationship to residence and the gender on the one hand and socio-economic conditions (rural-urban) on the other. Hence, these are discussed here.

Table 3.7: Infant Mortality Rates by sex and residence in India, 2010

Total			Rural			Urban		
Total	Males	Females	Total	Males	Females	Total	Males	Females
47	46	49	51	50	53	31	30	33

Source: Census of India website: http://censusindia.gov.in/vital_statistics/srs/Chap_4_-_2010.pdf

Table 3.8: Per cent change in average Infant Mortality Rates in India between 1998-00 and 2008-2010

Total			Rural			Urban		
1998-00	2008-10	% Change	1998-00	2008-10	% Change	1998-00	2008-10	% Change
70.0	50.0	–28.6	75.3	54.7	–27.4	44.3	33.7	–23.9

Source: Census of India website http://censusindia.gov.in/vital_statistics/srs/Chap_4_-_2010.pdf

From the above tables, it is seen that:

1. The infant mortality rate has decreased over a period of time
2. Infant mortality rate is more in rural area as compared to urban area
3. Infant mortality rate in rural area is decreasing faster than the in rural area
4. Infant mortality rate of females is more than the males

The possible reasons for the above observations are:

1. *The infant mortality rate has decreased over a period of time*: There is an improvement in socio-economic factors and availability of medical facilities.

2. *Infant mortality rate is more in rural area as compared to urban area*: The difference is due to better improvement in socio-economic factors and availability of medical facilities in urban area as compared to rural area.
3. *Infant mortality rate in rural area is decreasing faster than the in rural area*: This is because in earlier period the infant mortality rate in rural area was very much low. So, even same improvement in both areas will show the change in rural area in better light.
4. *Infant mortality rate of females is more than the males*: Historical as well as socio-economic factors are cited as reasons for this.

Life Expectancy at Birth

The life expectancy at birth indicates the average number of years a person is expected to live under prevailing mortality conditions. The following Table 3.9 gives Expectation of Life at Birth by sex and residence in India 1991-95 and 2006-10.

Table 3.9: Expectation of Life at Birth by sex and residence in India 1991-95 and 2006-10

Period	Mid year	Total			Rural			Urban		
		Total	Male	Female	Total	Male	Female	Total	Male	Female
1991-95	1993	60.3	59.7	60.9	58.9	58.5	59.3	65.9	64.5	67.3
2006-10	2008	66.1	64.6	67.7	64.9	63.5	66.5	69.6	68.0	71.4

Source: Census of India 2011.
Website: http://www.censusindia.gov.in/vital_statistics/SRS_Based/Introduction.pdf

From the above table, it is seen that:

1. Life expectancy has increased across sex and residence from 1991-95 to 2006-10.
2. Rate of increase in life expectancy is more in rural area as compared to urban area.
3. Life expectancy is more in urban area as compared to rural area.
4. Life expectancy of female is more than male.

The possible reasons for the above observations are:

1. *Life expectancy has increased across sex and residence from 1991-95 to 2006-10*: Life expectancy in general has increased because of improved medical facilities including immunization programme, improved food availability and slightly better economic condition of poor in relation to earlier much worse condition.
2. *Rate of increase in life expectancy is more in rural area as compared to urban area*: Earlier to 1991, life expectancy in rural area has been very low as compared to urban area. Therefore, the same factors as mentioned at sl. no. 1 above led to life expectancy in rural area more than the urban area.
3. *Life expectancy is more in urban area as compared to rural area*: This is because the medical facilities and economic condition of urban population are better than those of rural population.
4. *Life expectancy of female is more than male*: As longevity of female has been more than male since centuries, some scientists put genetic as one of the reasons. Biological difference is mentioned as another reason. Men take to smoking and alcohol more than women. Men work in more adverse environment compared to women. More men die of heart attacks compared to women. These are cited as possible reasons, but no conclusive reasons could be found for this.

United Nations chalked out eight millennium development goals for achieving by 2015. Regarding health, Infant Mortality Rate and Maternal Mortality Rate are among these goals. India will be failing to achieve both the goals going by the present progress on these fronts. The main reason for the failure is attributed to inadequate public healthcare services especially in rural area.

State Provision for Health

Healthcare in Rural Area

It is observed that healthcare in rural area is suffering due to poor infrastructure. Which include *pucca* road network, potable water supply, sanitation and reliable power supply to health centers. Absence of proper connecting road network is a major disconnect between rural and urban area. Poor infrastructure is a major hurdle to a flow of healthcare facilities to rural area.

In order to provide proper healthcare in rural area, National Rural Health Mission (NRHM) has been formed. The specific objectives of the mission are stated in the Framework for Implementation 2005-2012 which is given in the Box 3.4.

Box 3.4: National Rural Health Mission (NRHM) Framework for Implementation 2005-2012

On 12 April, 2005, the Government of India launched the National Rural Health Mission (NRHM) with a view to bringing about dramatic improvement in the health system and the health status of the people, especially those who live in the rural areas of the country. The NRHM covers the entire country, with special focus on 18 States where the challenge of strengthening poor public health systems and thereby improving key health indicators is the greatest. The Mission would help achieve goals set under the National Health Policy and the Millennium Development Goals.

The Objectives of the Mission

- Reduction in child and maternal mortality.
- Universal access to public services for food and nutrition, sanitation and hygiene and universal access to public health care services with emphasis on services addressing women's and children's health and universal immunization.
- Prevention and control of communicable and non-communicable diseases, including locally endemic diseases.
- Access to integrated comprehensive primary health care.
- Population stabilization, gender and demographic balance.

The Core Strategies of the Mission

- Train and enhance capacity of Panchayati Raj Institutions (PRIs) to own, control and manage public health services.
- Promote access to improved healthcare at household level through the female health activist (ASHA).
- Health Plan for each village through Village Health Committee of the Panchayat.
- Strengthening sub-centre through better human resource development, clear quality standards, better community support and an Untied fund to enable local planning and action and more Multi-Purpose Workers (MPWs).
- Strengthening existing (PHCs) through better staffing and human resource
- Provision of 30-50 bedded CHC per lakh population for improved curative care.

GoI Ministry of Health and Family Welfare
(http://jknrhm.com/Guideline/Frame_Work.pdf)

Healthcare for Urban Population

Private medical treatment in urban area has become so costly that only rich can afford it. For the rest, they have to depend upon state healthcare services. The state has therefore started to provide facilities for the poor in urban area in line with those in rural area. National Urban Health Mission (NUHM) has been formed for the purpose. The Framework for implementation October, 2012 for the same is given in Box 3.5.

Box 3.5: National Urban Health Mission (NUHM): Framework for implementation October, 2012

The urban population has increased to 377 million in 2011. Urban growth has led to rapid increase in number of urban poor, many of whom live in slums and other squatter settlements. As per Census 2001, 42.6 million people lived in slums spread over 640 towns/cities having population of fifty thousand or above.

Despite the supposed proximity of the urban poor to urban health facilities their access to them is severely restricted. This is on account of their being "crowded out" because of the inadequacy of the urban public health delivery system.

In order to effectively address the health concerns of the urban poor population, the Ministry proposes to launch a National Urban Health Mission (NUHM). The Mission Steering Group of the NRHM will be expanded to work as the apex body for NUHM also.

The NUHM would have high focus on: Urban Poor Population living in listed and unlisted slums; All other vulnerable population such as homeless, rag-pickers, street children, rickshaw pullers, construction and brick and lime kiln workers, sex workers, and other temporary migrants; Public health thrust on sanitation, clean drinking water, vector control, etc; Strengthening public health capacity of urban local bodies.

The National Urban Health Mission will provide flexibility to the States to choose which model suits the needs and capacities of the states to best address the healthcare needs of the urban poor.

All the services delivered under the urban health delivery system through the Urban-Public Health Centres (PHCs) and Urban-Community Health Centres (CHCs) will be universal in nature, whereas the outreach services will be targeted to the target groups (slum dwellers and other vulnerable groups). Unlike rural areas, Sub-centres will not be set up in the urban areas as distances and mode of transportation are much better here. Outreach services will be provided through the Female Health Workers (FHWs), essentially ANMs with an induction training of three to six months, who will be headquartered at the Urban PHCs. These ANMs will report at the U-PHC and then move to their respective areas for outreach services (including school health) on designated days. They will be provided mobility support for providing outreach services.

It would promote a community health volunteer-Urban Social Health Activist (similar as ASHA) or Link Worker (LW) in urban poor settlements and ensure the participation by creation of community based institutions like Mahila Arogya Samiti (MAS).

GoI Ministry of Health and Family Welfare
(http://pbhealth.gov.in/NUHM_Framework.pdf)

Following the launch of the National Urban Health Mission (NUHM) by GoI, the Maharashtra State announced on 02.03.2014 the launch of NUHM, the urban equivalent of the National Rural Health Mission (NRHM) launched in 2005. It focuses on urban poor especially slum dwellers.

Rajiv Gandhi Jeevandayee Arogya Yojana (RGJAY)

In India, a number of initiatives have been taken by the Government of India at the centre as well as states. The initiative taken by a typical state of Maharashtra is given here briefly.

The scheme has been formulated by the State of Maharashtra with the objective to improve access of Below Poverty Line (BPL) and Above Poverty Line (APL) families (excluding White Card Holder) to quality medical care for identified speciality services requiring hospitalization for surgeries and therapies or consultations through an identified Network of health care providers. It is planned to be implemented throughout the State of Maharashtra in phased manner.

The Scheme provides coverage for meeting all expenses relating to hospitalization of beneficiary up to Rs. 1,50,000/- per family per year in any of the Empanelled Hospital on cashless basis through Health cards or valid Orange/Yellow Ration Card.

Global Position about Health Indicators

In the global context, Infant Mortality Rate and Life Expectancy at Birth are the most important indicators to compare the socio-economic conditions and healthcare services prevalent in the country. Over a period of time, there has been steady improvement in Infant Mortality Rate and Life Expectancy at Birth in India. Number of factors seem to have contributed for the increase in the life expectancy. The main factors are universal immunization programme and changes in diet, along with prevention and treatment of infectious diseases.

Childhood vaccination has checked epidemics and saved number of lives. Earlier people had more children, and the chances of all the kids getting balanced diet were low. Increased awareness about family welfare has greatly helped this aspect. Life threatening diseases like diphtheria, tetanus and whooping cough have been eliminated completely. India has also been declared a polio free nation on 13.01.2014. The steps like providing clean drinking water, sanitation facilities and better control of non-communicable diseases are expected to help to increase life expectancy beyond the present level.

Although there has been steady Improvement in Infant Mortality Rate and Life Expectancy at Birth in India, India is still way behind other nations in these areas as will be seen from the comparison given below.

Infant Mortality Rate

Table 3.10 gives Infant Mortality Rate for a few representative countries.

Table 3.10: Infant Mortality Rate in 8 selected countries per 1000 live births

Country	*Infant*	*Under 5*
USA	6	7
UK	4	5
Japan	2	3
BRICS countries		
Brazil	13	14
Russia	9	10
India	44	56
China	12	14
South Africa	33	45

Source: UN Human Development Report 2014.
Website: http://hdr.undp.org/sites/default/files/hdr14-report-en-1.pdf

It will be seen from the above Table 3.10 that India's Infant Mortality Rate is highest among the countries mentioned above, especially much more than China.

Life Expectancy at Birth

Longevity as represented by the indicator-Life Expectancy at Birth is one of the three parameters used for arriving at the Human Development Index (HDI), which is used as a valid measure of the country's progress. Table 3.11 gives Life Expectancy at Birth for a few representative countries.

It will be seen from Table 3.11 that India's Life Expectancy at Birth is very low and especially much lower than China.

The above comparison indicates that much more has to be done to improve healthcare in India especially in rural area. In India, major challenge is poverty with about quarter of the total population of the country living below poverty line. The problem for these people is how

Table 3.11: Life Expectancy at Birth in 8 selected countries

Country	*Years*
USA	78.9
UK	80.5
Japan	83.6
BRICS countries	
Brazil	73.9
Russia	68.0
India	66.4
China	75.3
South Africa	56.9

Source: UN Human Development Report 2014.
Website: http://hdr.undp.org/sites/default/files/hdr14-report-en-1.pdf

to get two square meals. The nutritional aspect of the food becomes secondary to them when their primary requirement of food for satisfying hunger itself is not met.

In India, generally predominant factors in selection of food are: food being produced in one's geographical area, age old social customs and habits formed since childhood. It is of late that nutritional value in the food is somewhat being understood by the people. The awareness of this aspect is still much less in the rural area.

Inadequate Allocation of Funds for Public Health

Another problem is that the budget allocation to healthcare services is too inadequate to catch up with other nations referred above. India spends about 1 per cent of its Gross Domestic Product (GDP) on public health, compared to 3 per cent in China and 8.3 per cent in the United States.

Globalization puts more emphasis on economic progress and directly or indirectly puts premium on spending on social sector of which healthcare is one of the major components. Inadequate allocation of funds for public health resulted in dilapidated condition of government hospitals and clinics. The healthcare services in the rural area are the worst affected.

Global Trend: Managing Healthcare by the State

Changing Priority from Tropical to Life-Style Diseases

India has been fighting from the past with poverty-driven diseases such as malnutrition, anemia, miscarriages and other tropical diseases such as malaria etc. However, now under globalization, suddenly emphasis has shifted from tropical diseases to life-style diseases such as heart disease, diabetes, cancer, HIV/AIDS, obesity etc. As a fall out of early industrialization, developed countries are gripped with these diseases and they are persuading other countries too for according higher priority for combating these diseases.

Global Trend of Healthcare Services

World over, management of healthcare services has been the most intricate subject for the government for two reasons. Firstly, there cannot be any statistical measurement of satisfaction level of healthcare. As such any provision of healthcare by the state for the people will always fall short of people's expectations. Secondly, finding adequate resources, for providing required healthcare services *vis-à-vis* other sectors, has always been a problem for the state. Thus, even richest country like USA with highest per capita income, find difficulty in providing healthcare up to the satisfaction of the people. The healthcare plan of Obama administration which has gone quite far in extending the facility has also met with lot of criticism.

Obama Care—New Healthcare System in USA

Obama care is the unofficial name for The Patient Protection and Affordable Care Act 2010. It includes offering Americans a number of protections in regard to their healthcare and setting up a Health Insurance Marketplace where Americans can purchase federally regulated and subsidized health insurance. Though intended for the welfare of the not-so-rich, the protagonists and critics have taken diametrically opposite positions, i.e. in favour of and against the plan.

Further, Obama's plan to extend private health coverage to the uninsured also took off in November, 2014 as government-backed online insurance marketplaces opened their 2015 plans to millions of potential enrollees.

Healthcare in U.K.

Though there are slight variations in the healthcare system followed in the regions, i.e. England, Northern Ireland, Scotland and Wales, UK provides public healthcare for all citizens. The expenditure is met through general taxation. There is also private healthcare sector but it is comparatively much smaller. With high public spending on healthcare, UK is also experiencing the difficulty in managing it.

The lack of public satisfaction about healthcare systems in US or UK should not give an impression that the system in India is not to be found fault with. The people in the West are prosperous, they have social security and they have choices, whereas quarter of India's total population is living below poverty line and the poor have no choices. The process of globalization whose main emphasis is economic progress leaves little room for giving priority to public healthcare. The situation in India with regard to healthcare for the poor is thus really bad.

Conclusion

The infant mortality rate in India is very high. Malnourishment is the major cause of this. At the back of malnourishment is poverty which is rampant in rural area. Lately an idea of covering the poor people with suitable insurance cover is being toyed. However, providing health insurance cover is hardly a solution for the main problem of poor healthcare in the rural area. Against this background, it is necessary for the state to provide the rural people proper primary healthcare which should be easily accessible.

While almost all countries have tried to jettison internal and external resources for meeting basic requirements like food and shelter, providing adequate healthcare to people has remained an intractable problem. The budget allocation of funds for healthcare services is too meager to take care of actual requirement. India has specifically acute problem in meeting the requirement of healthcare for the ageing population. In private hospitals, healthcare is 4-5 times that of public health care. Unable to provide proper public healthcare to the needy, the State is coming up with health insurance schemes. In actual practice, these are poor substitute for the proper public healthcare, since, it is a herculean task to get the claims passed from insurance companies as the process involves lot of paper work for the care giving institutions. Too much emphasis of globalization on economic progress seems to be hitting hard social sector which includes health and education.

4
Globalization and Technology

ROLE OF DEVELOPING TECHNOLOGY

Prologue

Technology means study or practical use of applied sciences. While both technology and globalization have their own histories, technology prevailed even within geographical boundaries and thus even before globalization process set in. Globalization and technology are so much interconnected that the questions are often raised about the relationship between the two; the questions are whether technology is the cause of globalization or *vice-versa* and whether technology is the enabler of the globalization or *vice-versa*.

Role of Technology

Technology is like any other tool which can be used as the user wants to use. User can use it for constructive as well as destructive purposes. The nuclear science has provided many breakthroughs in the form of nuclear medicine alleviating the scourge of many diseases. At the same time the same very science is being used to produce atom bombs capable of annihilating the mankind. Therefore, the technology is use neutral. It would work as the user wants to use. By the same token, while technology provides many devices for human comfort, on psycho-social front technology may add to knowledge but by itself does not make man or woman wiser.

Technology has made far reaching changes in the mode of living of people. Thus, it has been instrumental in transforming the society to adapt to new patterns. Earlier, most of the people were engaged in agriculture and allied activities. Later, many of the people living on agriculture shifted to industries which came up as a result of industrial revolution. These shifts brought in life style changes in the society.

Information and Communication Technology

Just as industrialization brought in life style changes in the society, the advancement in information and communication technology during the last two decades made radical life style changes in the society. Due to the advancement of ICT, the contacts between the people living even at far off distances have increased tremendously. The mode of life of people has become faster than ever. With the advent of social media, many have started interacting and developing social relationship through face book without any face to face physical contact.

Technology has moved from its technical domain and transformed traditional society into a new network society. Manuel Castells (1996) argues that "this shift requires reconceptulizing many social processes and institutions as expressions of networks, moving away from conceptual frameworks organized around the notion of hierarchies." (Ritzer, 2012: 1961).

Digital Divide

Developed countries continued investing more resources in research and developed new technologies. Thus, they could reap the benefit through new technologies immediately. On the other hand, developing countries having no resources for research have to depend on the developed countries for transfer of new technologies. Thus, developing countries have a great disadvantage. The use of information and communication technology especially internet is widespread in developed countries. More than 90 per cent of the population in the developed countries uses internet facility as against just about 16 per cent in India. This abysmal difference in the usage of internet and other information and communication facilities is popularly termed as 'digital divide.'

Biotechnology in Agriculture

As there has been great advancement of technology in the field of physics, there has been great advancement in the field of biotechnology. Especially the bio-agricultural research in the seed has enabled farmers to improve productivity by leaps and bounds.

Technology in Medicine

The introduction of technology has made great revolution in the medical field. Nuclear medicine is one such latest tool. The investigative tools can now diagnose the disease more precisely. Besides producing effective drugs for medical treatment, surgeries are possible in every part of the body except brain in which success rate has been minimal. Heart surgery, knee joint and kidney replacement have become quite common. Thus, life has become bearable for the people who faced serious handicaps earlier. Ironically though medical science has found some remedies for the complex diseases, it shows its limitations in ailments like common cold which looks so simple.

Indian medical profession is intensively using advances in technology in medicine. More and more diagnostic centers with latest instrumentation in testing as well as surgical procedures are coming up. India has developed its reputation so much that people from West as well as Europe are coming to India for treatment. Of course cost factor is playing major role in this trend as treatment in India is much cheaper than in West and Europe.

Nuclear and Space Technology

India has made tremendous progress in nuclear technology and it has been acknowledged as a nuclear power. This would help India to build more nuclear power stations rather than depend heavily on coal based thermal power stations which produce harmful emissions. As regards space technology, India has successfully launched Manglayan in 2013 which is now orbiting the Mars making India the first country in the world to achieve the feat in the first attempt. With its progress in space technology, India is expected to tap global market in the field of putting satellites in the space.

Time-space Compression

Mankind has moved from one mode of transport to another with more speed from bullock cart/horse driven carriage, motor cycle, car, train and then planes to jet planes. Some time in future, travel to another planet by spaceship may become common. The new technology enabled movements ever faster and it appears as though distances between the places on the globe have reduced radically. David Harvey (1989) terms this as time-space compression. With time-space compression, it has been possible to achieve greater interconnectedness between the people living at a distance, facilitating the process of globalization.

Technoscapes

Arjun Appadurai (2005) describes a framework comprising five dimensions of global cultural flows one of which is technoscapes. Here technoscapes refer to global flow of technology, scapes refer especially to irregular shapes just as landscapes. The spread of technology has been quite uneven, developed countries having become rich with technology followed by others. The advancement of information and communication technology has enabled to move information across the globe with high speed. The information or financial transactions can now take place *via* Internet in split seconds. Also, people remain connected to each other irrespective of their location and distances on earth. Thus, technology has not remained isolated as a physical concept, but it has become very much integral part of the social process.

Will Robot Take over Human Being?

Many of the functions which were done routinely by human beings are being done by machines and computers. The speed of advancement of technology suggests that though human being will still remain relevant as a producer and operator of technology, most of the physical activities being done by him now could be done by the robot in due course. Japan has developed robot capable of doing almost all household works which can be timed. Efforts are also afoot to make robot capable of responding to various situations as thinking human being does. Already this principle is built in the guided missiles in which the missile corrects its course on its own automatically if any deviation from the course takes place in its position during the journey.

Drone, an Unmanned Aerial Vehicle (UAV), flies without a human pilot. It is operated by remote control. It is being extensively used for collecting meteorological/geographical data in difficult locations, reconnaissance mission and in combat operations to avoid the likelihood of the aircraft with pilot getting shot down by the adversary. Another example is driverless car capable of fulfilling the transportation capabilities of a normal car with driver. It is capable of sensing the external environment and running without a human driver. Presently they are in the prototype stage and in restricted use.

Artificial Intelligence

Distinguished physicist Stephen Hawking in December, 2014 warned that the development of full-fledged, autonomous Artificial Intelligence (AI) could spell doom for the human race. There are already super computers that can outsmart some of the functions of human beings. With the scientific work in progress, sooner or later a machine with AI will be developed which can think on its own. In this context, there is an apprehension that there will be little use of humanity, making it almost dispensable. But protagonists of AI contend that AI could be seen as just another service provider rather than seen as usurping power of thinking human being. Also whatever may be the effort put in by the mankind, it is just impossible to develop a robot matching the capability of a human brain.

Technology and Human Body

Through close interaction between the local and the global under globalization, a new reconfiguration has emerged which is termed as glocal. This change percolates further down to micro level, i.e. human body. More and more humans are coming out from the hard work in agriculture and manufacturing to softer jobs in the services sector such as information and communication technology. From body labour, there is a shift to mental work.

Technology has increased comfort level of human beings. But it has also brought some undesirable consequences. Physical labour is essential part of health and wellbeing. The physical labour is antidote to mental stress. When most of the activities are delegated to machines, the incidence of diseases related to stress such as obesity, heart ailment and host of other ailments is bound to increase. There will be more interconnectivity between man and machine rather than one human being with another. Already this is happening now with people getting more and more glued to TV resulting in less and less physical social contact.

Though it might be thought that the advancement of technology has diminished the role of (human) body, its social and related value retains paramount importance in globalization. Thus, even if technology advances, the function of human body will always be pivotal in the society because technology will be driven by the human bodies only.

Technology and Globalization Enabling each Other

The advancement of technology is being used to further the process of globalization. So also the globalization is accelerating the expansion of research and development giving birth to newer and newer technology. It is seen that both technology and globalization are promoting each other. Thus, rather than one being the cause of other, both are mutual enabler of each other.

Conclusion

Over the years India has made tremendous progress in all fields of technology, especially its progress in the specialized fields of electronics, information and communication technology, nuclear power and space technology is phenomenal.

It is noteworthy that the movement of technology and globalization has been simultaneous, side by side. Thus, both are enabling and complementing the progress of each other. Technology is use neutral in the sense that it is just a tool and it depends on the user how he or she wants to use it, whether for constructive or destructive purposes. Trust has acquired importance in this situation. When trouble makers use, the same very instruments (*i.e.* mobile phone, airplane, fiber optic technology etc.) which provide assistance to open society, for creating violence, it reduces the trust about technology though technology *per se* is not at fault.

Technology has made movement of information, people and goods faster. With time and space compression, the world has become pretty smaller. Technology has not remained isolated as a physical concept alone, but it has become integral part of the social life.

ROLE OF INFORMATION AND COMMUNICATION TECHNOLOGY—MEDIA

Prologue

Information and Communication Technology (ICT) is an integration of technologies of information, telecommunication (telephone and wireless) and includes print, cinema, radio, internet, computer, television, mobile phone etc. The term ICT is being used since 1980s but has become more popular since late 1990s.

With advancement of information and communication technology, there has been tremendous increase in the interconnectivity between the people across the globe. The process of globalization has resulted in time and space compression so much so that the world is being looked as a global village. Both globalization and information and communication technology are progressing apace. The natural question is whether there is any relationship between globalization and ICT and if it is there, which one is enabling the other, i.e. whether globalization is helping ICT to grow or ICT is enabling globalization to grow or both are enabling each other to grow?

Evolution of Present Media

The media represents the unique creative power of human mind. It is created for facilitating human discourse. The mass media is intended to reach a very large audience and area, as against the local media which caters to smaller population and local area. Chronologically media started growing with development of print media beginning late fifteenth century. As regards mass media in India, it started with the first newspaper 'Bengal Gazette' published by Englishman in eighteenth century. This was basically meant for the Englishmen who were working for East India Company. Later many newspapers came up during independence movement. The print media was followed by Cinema from about 1900, Radio 1910, Television 1950, Internet 1990 and Mobile phones 2000. Each mass media has its own characteristic content type.

After three officially known state powers namely Parliament, Executive and Judiciary, the press is most commonly known as the fourth power or the Fourth Estate. Freedom of press is given utmost importance in democracy because free press enables people to make informed choices rather than making choices in ignorance and acts as a check on the functioning of the government, politicians and institutions so that these act according to the responsibilities devolved on them. Although initially press was called as a forth power as it was the only media, later as the media expanded to number of forms such as radio, television, internet etc., the entire media is now being perceived as the fourth power. Media by its reach covers all aspects of life, i.e. social, economic, cultural and governance. In present times, computers, internet and television have made media as a very powerful tool to influence the public opinion.

Role of Media

Social Change

Communication is part of social system. Nobody can live in isolation.

Media has power to influence the attitude of human being. It can create new attitude. It has also power to enhance capability of human being. By way of comparing social ethos and norms of different societies, it can bring change in the existing social system. Media can talk about individual member's freedom, discuss merits and demerits of family pattern (patriarchal or matriarchal), rigidity of caste system, economic system, system of governance, value system, cultural aspect of the society and so on. The influence of media is seen from oriental culture getting influenced by the western culture, change in dress fashion, music etc.

Medium and the Content

The advancement of information and communication technology has made the world look like a 'global village' a term firstly used by Marshall McLuhan. Through instant interconnectivity possible now, any work or business can be conducted any time and from any place in the world.

In print media, content of the matter was the most important. However, with the advent of Television, medium has also become important, so much so that there is a question mark as to whether medium (TV) is more important than content (particular programme) or *vice-versa*. The influence of media can be gauged by looking at the people who are just glued to TV, even for no specific reasons, and irrespective of programme is worth seeing or not. Media has thus acquired powerful position in the modern society in shaping individual life and culture.

Impact of ICT

Information and communication technology has facilitated the organizations to do business from anywhere and anytime. ICT has enabled small to huge financial flows to take place instantly across the globe. While this has been of great help to business organizations, this has also led to many economic crises in the world. Thus, ICT as any other technology is only a tool and it depends upon how it is utilized.

Information and communication technology also helped NGOs. Prior to ICT, NGO movements were locally or regionally bound. However, after advancement of information and communication technology, the movements through national and worldwide networks helped to expand their field of activity. Another area which got boost with the advancement in information and communication technology is education. Educative programme through ICT is quite a popular mode in developed countries, though it is less popular in developing countries especially because there are no required facilities available in these countries.

Legitimacy of the State at Stake

Information and communication technology is playing pivotal role in changing the relationship between the state and the citizens. Previously, the state used to be the sole authority to respond to the needs of the citizens. But now there is so much information flow around the citizens that the very legitimacy of the state as a sole responder has become ineffectual. Earlier, the foreign trade was routed solely through state agencies like State Trading Corporation in India. Now, for most of the general goods, trading is done on internet directly by the concerned parties.

Earlier media used to display mostly advertisements and entertainment programmes. Many other subjects are being covered now by the media. For example, matters related to politics, religion, ethnicity etc. are getting prominence. Looking at the intensity of discourse taking place directly on global stage, one wonders whether the state is getting bypassed even over important issues.

Reach of ICT in Rural Area/Digital Divide

Digital Divide

The world is divided between those who have easy access and those who have no access. This difference is getting translated into social inequality, for example 'information is education.' The popular term for this divide is 'digital divide'. It is noteworthy that the 'digital divide' is widening firstly due to newer efficient and faster versions of ICTs coming up often as a result of constant research and development in this area, and secondly due to the aspect of affordability.

Though information and communication technology is spreading fast, its spread is not uniform not only nationally but even regionally and even in different groups. Developed nations are the first ones to have had it. Similarly, it is more dominant in urban area. The literacy and affordability are also factors in the spread of ICT. Thus, there is a divide between urban and rural, rich and poor, educated and illiterate and above all global divide between the nations in developed North and the nations in developing South.

In spite of India attaining unique position in the field of information and communication technology, the users of internet are barely 16 per cent of the total population. While educated and rich people are able to afford the facility, the poor people are unable to access the facility. Thus digital divide could not be bridged in India so far.

C-DOT: Technology to Rural Area

Earlier India was following the model of developed countries wherein emphasis was on creating teledensity which obviously means keeping these technologies urban bound. It was in mid 1980s that Rajiv Gandhi, the then young Prime Minister of India provided impetus to telecommunication and information technology and Centre for Development of Telematics (C-DOT) was set up in 1984 to develop state-of-the-art telecommunication technology. C-DOT facilitated rural population to get access to much needed telecommunication technology which was till then confined to urban population only (Karan, 2004: 124).

The New Telecom Policy (1999) was launched for developing rural communication and Vidya Vahini and Gyan Vahini programmes were launched for education purpose in rural schools. However, irregular power supply in rural area remains a major problem for running these programmes. The problem is being solved at some places by installing small diesel generating sets for providing uninterrupted power supply to computers.

e-Choupal

Earlier internet facilities were not available in rural area. In this context, ITC-a corporate organization is doing pioneering work in trying to provide internet based direct marketing facility called 'e-choupal' in villages. 'e-choupal' is a kiosk which is equipped with a computer that has internet facility. Telephone facility or wherever telephone facility is not available, VSAT stations have enabled internet facility even in remote rural areas. At some places, the problem of continuous availability of electric power for computer and internet operation is solved by installing small diesel generating sets. This has greatly helped agricultural business in rural area.

With e-choupal, villagers are now getting informed of the trend of market pricing of their produce and they have now more choices for selling them. They can now choose their own timing to sell the produce. Earlier rural population was entirely dependent for these on urban market which is invariably situated at a distance. With poor communication facilities like roads, it used to be extremely difficult to market the agricultural products. Now, wherever 'e-choupal' is located, villagers are finding agricultural business easy, i.e. without hassles.

Rural "e-governance"

Though the pace is slow, internet services are getting increasingly popular in rural area. In future, there may be number of internet cafes in villages as they are now in urban areas. While due to lack of education, older generation in rural area is not in a position to participate in e-services, younger generation is quite enthusiastic about these. Gradually India will emerge as a nation of cyber community.

Just as many of the services pertaining to urban area are computerized, there are number of services pertaining to rural area which can be computerized. The idea is to include those services which are basic in nature and required often by the common man so that he may not be required to approach bureaucracy for every matter. Some of these services are:

- Data about population
- Birth, death, marriage
- Caste
- Residence
- Land and revenue records
- People below poverty line
- People with *aadhaar* card
- People with ration card
- People eligible for pension and those who are getting pension
- Payment of house tax and other taxes
- Data about literacy/education and Health services
- Data about availability of toilet at home
- Data about agricultural services such as meteorological data, seeds, fertilizers, pesticides, market etc.
- Data about entitlements
- Data about employment/unemployment
- Information about various government projects/schemes
- Income
- Solvency
- Legal heir

As an example, the project named e-district project was implemented sometime back in two districts namely Ganjam and Mayurbhanj in Odisha state (India) on pilot basis and the certificates like caste, residence, solvency, income and legal heir are being received online in both the districts.

Social Networking—New Development

Social Networking Sites

Any two people on the globe can make contact through a chain of intermediaries. A person joins one of the social networking sites. He invites people he knows to join. Those people invite their contacts to join. Thus a process repeats for each person. Conceptually, any person can make contact through anyone they have a connection to, and so on. Social networking thus establishes internet communities that enable people to make contacts, though they might not have met before.

Of late, social networking sites on internet are becoming more and more popular for communication and making friendship. Among popular ones are 'facebook.' Social networking sites provide instant connectivity with viewers, which was not possible through print media. These sites are becoming extremely popular with the younger generation. The relationship is now being developed through these sites rather than physical contact. There are certain advantages as well as disadvantages in this type of interaction. The advantage is that no big effort is required in communication and one can be communicating several persons at a time. The disadvantage is that many instances of abuse and duping one another are reported regularly in the press.

Another category of media being used are tweeter and blogs. Interestingly, many well meaning politicians who were earlier seen as conservative in using such media have also started using aforementioned sites. The peculiarity of the sites is that these do not produce any material by themselves and the users of the sites are both consumers and the producers.

Digital Social Networking

Digital networking is real time networking. Social networking is now being accessed through mobile/cell phone which means the facility has become easy to avail. Some sociologists contend that the use of digital social networking is not undermining the relationship in the communities though they are decreasing face to face contacts between individuals. They say there is more integration in the community as increased interaction through internet is strengthening the community feeling.

The advantage of internet and cell phones is that they facilitate local community members to connect easily with the people situated at a distance anywhere on the globe. They contend that the relationship is only changing the form from physically local bounded communities to globally extended communities (Ritzer, 2012: 438-39). New technologies are also being incorporated into more routine aspects of daily social life. The critics of digital social networking, however, contend that the technology has more disadvantages than advantages and it is being misused by unscrupulous people to foment trouble in the societies which otherwise are peaceful.

Global Reach

Global Village

With advanced information and communication technology, there has been time and space compression. People situated in one part of the globe are able to connect with the people in the other part of the globe easily and instantly. "Marshall McLuhan's theories of media emphasize the way in which technological development changes society, culture, and the individual. His coining of the term 'Global village' thus conveys how the world was becoming smaller, more connected, and social distance ended."

Relationship between Globalization and ICT

Globalization encompasses multiple aspects of society. However, it mainly refers to free flow of trade, capital, technology and labour. Trade includes production as well as market. All these activities are facilitated by the information and communication technology. The demand on ICT will increase as the globalization expands. This demand spurs the research and development activity in the field of ICT. Thus, globalization and information and communication technology are highly intertwined and both are advancing the cause of each other.

Downside of Mass Media

The purposeful role of media has been well explained earlier. However, like any other technology, media can be used either for facilitating human lifestyle or for wrong purposes. Many a times, there are big advertisements about the products which are of spurious nature and people are misled by these advertisements into buying such products. Similarly, television is used for giving slant news which again can mislead the people. Many times, the media gives manipulated version of the event which is far from reality.

The influence of media affects politics greatly. The phenomenon of paid news has become quite common. The diktat and the policies of those who own media affect the neutrality and objectiveness of the reporting. Instead of depicting the opinion of masses, the media starts acting as opinion maker. The trial by media is quite popular term in describing the event in a partisan manner, same commentary running continuously for days.

People expect media to be potential educator since it has capability to provide educational programme. However, in practice, actual educational content shown by media is insignificant compared to space and time given to advertising and entertainment.

There are instances of displaying images on internet which lead to fomenting ethnic or religious conflicts which have potential to cause even wars between the nations. Combating wrong use of internet or detecting cybercrime has been found to be extremely difficult.

The emphasis on depiction of catchy lifestyle of elite class through mass media especially TV has profound impact on common masses turning them to imitating that kind of lifestyle and spending more money for that purpose even though their earning may be modest.

Thus, there are both advantages and disadvantages of mass media and it depends upon the user how he wants to use it.

Conclusion

With the advent of information and communication technology, the interconnectivity between the people situated at a distance on the globe has tremendously increased. This has led to unimaginable time and space compression. On the economic front, this technology has facilitated the organization to do business from anywhere as well as anytime. ICT has enabled small to large financial flows instantly across the globe. While this has been of great help to business organizations, this has also led to flourishing speculative business and occurrence of many economic crises in the world. Thus ICT as any other technology is only a tool, and it depends how it is utilized.

In the famous words of Marshall McLuhan, the world has now become a 'global village.' ICT has reduced earlier face to face social contact between the people. While some sociologists contend that this has led to reduction in real community feeling, some sociologists contend that instead of reduction in community feeling, only the relationship has changed the form from physically local bounded communities to globally extended communities. In any case, mass media is playing its role in developing modern society. Apart from entertainment, as a part of democracy, it is disseminating news and depicting events enabling the public and the state to draw their own conclusions. It is bringing out events about which people other than those who are witnesses would never have known anything.

Like any other technology, media is also (mis) used for giving manipulated version of the event and sometimes even disturbs the prevailing peaceful atmosphere. It is extensively used for marketing the products which may not be genuine or fashions which may not be truly in the best interest of the society. Women are shown more as fashion models rather than depicting their real major role in nation building.

Regarding the question as to whether there is any relationship between the globalization and ICT, it is observed that both are highly interwoven and both are advancing the cause of each other.

5
Globalization and Development Process

MIGRATION AND URBANIZATION

Prologue

Migration is defined as a move from one migration defining area to another, involving a change of residence. The term internal migration is used to denote migration (change of residence) within national borders. Nomadic movements are not generally called migration as the nomads do not settle in a new place. Migration happens due to both economic and social reasons. From olden times, people used to migrate for seeking better livelihood or to avoid social discrimination and conflict.

Migration is an age-old phenomenon. Migration of people took place at different times in the northwestern Indian subcontinent. Political development is another cause of large scale migration. Partition of India in 1947 is estimated to have caused migration of nearly 10 million people. There is a steady migration of rural population to urban area. The relevant point for discussion here is whether globalization is hastening the process of migration of rural population, resulting in rapid urbanization?

Rural-Urban Migration: Magnitude, Reasons and Social Aspect

Table 5.1 shows the rural-urban distribution of population as per Census of India 1991, 2001, 2011.

It will be seen from Table 5.1 that there has been steady decrease in the percentage of rural population and increase in the urban population from 1991 to 2011. Also the rate of decrease in the percentage of rural

Table 5.1: Rural and Urban Population 1991-2011

Census year	*Percentage of Total Population*	
	Rural	*Urban*
1991	74.30	25.70
2001	72.18	27.82
2011	68.84	31.16

Source: Census of India 1991, 2001, 2011
Website: http://censusindia.gov.in/2011-prov-results/paper2/data_files/india/Rural_Urban_2011.pdf

population as well as increase in the urban population is increasing. Urbanization is occurring either due to outgrowth of population of the same place or inward coming of people from other places. Among these factors, migration of people from rural to urban area is playing major role in urbanization.

Industrialization in India is estimated to have led to 100 million circular migrants, as these migrants though moved to urban area lack of shelter and social security and many of them keep houses in their old places of residences. Most of these people go back to their villages to work during agricultural season and come back to new places again, phenomenon known as circular migration.

In modern globalization times, due to ease of transport and communication, migration from hinterland has become a part of universal process of urbanization and industrialization. In most countries, it has been observed that industrialization and economic development has been accompanied by large-scale movement of people from villages to towns, from towns to cities and from one country to another country.

Urban growth is the result of, besides net rural-urban migration, a number of factors such as natural increase, net increase in new towns and jurisdictional changes. In India, internal migrants touch 400 million in the 2011 census, which figure is twice of China's estimated 221 million. Residency system prevailing in China restricts migration of rural people to urban area. China has now decided to adopt residency reforms to ease migration to tame the anger in rural population.

It is estimated that rural-urban migration has contributed to about 20 per cent of increase in urban population. Though migrants contribute about 10 per cent to the national GDP, they are excluded from urban fore-planning initiatives and have to face innumerable problems in settling down in urban area. It would not be exaggeration to say that from the standpoint of city-dwellers the migrants are unfortunately portrayed as a "burden" to society. According to UNESCO's report June 2013 '*Social Inclusion of Internal Migrants in India*,' migrants are given very low priority, most of them are denied basic rights with respect to facilities pertaining to shelter, healthcare, education to children etc. and existing policies have failed to provide legal or social protection to this vulnerable group.

Natural migration of rural people opted voluntarily for seeking better employment opportunities in urban area can be understood and the surge of population in urban area can be mitigated by way of improving infrastructure in urban area. However, distress migration, because there is no choice available in rural area on account of socio-economic conditions, is certainly a blot on the society and the state. For example, discrimination on the basis of caste impels youth to migrate to urban area where there is practically no discrimination on the basis of caste. Similarly, the pathetic quality of education and healthcare facilities in rural area urge people to move to urban area. This situation in rural area can only be mitigated by social change and providing economic support by the state. In this context, MGNREGA with all its shortcomings has been found to be very useful in mitigating the hardships in the rural area.

Development of *Rurban* Centres/Cities

Rurban Centres

Apart from two broad categories, i.e. rural and urban, we can envisage a third category called *Rurban* representing the intermediate scenario. *Rurban* can also be seen as rural area with a sort of urban flair to it or with all of the commercial needs of rural, but with far less urban concrete. At one end of the paradigm there is no major occupation other than agriculture in the rural area and at the other end there is over concentration of industries in urban area. This has resulted in an unbalanced development in the regions. On the one hand it is said that there is a difficulty in providing infrastructure in every village. On the other hand the cities are getting so much overpopulated that there is always a serious problem of providing adequate civic amenities like clean drinking water, electricity, sanitation facilities.

Development of growth centres called *Rurban* will reduce the distance-space and economic gap between village and urban centres. These centres will serve dual purpose as nearest markets for the rural products and ready raw material inputs to small industries. The entrepreneurs can be encouraged to set up at these places small industrial units such as soap making, paper making, electric motor winding, auto repairing, fruit processing, handloom and carpet making etc.

Cities

Under globalization, we observe the huge contrast around. There are ultra rich and extremely poor people. There are privileged and disadvantaged people. The process of globalization is better seen happening in Cities. Cities comprise both, people with affluence as well as poverty, high rise buildings as well as slums. On one hand, there are big companies and business magnets and on the other hand there are small petty shops on the footpath and rag pickers. City is thus a mirror of life in contrast. Such huge contrasts sometimes turn the place into unseemly conflicts.

Rush of Hinterland Population Shifting toward Cities

The town and country planning departments do not envisage population shift of the scale and their planning has often been based on how to mitigate the current situation rather than planning for the future growth. The vested interest forces also play spoilsport role in the unplanned growth. They put stumbling blocks as they fear that their unauthorized encroachments will be removed. The managements of Municipal Corporations have not been able to keep pace with the expansion of spatial (horizontal) as well as vertical (flat system) growth of the residential complexes and business establishments. The civic bodies in the cities have not been able to cater even basic facilities like roads, shelter, clean water, sanitation etc. to the residents and business establishments. The result is that the cities like Mumbai, Delhi, Kolkata etc. are becoming nightmare cities with increasing slum areas. Due to inhuman living conditions, such places become breeding ground for crimes.

The transport system in cities is most chaotic particularly due to encroachments alongside the roads by the people with vested interests. The environment in the cities is most polluted because of fumes from vehicles and emissions and effluents from industries.

Advancement in information and communication technology allows us to work from anywhere. We can do office work even sitting at home. It was, therefore, thought that cities will lose their stature with the advancement of technology as it will be possible to do any job from anywhere, i.e. even from village on town. However, this has not happened and growth of cities continued unabated. The headquarters of business corporations are situated in cities. The strategic and management functions, planning and control functions are operated from headquarters. Marketing happens in cities. The headquarters of the organization is thus a nerve centre. It is from here that the subsidiaries spread over the globe are advised and controlled. Alongside specialized high income jobs, there are also low wage earners in cities. With socio-economic and cultural activities concentrated in city, it is almost a replica of the world.

By the very nature of intense economic activities in cities, cities have duel relationship. They are intimately connected with the economic system of the region in which they are situated. In fact to start with, places become cities on the strength of the economic system surrounding it. In course of time, economic system of cities gets interconnected with global economic system. The basic infrastructure and environment for setting up global business in a city is provided by the state support. In this way, cities get into dual relationship—one with the hinterland and the other with global system.

However, there is also some kind of disconnect between the two. This duel relationship resulting in disconnect can even be seen between cities and suburban system around. While the suburban system around represents traditional regional economic system, cities may represent more of the global economic system. For example, worker-management relationship and the level of wages in cities may vary widely from the suburban area in which the city is situated. The wages in cities will be much higher than in the suburban area.

China and India with Regard to Urbanization

For all important demographic related issues, the comparison between India and China is inescapable for two reasons. One reason is that both countries have large population to cater to. Another reason is that both countries have got independence from foreign domination more or less at the same time. However, there is an important difference in one aspect between the two countries and that is the system of governance. In China there is only one party, i.e. communist party ruling the country and thus there being no opposition, there is an authoritarian regime in China. In India there is a democratic form of governance. With strict adoption of one child norm, China could control the population growth. On the other hand, the method of birth control through family planning even for two or three children met with stiff resistance in India.

Both countries have had agriculture as the mainstay and rural population earlier accounted for more than seventy-five per cent. However, with industrialization in urban area, there has been shift from rural to urban area. In earlier times, the shift has taken place at a fast pace in China as compared to India as China created urban infrastructure speedily. With authoritarian rule, China did not face any difficulty like land acquisition etc. for creating infrastructure, whereas in democratic country like India, there have been many difficulties.

China, after decades of infrastructure build up unfettered by urban political concerns, now has an urban infrastructure capable of absorbing ten million new rural migrants a year into the urban economy. Combined with its low birth rate, China can expect that by 2050 its urban population will be 75 per cent of the country's total, compared to less than 40 per cent now. India, by contrast, will be unable to accommodate more than two million persons a year into urban areas, a rate lower than the rate at which the rural population is growing. Hence, even by 2050, India will still have largely a rural population. (Dossani, 2008: 233).

One area in which emphasis can be laid to tame the high rate of migration from rural area is to give fillip to rural industrialization. In this context, development of cottage and small scale industries can play an important role. However, with the advent of globalization, the efforts to encourage development of cottage and small scale industries have not met with significant success as these rural industries are unable to face stiff competition with regard to costs and prices of products from mass production methods adopted by large factories. Best that they can do is to function as ancillaries to feed specific components to main production units.

Conclusion

Industrialization around urban area and non-viability of agriculture are the main causes for large scale migration of rural population to urban area. The scale of migration is more in youth population. With availability of enthusiastic hard working youths, cities are acting as hubs for the activities of MNCs. On the other hand, rural area has lost the charm it possessed in earlier times. Under globalization, old people in rural area are the worst affected because when younger generation leave the rural place, old joint family system gets broken. There is no support system to take care of the old people at a time when they require help most.

The high rate of increase in population in cities in which major role is played by migration of rural population, has led to a complete mismatch between the increasing population and the civic infrastructure available to sustain it in urban area. Further, availability of jobs also does not keep pace with the requirement. This situation has led to increase in slums and crime rate in cities.

Coming to the question as to whether globalization is hastening the process of urbanization, the answer is yes, as it is seen that there is increase in the rate of rise in urban population as shown in the table given above. The logical reason for this is that the rate of increase in business under globalization is more than what it was there two decades back.

MEANINGS OF DEVELOPMENT

Prologue

There has always been a difficulty in finding the uncontested meaning of development. Though globalization comprises all facets of life, under globalization economic development gets more prominence. In this context, does economic progress mean development or does it relate to overall progress and well being? If it is assumed that under globalization development has taken place, the next question is whether all nations have gained from globalization equally or some nations have gained more than others. What could be the factors for different stages of development and is globalization related to the stage of development that a nation is in? There has been no uniformity in the level of industrialization of different nations. In the light of this, could level of industrialization be the determining factor for different stages of present development or there are also other factors? In order to get answers to all these questions, it is necessary to know in the first place what development is.

Definition of Development

The most familiar definition of development is that given in the Brundtland Commission report, *Our Common Future* (1987): "development which meets the needs of the present without compromising the ability of the future generations to meet their own needs". Another definition, from the Real World Member Forum for the future is: "sustainable development is a dynamic process which enables all people to realize their potential and improve their quality of life in ways that simultaneously protect and enhance the Earth's life-support systems" (Palanithurai and Ramesh, 2011: 5).

Human Development Index (HDI)

The question as to how should we measure the real progress of the country and its people has been engaging the attention of various world organizations. It was felt that either Gross National Product (GNP) or Gross Domestic Product (GDP) alone could not be considered a valid measure of progress as these reflect mainly economic aspects and therefore not enough to reflect the status of the progress in a comprehensive way. In this context in early 1990s, United Nations Development Programme (UNDP) brought out Human Development Index (HDI) as a valid measure of the country's progress. It encompasses three major components. The education due to its unique importance is one of these components, others being longevity (indicator of health) and per capita GDP.

Thus HDI is calculated as an average of the sum of three indexes namely educational attainment, longevity and income. Individual Index is calculated from the equation:

$$\text{Index} = \frac{\text{Actual Value} - \text{Minimum Value}}{\text{Maximum Value} - \text{Minimum Value}}$$

Minimum and maximum values are fixed for each indicator.

Definitions of Terms Related to HDI

Human Development Index (HDI): A composite index measuring average achievement in three basic dimensions of human development—a long and healthy life, knowledge and a decent standard of living.

Life expectancy at birth: Number of years a newborn infant could expect to live if prevailing patterns of age-specific mortality rates at the time of birth stay the same throughout the infant's life.

Mean years of schooling: Average number of years of education received by people ages 25 and older, converted from education attainment levels using official durations of each level.

Expected years of schooling: Number of years of schooling that a child of school entrance age can expect to receive if prevailing patterns of age-specific enrolment rates persist throughout the child's life.

Gross national income (GNI) per capita: Aggregate income of an economy generated by its production and its ownership of factors of production, less the incomes paid for the use of factors of production owned by the rest of the world, converted to international dollars using PPP rates, divided by midyear population.

On the above basis, the HDI ranking of 10 selected countries out of 187 countries covered by the Human Development Report 2014 is given in Table 5.2 below.

Table 5.2: UNDP Human Development Report 2014: Human Development Index 2013

Country	*HDI 2013 Rank*	*Life expectancy at birth (years) 2013*	*Mean years of schooling (years) 2012*	*Expected years of schooling (years) 2012*	*Gross National Income (GNI) per capita (2011 PPP$) 2013*
US	5	78.9	12.9	16.5	52,308
Germany	6	80.7	12.9	16.3	43,049
UK	14	80.5	12.3	16.2	35,002
Japan	17	83.6	11.5	15.3	36,747
France	20	81.8	11.1	16.0	36,629
Russian Federation	57	68	11.7	14.0	22,617
Brazil	79	73.9	7.2	15.2	14,275
China	91	75.3	7.5	12.9	11,477
South Africa	118	56.9	9.9	13.1	11,788
India	135	66.4	4.4	11.7	5,150

Source: UNDP Human Development Report 2014: Human Development Index 2013.

Website: http://hdr.undp.org/en/content/table-1-human-development-index-and-its-components

It is seen from Table 5.2 that India ranks as low as 135 out of 187 countries. Even leaving developed countries, Brazil, Russia, China and South Africa of the group of BRICS countries are also ahead of India. The ranking of India is low much because of low level of adult education and per capita income.

Development is generally linked to economic progress but it is much more than merely economic progress although economic progress is an important component of the development. However, it will be seen from the HDI that it is related to social aspect also. Amartya Sen, Nobel Laureate takes a still broader view of development. He says development is multifaceted, and links it to the process of expanding the real freedom enjoyed by the members of the society.

Development Discourse

Adulthood/Childhood

Akhil Gupta (1998) in his book, '*Postcolonial Developments*' uses simile of development and underdevelopment/developing stage to adult and childhood. Past from the colonial era, we as belonging to underdeveloped world seem to be carrying old nostalgia. Development is generally related to economic progress. In this sense, development or underdevelopment denotes good economic condition or poor economic condition respectively. This is however a narrow meaning of the term development. It is also related to social status. Thus development or underdevelopment also denotes two different identities. Development indicates higher social standing, i.e. adulthood and underdevelopment in the eyes of developed nations indicates lower social standing, i.e. childhood. This is based on the concept that child gets developed with experience and time. Developed countries before they attained the present status had undergone various levels of socio-economic and political developments. In the same way, developing countries are following similar trajectory. Thus, the word development is indicative of who were born earlier and became adult. By this concept, the developing countries are seen as children born now and as their economies grow, they are on the development path indicating that they are on the way of becoming adult.

Developed and Underdeveloped: Forms of Identity

Developed and underdeveloped can be seen as forms of identity. When we deal with the global financial institutions, i.e. IMF, WB or WTO, through use of the terms—development or underdevelopment—developing countries become the subject of control by the developed countries. Development implicitly indicates dependency or control of the underdeveloped by the developed and thus development and underdevelopment create social identities.

Relationship between Globalization and Development

The countries which started early on the path of industrialization have definite advantages over others who started late. Thus, US and Europe have the economic advantage all along as they took to industrialization earlier. Even in Agriculture sector, by providing large subsidies, they are better off than developing countries. The time gap between developed and developing countries regarding the stage of development created a sort of hierarchy and economic inequality in favour of developed countries.

Under the same process of globalization, we find different outcomes in terms of economic progress of various nations. These different outcomes do not seem to be related as much to the extent globalization process has been adopted, but it is related to the capacities built up to get the maximum benefit of globalization. For example, if any nation pays attention to skill development, that nation will be able to get more benefit out of the process of globalization. Similarly, that nation will be able to benefit more from globalization which develops infrastructure so as to attract setting up of global business centers. Sanctity of contracts and the system of jurisprudence also matter for global business players. Favourable political environment is another important factor to attract global business. Thus, benefit from globalization will vary according to related structural capacities built by the nations.

While there may be some truth in putting the blame for the poor plight of disadvantaged society on globalization, but the globalization cannot be blamed entirely for its plight. It also matters how a society and the state manage its affairs rather than attributing its problems solely to global economy. There are many inherent internal governance problems responsible for the poor plight such as non-sensitive authoritative government, overregulation of economy, corruption etc. If these inherent problems are solved, society may find globalization helpful for development of the society.

The proponents of globalization contend that a lot many opportunities are made available by the process of globalization. Those who aspire for development are required only to liberalize their economy and utilize the opportunities thrown open by the process of globalization.

However, the critics of globalization contend that there is dichotomy between globalization and development as both do not go hand in hand. They on the contrary contend that under globalization poor starts depending more and more on the global economy and thus become subservient to it.

Critics contend that globalization could not bring a feeling of contentment in general. They point out that many people in the countryside remember their old days and believe that they were more contended in the past than they find now in modern times. They think that the staple food that they were eating in the past was far more pure, tasty and nutritious than hybrid variety now. This perception negates the conception that the modernized state has brought more satisfaction in the rural area.

Thus, development is seen as a test for measuring the success of globalization.

Post-development View

The description of the development as given above is contested by proponents of post-development theory. Post-development theorists contend that present view of development is a creation of Western and European nations. It is more in the nature of their own academic, social, economic and cultural context. It reflects the relationship between the West and the rest as developed and underdeveloped, superior and inferior, thus, creating hierarchies. It is based on the systems of capitalism and industrialism which are not sustainable in the long run because of the limited availability of resources.

Post-development theorists on the other hand advocate that the development should be based on and suiting to local, social, cultural and historical context. As an example, there are many people particularly in rural area who strongly believe that earlier times were better and they were more contended in those times. They express that the food they used to eat during old times was tastier as against present insipid food. The social relationship was more genuine. There was respect for the values. As against those times, under present context of development, there is undue primacy to economic status, material progress has acquired more importance. Age old traditions are being seen as impediments in the way of progress.

It will be seen from the above contentions of development and post-development theories that there is a vast gulf between the two theories and the perception of their theorists. The thrust of the arguments lead us to consider that development cannot be seen from the prism of Western and European view of development and it should also be seen in the context of local socio-economic, cultural and historical context.

Conclusion

As mentioned in the beginning, it is difficult to define development. It depends upon the field of reference. Here we are restricting the meaning of development as growth or progress with reference to globalization. Since, globalization is generally perceived more in the context of economic progress, there is a general notion that economic progress means development. But this is not correct. By restricting the meaning of development to economic progress, we are narrowing its real meaning. Development touches upon every aspcct of life such as social, economic, political, cultural etc. Education for example is a key to development. The development of value systems, freedom of expression, freedom of following one's religion etc. also form the part of development. The broader meaning of development will have, therefore, to be holistic, though economic aspect may overshadow others as it does with reference to globalization.

The countries, in which industrialization started earlier, have lead in becoming developed countries economically earlier. At social level, developed and underdeveloped mean different identities, similar to adulthood and childhood. By this concept, developed countries tend to assume that that they have attained adulthood and developing countries are yet in the childhood stage.

There is no consensus about the kind of relationship existing between globalization and development. In fact, critics of globalization contest the proposition that globalization leads to overall development. They point out that while globalization may have led to some economic progress but under globalization the importance of social and value system is diminished.

In order to get the best benefits on economic front from globalization, it is contended that prior structural arrangements like infrastructure, skill development, conducive political environment etc. have to be in place. Lastly development is not a temporal arrangement, but it is supposed to last long and self-sustainable.

IMPACT OF GLOBALIZATION ON ECOLOGY/ ENVIRONMENT/SUSTAINABILITY

Prologue

According to environmentalists, if the present trend of environmental pollution continues, it will be unsustainable for all species in the world, including human beings. This view is upheld by Intergovernmental Panel for Climate Change (IPCC), the leading international body for the assessment of climate change established by the United Nations Environment Programme (UNEP). It is generally believed that though globalization pervades many aspects of the world, its emphasis is more on the economic progress. Economic progress involves use of natural resources, some of which are renewable and some are non-renewable. In the process of industrialization and other uses, the environment is getting affected adversely. If industrialization and other uses are considered necessary for development, how do we balance the economic progress and its impact on the environment?

The critics of the environmentalists argue that the impact of economic activity on environmental pollution is overstated. The consensus is, however, converging on the view that any development hereafter should be sustainable development in the long run and if it is not, it is better to forgo such development. But what is the meaning of sustainable development and how do we achieve it?

Definition

There are number of definitions of sustainable development, but the most widely used one is from the report of World Commission on Environment and Development, later named as Brundtland Commission, presented in 1987. It states that:

> "Sustainable development is development that meets the needs of the present without compromising the ability of future generations to meet their own needs. It contains two key concepts:
>
> - the concept of "needs", in particular the essential needs of the world's poor, to which overriding priority should be given; and
> - the idea of limitations imposed by the state of technology and social organization on the environment's ability to meet present and future needs."

Thus, sustainable development seeks social and economic progress for all generations within the finite natural resources.

Seriousness of Problem/Report of Intergovernmental Panel for Climate Change

Looking to the major shift in climate certainty, there is a growing concern about the impact of present unrestrained nature of development that is taking place world over. Intergovernmental Panel for Climate Change

Box 5.1: Intergovernmental Panel for Climate Change (IPCC)

The Intergovernmental Panel for Climate Change (IPCC) IPCC 5th Assessment Report "Climate Change 2013" accepted on 26 September, 2013 in Stockholm, Sweden brings out many important issues.

- Warming of the climate system is unequivocal, and since the 1950s, many of the observed changes are unprecedented over decades to millennia. The atmosphere and ocean have warmed, the amounts of snow and ice have diminished, sea level has risen, and the concentrations of greenhouse gases have increased.
- At the end of the century it is very likely that the average temperature will be at least 1.5 C higher than in the late 1800s. There will be frequent heat waves and for longer periods. Dry parts of the world will become drier, while it will rain more where the climate is more humid.
- Since the oceans are getting warmer and the glaciers are melting, sea level will continue to rise. The amount of carbon dioxide is 40 per cent higher than before the industrialization began.

The only way to prevent climate change is to make drastic and long-term reductions in our greenhouse gas emissions.

(http://felixonline.co.uk/features/3913/ipcc-climate-report-2013-an-ultimate-warning/)

(IPCC) has been charged by the United Nations to study this matter in depth and their findings are given in the latest 2013 report on climate change (Box 5.1).

Sources of Pollution—Non-Agricultural

Greenhouse Gases

Due to early industrialization and extensive use of fossil fuels in developed countries, there has been steep increase in green house gases which consist of carbon dioxide, methane, nitrous oxide, and ozone. Greenhouse gases greatly affect the temperature of the Earth. On the other hand, the quantum of greenhouse gases produced by developing countries is much less. For example per capita production of greenhouse gases in USA is ten times that of India. This puts responsibility for reducing greenhouse gases more on developed countries than developing countries.

Ozone Depletion

Ozone is a molecule consisting of three oxygen atoms (O_3). It has irritating and corrosive properties. Ozone has two types depending on where it is situated. A small percentage of ozone is found near the earth's surface which is termed as 'bad ozone' because of its characteristics. However, most of it is found as a layer in stratosphere that extends between 15 and 35 km above the earth's surface. This ozone is termed as 'good ozone'. It is termed as good because its layer acts as a barrier which absorbs 97-99 per cent of the sun's high frequency UV radiation. Ozone is all the time created as well as destroyed. It is necessary to keep the balance of ozone in the stratosphere.

There are certain substances emitted by the processes used by human beings which deplete the ozone. A class of volatile organic chemicals known as chlorofluorocarbons, or CFCs is considered as bad for the ozone. For example Freon gas which belongs to this class which is used as refrigerants has destructive effect on the ozone. Scientists hold the view that the depletion of ozone will have wide ranging bad effects on earth which include increase in skin cancer, cataracts, suppression of immune systems, reduction in the growth of phytoplankton (photosynthesizing microscopic organisms) in the oceans and bodies of fresh water, cooling of the stratosphere, with possible climatic effects (Ritzer, 2012: 1631).

Sources of Pollution—Agricultural

In agriculture, the use of pesticides and chemical fertilizers consisting of nitrogen, potassium and phosphorus is steadily increasing. This is resulting in effluents carrying residues of pesticides, nitrogen, potassium and phosphorus. The use of such contaminated surface water affects wildlife as well as other species. Further, overconcentration of nitrogen and phosphate in surface water causes growth of algae *vis-à-vis* other aquatic forms of life.

There is a risk of finding traces of the aforesaid residues in food being consumed by the human beings affecting health of the people. This is the reason for quite number of people opting to switchover to use organic food in place of food produced by using chemical fertilizers and pesticides in agriculture.

Expansion of agriculture and industrial development is leading to over-reduction of vegetative cover. Such over-reduction of vegetative cover is affecting habitat of wildlife. This is evident from the reports of wild cats and other wild animals roaming in the vicinity of villages.

Acid Rain

Industrialization started in West and European countries in the nineteenth century mainly used coal for production of energy. Coal contains mainly carbon and some percentage of sulfur. After combustion, CO_2 and SO_2 gases are formed which are released in the atmosphere. After getting dissolved in water vapour, the combination becomes acidic (pH< 7). Further, surface water containing residues of chemical fertilizers and pesticides used in agriculture in ultimate stage, i.e. by way of evaporation etc. also becomes acidic in the atmosphere. All these elements, together dissolved in water vapour, form acid rain. The process thus explained has become prominent from twentieth century onwards. The rain with more concentration of acid has capacity to dissolve limestone and even form caves in the rocks.

Bio-fuels

The process of globalization is encouraging a shift in agriculture in developing countries from staple produce to producing bio-fuels such as corn, sugar, palm oil, *jatropha*. Some people argue that the production of bio-fuels has bad impact on ecology. Philip McMichael says while the protagonists of globalization term this shift as development of alternative green fuel, critics term this as shift to industrial agriculture which is beyond the reach of common farmer, ecologically unfavourable, and displacing traditional staple food crops (46 Ritzer, 2012: 44).

Overuse of Natural Resources under Globalization

Though North emphasizes South to undertake development that is sustainable, it does not mind relaxation of environmental norms by the South if it serves the interests of the North. For example, meat, beef, lamb, pork or fish are imported by North from South because breeding of these species creates environmental burden.

CO_2, methane and nitrous oxide are the primary green house gases in the atmosphere. Among these, especially long time presence of CO_2 leads to climate change. The burden of CO_2 is continuously increasing as coal based thermal power stations consume large quantities of coal. The green house gases like CO_2 absorb infrared rays of sun and trapped heat raises temperature of the earth, which is dangerous for the species on earth. The species on earth are paying the price for industrial development which is driven vigorously by the process of globalization.

Since there is strong resistance in developed countries for setting up new industrial units because of environmental problems, there is a trend to locate new industries in developing countries, if necessary even by relaxing their own environmental norms. Industrialization changes the traditional livelihood of people from agriculture to industry and relaxing environmental norms further affect health of the people.

As mentioned, the overuse of natural resources for industrial purposes is leading to loss of biodiversity, increasing concentration of CO_2, NO_2 and SO_2 in the atmosphere, acidification of rain water and oceans, deforestation, decline in fresh water, climate change etc. The process of globalization is continuously enlarging the scope of the use of natural resources. According to critics of globalization, the overuse is so extensive that its effect is crossing planetary sustainability and thus making living on earth increasingly unsafe.

The growth of economy is accompanied by increasing consumption of natural resources and damage to environment. Let us illustrate this by an example of forest trees. We cut trees for producing paper or using them as fuel. There are two options. One option is planting new trees in as many numbers as we cut. This will maintain balance in the ecology and serve long term interest of the society. On the other hand if we cut the trees but, for immediate benefit, do not plant new ones because the process requires effort and expenditure, very soon the forest will be lost, disturbing the ecology. Such action may lead to drought etc.

Forests are useful as they absorb carbon dioxide which is harmful for living beings. But industrial development is reducing forest cover. This is resulting in the climate change. The climate change is also in the form of change in the intensity of seasons including pattern and quantity of rain which affect agriculture, living species and biodiversity.

Rural hinterland is giving way to urban complexes posing new set of environmental problems. The phenomenal increase of petrol/diesel driven vehicles, and power stations/industries consuming huge quantity of fossil fuel, producing ash and emitting harmful gases etc. are exceeding carrying capacity of the biosphere. Ever increasing ecological problems associated with economic growth imperative are posing huge challenges to mankind.

The global companies when they set up works in developing countries take into account costs required to produce the product, but they largely underestimate the socio-environmental costs involved such as mitigating problems arising from displacement of people, increasing pollution etc. This results in spoiling the existing environment. As regards developing countries, for development purpose, they are in dire need of the capital and, therefore, they perforce agree for the terms set by the developed countries.

Relationship between Growing Income and Environmental Pollution

Environmental Kuznets Curve (EKC)

The Environmental Kuznets Curve (EKC) depicts relationship between environmental quality and economic development. According to Environmental Kuznets Curve (EKC), at first various indicators of environmental degradation tend to get worse as modern economic growth occurs until average income reaches a certain point over the course of development. Thereafter, indicators of environmental degradation fall with increasing per capita income. However, the KEC is found to be true only in few cases. As the globalization proceeds, there has been reduction in emission of sulfur dioxide that causes acid rain and particulate matter that causes lung cancer. But there is no improvement in the quality of surface water that contains coliform bacteria and emission of green house gases (GHGs) in the atmosphere that deplete ozone layer in the stratosphere (46 Ritzer, 2012: 1945).

Relationship between Growing Income and Environmental Pollution

The relationship between growing income and environmental pollution is a matter of intense discussion. Environmentalists hold the view that as the globalization proceeds, there will be more industrial activity which will increase environmental pollution. On the other hand, protagonists of globalization argue that as the incomes rise, there will be emphasis on development of eco-friendly technologies which will enable to reduce environmental pollution. For example, thermal power stations which consume coal with increased sulfur content and thus emit high concentration of SO_2 are required to install de-sulfurization plants. A lot of research and development activity is going on in this field and in times to come, every installation which emits pollution will be required to install devices to counter pollution.

Lack of Convergence in Approach to Implementation of Food Safety Laws

The Agreement on the Application of Sanitary and Phytosanitary Measures, also known as the SPS Agreement was negotiated during the Uruguay Round of the GATT and came into force in 1995. Under the SPS agreement, the WTO sets constraints on member-states' policies relating to food safety (bacterial contaminants, pesticides, inspection and labelling) as well as animal and plant health (phytosanitation). There are three standards' organizations which set standards that WTO members are required to base their SPS methodologies on.

However, there is a difference in the approach to the implementation of the measures, depending upon whether the country is exporting or importing. On the one hand, the exporting countries feel that the importing countries are framing levels of acceptance to block the imports. On the other hand, importing countries feel that their sovereignty about deciding what is best for their country is compromised by the standards. While USA contends that the restrictions in SPS measures should be based on scientific principles and not maintained without sufficient scientific evidence, European Union favours precautionary principle which may be based on public perception about some technological development that is perceived as a threat to human health or ecological balance (Solbrig, Paarlberg, and Castri, 2001: 394). European Union contends that sufficiency of scientific evidence is always questionable and therefore it espouses the precautionary principle based on public perception.

Remedial Measures/Importance of Sustainable Development

Sustainable Development

Though development has been defined as sustainable if it satisfies present-day needs without compromising the capacity of future generations to satisfy their own needs, unfortunately most of the people think more about well being of people in the contemporary world than take a futuristic view. This thinking emerges mainly from two factors. One is the urge for pursuing development at any cost. Second is greed for expanding business empires. The policy of development at any cost and greed for expanding business empires affect environment adversely. In both cases, mostly the businessmen do not own social obligations toward people who are getting affected by their business.

What has happened in Uttarakhand State in the Himalayan mountain range of India in the month of June 2013 is an eye opener for what can happen if the concerns of ecological balance are not addressed. During the deluge thousands of people have perished and lakhs of houses have been washed away by the river floods. Though the damage happened because of the scale of nature's fury in terms of cloudburst and rains, but the scale of damage could have been reduced if steps would have been taken to maintain the ecology of the area.

In the name of development of area some things were done which should have been avoided. For constructing or widening the roads there are two options. One is by felling deodar trees and mountains being cut. Second option is building walls on the sides by stone pitching and filling the earth. The former has been adopted instead of the latter one which is better option. Further, construction of buildings along the riverbanks took place which did not allow water to pass quickly. Development of urban areas took place without regard to drainage system. All these deviations finally resulted in a tragedy. This is a classic example which highlights the importance of sustainable development.

Importance of Bio-Diversity

Ecological balance is essential for sustenance of all living species. Inter-linkage between species is a characteristic of biodiversity. A significant change in the form of numbers or extinction of any specie upsets the ecological balance. Thus, human beings cannot get away with any kind of environmental damage without affecting them in course of time.

The Convention on Biological Diversity (CBD) took place at the Earth Summit in Reo de Janeiro in 1992 with the objectives of

1. Conservation of biological diversity
2. Sustainable use of its components; and
3. Fair and equitable sharing of benefits arising from genetic resources

The bio-diversity strategies and action plans were drawn up at the convention to achieve the above objectives.

Kyoto Protocol

The Kyoto Protocol is an international treaty framed in 1997 by 192 parties in Kyoto, Japan committing State entities to reduce their greenhouse gas emissions. The protocol enunciates principle of Common but Differentiated Responsibilities putting the obligations to reduce the emission on the developed countries. Industrialization has first started in the countries in the North. Thc development of these countries was associated with huge carbon emissions in the atmosphere. Developing countries have started industrial development since last few decades only. If carbon emissions arc to be restricted now, this will hit development in the countries in the South. The countries in the North will not suffer as much since development has already taken place there. Another aspect is developing countries are economically poor. These aspects have been duly acknowledged in the Kyoto protocol. Though it does not call for developing countries to share the burden of carbon emissions, the developed countries do insist on reducing emission levels by developing countries too.

The Protocol came into force formally in 2005. The Protocol's first commitment period ended in 2012. Second commitment period was proposed in 2012, known as Doha Amendment, seeking Europe to commit to reduce CO_2 reductions until 2020, but the Amendment is yet to be ratified. Discussions are in progress to prepare post-Kyoto legal framework that would require all major polluters to pay for CO_2 emissions. United States, China and India expressed that they would not ratify any treaty that will bind them legally to reduce CO_2 emissions. China and India contended that they are presently in development stage and it is but natural that emission of CO_2 gases is unavoidable.

However, in November 2014, U.S. and China agreed to a deal according to which US will reduce emission by 26-28 per cent below its 2005 level by 2025 and China will cap its overall emissions by 2030 or earlier by way of increasing the share of non-fossil fuel energy sources in its overall energy mix to 20 per cent. China proposes to switch over from fossil fuel energy sources to wind, hydro, biofuel and nuclear power. India's share of global carbon emissions in 2013 was 7 per cent compared to China's 28 per cent and the US's 14 per cent. CO_2 emission in per capita terms, India's emission is 1.7 tons, China's 6.2 tons and US's 17.6 tons. Though lowest among three countries, India stands as world's number three emitter and this is certainly a matter of concern.

China's unprecedented growth so far is accompanied by high use of fossil fuel energy and consequently there has been growing anger among the Chinese people about the high level of pollution. It is reported that in 2012 alone, nearly seven lakh people died prematurely because of industrial pollution.

India has a dual problem. On one side, India has a quarter of its total population below poverty line. It badly needs economic growth and it needs to provide employment to increasing youth population through enhancing industrialization. On the other side, enhancement of industrialization will increase pollution unless there is quantum shift to non-fossil fuel energy sources. However, now that two of the three major countries opposing reduction of emission have agreed to limit their future emissions, India will be hard pressed to commit to reduction in emissions as all nations are expected to restrict emissions.

Lima Summit

The contentious issues were taken up in the annual UN climate summit of 194 countries in Lima in December, 2014. However, while the deal was concluded, including agreement for the first time that all countries (not only developed countries) must cut greenhouse gas emissions, most of the contentious issues have been deferred for UN climate talks to be held in Paris in 2015. The aim of climate talk is to find ways to prevent global temperatures rising more than 2°C over pre-industrialization levels, which otherwise would risk triggering catastrophic climate change. In this context all countries are required to submit 'intended nationally determined contributions (INDCs)' to achieve the aim. The magnitude of the contributions is to be determined by the country itself.

The deal between US and China—two largest emitters means that the scheduled UN climate talks in Paris in 2015 could now move toward producing a post-Kyoto Protocol agreement that will take effect in 2020.

US' Comprehensive Environmental Response, Compensation, and Liability Act

The Comprehensive Environmental Response, Compensation, and Liability Act (CERCLA), commonly known as Superfund, was enacted by US in 1980 and amended in 1986. This law created a tax on the chemical and petroleum industries and provided broad Federal authority to respond directly to releases or threatened releases of hazardous substances that may endanger public health or the environment. The law authorized the Environmental Protection Agency (EPA) to identify parties responsible for contamination of sites and compel the parties to clean up the sites. Where responsible parties cannot be found, the Agency is authorized to clean up sites itself, using a special trust fund. It is time to have similar law in India to tax those industries which release hazardous substances and use the money on cleaning up the sites.

Green Climate Fund

Conference of Parties established Green Climate Fund (GCF) as an operating entity of the Financial Mechanism to assist developing countries, especially those developing countries particularly vulnerable to the adverse effects of climate change, in mitigating emissions and adapting to impact of climate change. The fund will contribute to the achievement of the ultimate objective of the United Nations Framework Convention on Climate Change. Rich countries are supposed to contribute to the fund. Goal is to make a corpus of $100 billion to developing nations from 2020. In November 2014, US pledged $3 billion and Japan $1 billion to the Green Climate Fund.

Conclusion

The growth of industrialization which is part of globalization process is accompanied by the increase in the environmental pollution. Since industrialization has first taken place in the developed countries in the North and their population density is lower compared to countries in the South, per capita production of greenhouse gases in developed countries is much higher than developing countries. The labour in the South is much cheaper than in the North and people in the North are very conscious about the environmental aspect. Therefore, North favours establishing manufacturing works/factories to be locaed in the South, if need be, even by relaxing environmental laws.

The globalization is leading to overuse of natural resources. Industries, automobiles etc. are increasing the emission of GHGs in the atmosphere which according to scientists is depleting ozone layer in the stratosphere. This will have very deleterious effect on the life on earth. In agriculture, the use of pesticides and chemical fertilizers consisting of nitrogen, potassium and phosphorus is steadily increasing. This is resulting in effluents/surface water carrying residues of the hazardous chemicals.

The relationship between growing income and environmental pollution is a matter of intense debate. Environmentalists hold the view that as the globalization proceeds, there will be more industrial activity which will increase environmental pollution. On the other hand, protagonists of globalization argue that as the incomes rise, there will be emphasis on development of eco-friendly technologies which will facilitate reducing environmental pollution.

In the age of keen competition, global companies do not take into account socio-environmental costs. With growth of economy as a major imperative, increasing ecological problems associated with economic growth are bound to pose huge challenges to make growth of economy ecologically sustainable.

Though Kyoto Protocol for reducing emission of CO_2 gases came into force in 2005, there has been no progress thereafter. United States,

China and India did not wish to ratify any treaty which will legally bind them for reducing emissions. Both China and India contended that they are presently in developing stage and at this time they cannot afford to commit legally for any reduction of gas emissions. However, in November 2014, US and China entered into a joint climate deal to limit emission of greenhouse gases. Thus India will now be under pressure to follow suit.

6
Globalization and Political Structure/Nation-State/ Nationalism/Democracy

Prologue

Historically, the concepts of nation-state and nationalism came to be known from the time of French Revolution (1789-1799). During that period there was radical social and political upheaval which left deep imprint on French as well as world history, marking the decline of powerful monarchies and the rise of democracy and nationalism. The terms like citizenship, legal rights and responsibilities of citizens are borne out from the idea of nationalism.

In earlier times, nations were free to follow their economic policies independently. However, the process of globalization called for far reaching adjustments in the policies. The critics of globalization term this as infringement of the concept of nation-state. On the other hand, the proponents of globalization contend that the nation-state does not lose its authority of governance, but it undergoes transformation with respect to its functions. Thus in the context of globalization, there is an intense debate on the issue of the autonomy of a nation-state.

History of the Term Nation

William I Robinson writes "The nation-state is a historically-specific form of world social organization in the process of becoming transcended by globalization. Historic structures may be transcended by their destruction and replacement. This is how, for instance, the historic structures of monarchy and feudalism in France were superseded. Such structures may also be superseded by transformation through incorporation into emergent new structures. This was the route through which monarchic and feudal structures were transcended in England. Hence, there are monarchical and feudal residues in England that we do not find in France." (Ritzer, 2010: 197).

French Revolution

Earlier, nation-state was a sort of loose confederation of various communities living within geographical boundary. As mentioned, the concept of nation-state and nationalism are the product of the French Revolution and the notion of citizenship, of being a person carrying certain legal rights and responsibilities, has germinated from the idea of nationalism. Citizenship carries with it rights like rights of individual freedom such as freedom of speech, freedom to follow his faith, and political rights allowing the citizen to participate in the political process etc.

Nation-state

Though nation and state are two different terms, in the context of globalization nation-state is used as a singular term. The nation refers to a social group with common cultural and ethnic identity and serves as a sovereign territorial entity. The state refers to geopolitical entity offering a centralized form of governance with an organizational structure. Nation-state formation took place at different times in different parts of the world. The Nation-state is thus an integration of cultural and ethnic identity and the organizational structure, serving as a sovereign territorial entity. Globalization transcends the nation-state (Ritzer, 2010: 141).

Impact of Globalization on Nation-state—Different Interpretations

Global and local are two ends of the paradigm. Distinguishing spatially, global can be said to lie outside the nation-state and local inside it. However, in this interconnected world under globalization, all three namely global, nation-state and local impinge continually on each other (D 18 Gupta, 1998: 25).

There are several arguments about the impact of globalization on the nation-state. These are on the following lines:

- The authority of nation-state is diluted; unique position of nation-state is compromised
- Nation-state retains power in spite of globalization; the statement that globalization causes demise of nation-state is overstatement
- Impact of globalization varies from one nation-state to another

Impact of globalization on the nation-state will also be viewed differently depending on the agency viewing it, i.e. whether agency is government, public or the civil society. Thus, nature of impact of globalization on the nation-state is most contested.

Earlier nation-state was independent entity. It had full control over economy. However, with the advent of globalization, many people believe that the globalization has compromised the unique position of the nation-state. There are two sets of opinions about this development. Some people believe that the change has happened because market and economy got globalized and some people attribute this to advancement of technology.

State is the site where the development of globalization takes place. With the process of globalization, the functioning of the state does not remain as it was before. It undergoes transformation as it has to maintain balance of power between the forces operating within the nation and outside. These forces relate to various aspects of society such as social, economic, and cultural etc. Thus, large body of sociologists contends that the state neither becomes irrelevant, nor any new adaptation replaces it. On the other hand, there is a deep transformation in its functioning.

Globalization has its impact on political front also. Politics does not remain now tied only to local or national perspective. The socio-economic policies which hitherto could have been pursued independently are affected by the process of globalization. They are modified taking into account impact of globalization. The critics of globalization see this as loss of autonomy in the functioning of the state and the political parties.

Global Organizations and Treaties

The globalization on the one hand creates and maintains global institutions such as WTO, WB, MNCs etc. and on the other hand influences the economic policies of the nation-state. Globalization creates conditions for accumulation of capital in the global economy which is so necessary to carry forward the process of globalization.

The utility of the Global Summits are interpreted in different ways. While, proponents contend that the world is building a consensus on the understanding and resolution of critical issues facing mankind, opponents see these global summits or treaties as neo-colonialism and argue that they impinge on the sovereignty of the nation-state and not necessarily bring improvement in the condition of the rural poor.

Impact on Agriculturists

Agriculturists constitute substantial population in every country. Earlier, agricultural economy was tied up with that of nation-state and agriculturists experienced certain degree of certainty. Now, the economic aspect of globalization which bypasses nation-state adversely affects these certainties which existed earlier.

Globalization means market economy. The proponents of globalization contend that globalization is beneficial for the farmers as they can now access market throughout the world. The accessibility of global market could now be possible due to advancement in information and communication. They can also take produce directly to market instead of depending upon middlemen.

Nationalism

Nationalism is understood as solidarity based on shared descent and shared culture. Nation comprises several ethnic groups and nationalism transcends ethnicity. In postcolonial nation-states, with independence, nationalism is a rising sentiment. It is more community oriented unlike in developed countries where sentiment of individual liberty is more preponderant. In postcolonial developing nation-states, people hold the view that the social includes well being of individual but contrary is not necessarily true.

It is generally held that interconnectedness due to the process of globalization would weaken the sentiments of nationalism and promote the sentiments of internationalism. However, situation at the ground level does not support this view. People in every country increasingly think that their country's position is always righteous *vis-à-vis* other countries and this is even leading to conflicts. This indicates that there is increasing reassertion of nationalism. Marxists are, however, critical about the idea of nationalism as they think that the idea of nationalism is a diversion from their concept that the workers as a class throughout world are one entity (el-Ojeili and Hayden, 2006: 157).

National Identity

National identity refers to people deriving self recognition out of a shared feeling of belongingness to the nation. It is interesting to note that people carry national identity even when they do not know each other, might not have seen each other or might not have any contact with each other. Another interesting thing to note is that people have national identity even in the face of cultural and ethnic diversity. This means national identity transcends differences in cultures and ethnicity.

Both political and cultural processes create national identities. There is, however, a difference between the identities created by political process and cultural process. Political process creates national identity through diktat by the party and its leaders, i.e. top down process. Cultural process creates identities through natural, i.e. bottom up process. Let us take the example of singing of national anthem at the time of starting of the classes in the school. It is a rendition of the history of nationhood and evokes emotional chord. These are used as symbols for binding the people together.

Some sociologists make a distinction between the contribution of society and the contribution of state toward the rise of power of the nation-state. The people in developed countries favour liberalization of economy and other aspects of life and less governance by the state. However, in developing countries, the state has to play an important role. Some sociologists opine that the rise of power in developed country say country like USA is largely on account of its society rather than the contribution of nation-state.

Corruption

Political Corruption

Economic side of corruption which affects business transaction cost has been dealt in the topic Global Economic Process. Here, political side of corruption is being dealt. Corruption is misuse of office. Some thinkers hold the view that some type of corruption is helpful. Hutchcroft (1997) expresses the view that corruption to expedite a public service is different from corruption to distort the delivery of service and is beneficial in otherwise sclerotic (opaque or non-transparent) systems.

Corruption has become a sensitive issue in India because it is all pervasive. In developed countries, there is practically no corruption at the lower level and thus common man is not affected. But in developing countries, there is corruption at all levels and therefore common man is affected.

It is held that corruption starts from the top and that includes the law makers. The major reason cited for unclean politics is that politicians have to spend huge sums of money during election. To make elections accessible to people of modest means, India has set a limit of Rs. 70 lakhs for the election expenses for the post of Member of Parliament. However, it is gathered that generally the actual expenses are much more. Further, the candidate has to face election every five years and so the necessity of having money at every electopn. The money has to be mostly arranged from the personal account and some support is given by the political party to which he belongs. The party itself is getting money in the form of donations from the private companies and contributions of small nature from party sympathizers. Companies can donate up to 5 per cent of their last three years' profits to political parties.

Since the amount of money legally allowed to be spent is in large variance with the actual amount spent, the situation leads to candidate arranging and spending the difference in illegitimate manner. This breeds corruption. Therefore, there is an urgent need to bring necessary reform in funding the election expenses.

Bureaucratic Corruption

In developing countries, there is a feeling that corruption in bureaucracy hurts society more than political corruption because the common man gets his first contact with bureaucracy for getting anything done from the state. There is a general perception that it is difficult to get things done without advancing money even when they fit into the rule. In this respect rural people are the worst sufferers as most of them are illiterate and can be exploited easily. The official concerned does not even admit this as corruption; instead he uses a respectful term *Suvidha Shulka.* As per Corruption Perception Index (2014) brought out by Transparency International-organization based in Berlin, in a total of 174 countries, India ranks as lowly 85.

Computerization of Records

Computerization of records has made tremendous improvement in combating corruption in India because under the scheme people have easy access to the records and they can point out if there is any discrepancy between the physical status and the record. The records include: land and revenue records; people below poverty line; peoplc with *aadhaar* card; people with ration card; people eligible for pension and those who are getting pension; certificates of birth, death, marriage; data about entitlements; data about employment/unemployment; information about various government projects/schemes; data about agricultural services such as meteorological data, seeds, fertilizers, pesticides, market etc.

Earlier computerization of records was done regarding services in urban area only but gradually records have been built up for the services even in rural area. This system gives big relief to the common man. Notwithstanding computerization of aforementioned records, people have still to go physically to state offices for innumerable matters including settling of disputes.

Right to Information Act, 2005

In order to promote transparency and accountability in the working of every public authority, Indian government has enacted a law: Right to Information Act, 2005 (modified up to 1st February, 2011). The Right to Information Act (Box 6.1) empowers all Indian citizens to seek information from public authorities. These include central, state and local governments, Parliament and state legislatures, judiciary, police, security forces and all bodies substantially financed by the government.

Information One can Seek

Records, documents, memos, mails, press releases, circulars, computer-generated material, orders, log books, contracts, reports, papers, or electronic data.

Filing an Application

Address the application to the Public Information Officer (PIO) of the department concerned enclosing the proof of payment of application fee of Rs. 10/-.

Deadlines

Reply within 30 days; 48 hours where life or liberty is involved; 35 days where request is given to Public Information Officer; 40 days where third party is involved.

Box 6.1: Right to Information Act, 2005
(Act No. 22 of 2005)
[As modified up to 1st February, 2011]

An Act to provide for setting out the practical regime of right to information for citizens to secure access to information under the control of public authorities, in order to promote transparency and accountability in the working of every public authority, the constitution of a Central Information Commission and State Information Commissions and for matters connected therewith or incidental thereto.

4. **Obligations of public authorities**—Every public authority shall—

(a) maintain all its records duly catalogued and indexed in a manner and the form which facilitates the right to information under this Act and ensure that all records that are appropriate to be computerised are, within a reasonable time and subject to availability of resources, computerised and connected through a network all over the country on different systems so that access to such records is facilitated;

(b) publish within one hundred and twenty days from the enactment of this Act,—

(i) the particulars of its organisation, functions and duties;

(ii) the powers and duties of its officers and employees;

(iii) the procedure followed in the decision making process, including channels of supervision and accountability.

5. **Designation of Public Information Officers**—Every public authority shall, within one hundred days of the enactment of this Act, designate as many officers as the Central Public Information Officers or State Public Information Officers, as the case may be, in all administrative units or offices under it as may be necessary to provide information to persons requesting for the information under this Act.

6. **Request for obtaining information**—A person, who desires to obtain any information under this Act, shall make a request in writing or through electronic means in English or Hindi or in the official language of the area in which the application is being made, accompanying such fee as may be prescribed, to—

(a) the Central Public Information Officer or State Public Information Officer, as the case may be, of the concerned public authority;

(b) the Central Assistant Public Information Officer or State Assistant Public Information Officer, as the case may be, specifying the particulars of the information sought by him or her:

7. **Disposal of request**—The Central Public Information Officer or State Public Information Officer, as the case may be, on receipt of a request under section 6 shall, as expeditiously as possible, and in any case within thirty days of the receipt of the request. either provide the information on payment of such fee as may be prescribed or reject the request for any of the reasons specified in sections 8 and 9:

12. **Constitution of Central Information Commission**—The Central Government shall constitute a body to be known as the Central Information Commission to exercise the powers conferred on, and to perform the functions assigned to, it under this Act.

> 15. **Constitution of State Information Commission**—Every State Government shall constitute a body to be known as the (name of the State) Information Commission to exercise the powers conferred on, and to perform the functions assigned to it under this Act.
> 18. **Powers and Functions of Information Commissions**—It shall be the duty of the Central Information Commission or State Information Commission, as the case may be, to receive and inquire into a complaint from any person—
>   (a) who has been unable to submit a request to a Central Public Information Officer or State Public Information Office;
>   (b) who hits been refused access to any information requested under this Act;
>   (c) who has not been given a response to a request for information or access to information within the time limit specified under this Act.
>
> http://righttoinformation.gov.in/rti-act.pdf

Emergence of Global Civil Society and NGOs

The efforts of state alone are not adequate to meet the requirement of development. Moreover, people find difficulty in approaching the state for each and every matter. They are more open to informal organizations. Achieving the goal of development calls for multidimensional and multilevel approach. In this context, Non-Governmental Organization (NGO) can bridge the gap between the government and the public and thus NGOs can play important role. They can get the funds from any source i.e. private or public. Since, they are not directly controlled by the state, they can adopt innovative ways to solve the problems of the people.

With the advent of globalization, it is contended that polity at local level and the civil societies are becoming prominent. Also the global civil society assisted by new technology is becoming more assertive. This development is interpreted as a check on the state and having impact on the functioning of the hitherto autonomous state. Some call this development as emergence of pluralized form of governance.

However, not all NGO's are working with sincerity. There are umpteen reports about misuse of private and public funds by these organizations. Further, there are reports about extracting money from people or institutions by blackmail or threat of lodging false complaints against them.

Comparison of China and India

There is a general opinion that social and economic institutions largely function well in developed countries. On the other hand, in developing countries, the vested interests take hold of the reigns of the institutions and their functioning is undemocratic. The developing countries also tend to get engaged in areas of business which they should not be there. It is said that in India, while the effectiveness of state is less in social sector which include health, education etc., its presence is more than desirable in economic area (Dreze and Sen, 2002: 346). Presently, there is a far cry for minimum government and maximum governance.

There is a lot of interest in the people in knowing the reasons of China getting much ahead of India in economic field in the light of both countries attained the independence from the Aliens at the same time. China developed conditions such as development of infrastructure etc. in their country ahead of embracing globalization. China adopted liberalization policies in 1978, earlier than India, which adopted the policies in1991. China took various reform measures which resulted in progress on certain fronts like manufacturing and exports. Therefore, China could derive benefit from globalization better than India.

Some people ascribe China's economic development to authoritarian rule, for example no civil society can block the project in China in the name of environmental impact. For a democratic country like India, it is difficult to take drastic reform measures as there is immediate outcry against any drastic measure. Thus, it appears that in India although there is a great room for improving the condition of development, its speed cannot match with that of authoritarian country like China. However, it is not necessary that everything is fine with the authoritarian rule. Many of the failures of the authoritarian regimes are not allowed to be surfaced lest people know about them and criticize the regime. Thus, it may not be in the interest of India to imitate the social, economic and political model of China simply because it is much ahead in the economic field.

Isomorphism/Geopolitics

Geopolitics

The world is broadly divided into two categories: The North is economically and politically powerful compared to South. It appears as though, the geography (area within boundary) and the politics therein combined together as geopolitics determine the form of the state and wielding of power. Swedish social scientist Kjellen (1917: 46) was the first one to coin the term Geopolitics According to George Steinmetz, the word Geopolitics points to the interface between two distinct ontological realms and scientific disciplines, geography, and politics. Geopolitical thinkers emphasized the effects of physical geography and spatial location on the growth and the decline of states and on military and foreign policies (Ritzer, 2012: 800-01)

It is observed that the West adopts certain policies which amount to liberalization as well as regulation. For example, developed countries while welcoming professional or skilled persons from developing countries, adopt policies which do not allow immigration of unskilled persons. Apparently the underlying idea of theirs seems to be that while skilled persons enrich the country, labour in great numbers may change the demography apart from taking away the jobs of their countrymen.

Isomorphism

Karen Jeong Robinson coins the term isomorphism which refers to specific organizational form of the contemporary nation-state becoming the standard form of organizing societies around the world. Isomorphism refers to similarity. It is observed that there is a kind of broad similarity in constitutions, national policies and economic and social agenda adopted by the nation-states. Nation-states take a cue from each other's policies and programmes and try to internalize what suits them. Isomorphism is getting promoted not only by the efforts of the nation-states but also by the contribution of international non-governmental organizations (INGOs) (Ritzer, 2012: 1217).

Conclusion

The concept of nation-state and nationalism are the product of the French Revolution of 1789. The notion of citizenship, i.e. being a person carrying certain legal rights and responsibilities, has germinated from the idea of nationalism.

Citizenship carries with it rights like rights of individual freedom such as freedom of speech, freedom to follow one's faith, and political rights allowing the citizen to participate in the political process etc. The Nation-state is an integration of cultural and ethnic identity and the organizational structure, serving as a sovereign territorial entity.

Earlier, nation-state was independent entity. It controlled economy. However with the advent of globalization, there is intense competition on economic front. Many people believe that the globalization has compromised the unique position of the nation-state. The socio-economic policies which hitherto could have been pursued independently are affected by the process of globalization. Globalization has its impact on political front also. Politics does not remain now tied only to local or national perspective. Thus, there is some loss of autonomy in the functioning of the state and the political parties. In this interconnected world, all three namely global, nation-state and local impinge continually on each other. Critics of globalization see the global treaties as neo-colonialism and argue that they impinge on the sovereignty of the nation-state and not necessarily bring improvement in the condition of the poor. Globalization thus transcends the nation-state.

On the other hand, protagonists of globalization contend that globalization promotes democracy. Under globalization, the nation-state does not wither away or lose its significance but it undergoes transformation with respect to its functions. Rise of a feeling of nationalism and national identity also indicate the significance of a nation-state.

The informal networks, i.e. NGOs play important part in assisting the State in governance because the people are more open to informal organizations like NGOs. However, it is observed that many a times civil society which is acquiring a global status goes overboard in opposing even fair actions of its own nation-state.

Though China and India have attained independence more or less at the same time, China has done better than India in the economic field. In this context, a question is often asked as to which system is better, i.e. whether a nation-state with authoritarian rule that is existing in China or democratic set-up that is in India. People differ in their perception about both the systems. There are advantages and disadvantages of both systems.

Finally, on a philosophical plane, one important question arises, i.e. whether nationalism can go hand in hand together with globalism or they are antagonistic to each other? The answer can be found by considering a simile like this in simple terms. Member of a family is supposed to operate within a circle of family. Family is supposed to operate within a circle of society. Society is supposed to operate within a circle of nation-state. Similarly, nation-state is supposed to operate within a circle of globe. All these will operate harmoniously provided there is a genuine compromise or inclusive approach on the part of each entity and there is no element of exploitation by one entity of another. It is when there is no genuine compromise or inclusive approach and there is an element of exploitation by one entity of another that nationalism goes counter to globalism or *vice-versa.*

7
Globalization and Culture

CIVILIZATION AND RELIGION

Prologue

In this highly interconnected world, there is increasing economic as well as socio-cultural relationship between the societies across the world. The relationship has both positive as well as negative connotations. On the one hand, there is a sharing of socio-cultural values and on the other there are sporadic socio-cultural clashes in the context of religion. This begs the question as to whether globalization is leading to multiculturism or the view taken by Huntington that there is increasing preponderance of clashes between major civilizations.

Definition of Civilization

Oxford Dictionary gives a meaning of civilization as advanced stage of social development; civilized conditions or society. Webster dictionary gives a meaning of civilization as: a relatively high level of cultural and technological development; the culture characteristic of a particular time or place; refinement of thought, manner, or test; a situation of urban comfort.

Samuel Huntington defines a civilization as 'a cultural entity', tied to language, customs, institutions, and self-identification. Some sociologists distinguish between culture and civilization saying that the culture represents a natural, pre-rational folk-spirit, civilization represents more rational and material progress.

Civilizations are not confined to the nation-state boundaries. It is often seen that civilizations are spread over number of nations.

Indus Valley Civilization and Indian History Thereafter

While discussing socio-economic and cultural changes in society it is necessary to know the civilization and history of the nation to which that society belongs. The earliest picture of India's past is known from the remains discovered at Mohenjo-daro in Sind and at Harappa in the Western Punjab. Historian Sir John Marshall under whom the excavation took place tells that the civilization hitherto revealed both at Mohenjo-daro and Harappa is age old with many millenniums of human endeavour behind it and that India must henceforth be recognized, along with Persia, Mesopotamia, and Egypt. Some historians put the beginning of the Indus Valley civilization as 3000 years BC.

There is one feature which is central for flourishing of civilization and that is availability of water. Obviously for meeting the basic requirement of water, the settlements in olden times were either near the banks of rivers or where the rain water could be harvested. The deurbanization or decline of Indus Valley Civilization like other Bronze Age civilizations across the world-civilizations of Greece and Crete, the Old Kingdom of Egypt and the Akkadian Kingdom of Mesopotamia—are attributed probably to the period of widespread aridification due to weakening of monsoons.

Out of the great cultural synthesis and fusion that took place between the Aryans and the Dravidians who were probably the early representatives of the Indus Valley civilization, grew the Indian races and the basic Indian culture.

Out of the conflict and interaction between the races arose the caste system which in the course of succeeding centuries was to affect Indian life so profoundly. One book of inestimable value is Kautilya's *Arthashastra* of the fourth century BC, which gives details of all aspects of society, i.e. social, economic, political, and military organization of the Maurya Empire.

The period of Gupta Empire in fourth and fifth century AD has been called as Golden Age of India and was marked by great achievements in science, art, and literature. The period is noted for initiation of decimal numeral system and scholars as Kalidasa, Aryabhatta. Strong trade ties also made the region an important cultural centre and established it as a base that would influence nearby kingdoms and regions in Burma, Sri Lanka, Maritime South-east Asia, and Indochina.

Muslim rule started in some parts of north India in the thirteenth century. Among different Mughal rulers, Akbar—Emperor from 1556 to

1605 AD is known as the greatest ruler of the Mughal Dynasty. In order to extend his power and influence over the entire country, cutting across religious orthodoxy, he worked for bringing religious harmony and to this end he promulgated *Din-i-Ilahi*, a creed attempting to unify Islam, Hinduism, Zoroastrianism, and Christianity. Thus, the foundation for a multicultural empire under Mughal rule was laid during his times. After Akbar, the Mughal Empire suffered a gradual decline in the early eighteenth century, which provided opportunities for the Maratha Empire under the leadership of Chhatrapati Shivaji to exercise control over large areas in the subcontinent.

Then came the British presence in India. Beginning in the late eighteenth century and over the next century, large areas of India were annexed by the British East India Company. Dissatisfaction with Company rule led to the Indian Rebellion of 1857, after which the British provinces of India were directly administered by the British Crown. Later developments like freedom struggle of Indian people successfully led by Mahatma Gandhi and other leaders culminating in independence of the country in 1947 are well documented and within the domain of public knowledge.

A Clash of Civilizations

Samuel Huntington (in an article in the journal Foreign Affairs, 1993) claims that world is entering a new period. No longer will conflict pivot around ideology or politics as it did for most of the twentieth century, with communism, fascism, and liberal-democracy fighting for adherents. He claims the world will be shaped most importantly by the clashes between eight major civilizations: Western, Confucian, Japanese, Islamic, Hindu, Slavic-Orthodox, Latin American, and African.

According to Huntington, the global interconnectedness which has catalyzed the process of globalization will itself increase the clashes between civilizations. Though he mentions about the clashes between eight major civilizations, he highlights the concern especially about the clashes between Western and Islamic civilizations, giving the reasons that western ideas, values, democracy etc. do not go down well with Islamic civilization. (D 15 el-Ojeili and Hayden, 2006: 168) (D 46 Ritzer, 2012: 212). Besides clash with Islamic civilization, Huntington hints about clash with Sinitic civilization based on growing global economic and military power of China.

Huntington's article (1993) and his subsequent book (1996) on "A Clash of Civilizations" became a subject of great debate throughout world.

While many shared his views, the critics find him predicting a pessimistic future. Notwithstanding multiple views on the subject, to Huntington, coordinated terrorist attack on September 11, 2001 in USA was seen as confirmation of his views expressed in 1993 about the clash of civilizations.

Globalization, modernity and liberalism are normally associated with political economy. According to this view the world is moving by the wind of political economy and every other aspect is directly or indirectly determined by it. Huntington, instead, brings civilizations or cultural identities to the center stage and highlights that developments in this area will shape the future of the world. Thus, the view of Huntington about centrality of civilizations and the generally held view that main platform of globalization is political economy and its impact on local culture, have become a subject of intense debate and research. According to Huntington, the status of civilizations or cultural identities will determine the shape of all other aspects of society (46 Ritzer, 2012: 212).

The period of globalization has seen many ethnic clashes around the world. These clashes get instantly highlighted in the wake of advancement in information and communication technology. But the fact is that side by side of these sporadic clashes, the people around the world are living peacefully and such facts are rarely highlighted by the media. For example, save some incidents of violence, there is multiculturalism flourishing in USA and flourishing peacefully. May be this is happening due to mature democracy existing there. Even Huntington also acknowledged the hope about understanding between cultures, though with qualification.

The clash of civilizations occurs due to rise of fundamentalism. The rise of fundamentalism is attributed, among other factors, mainly to the failure of nationalist secular rulers who are unable to satisfy the hopes and aspirations of the people, as they preside over corrupt, undemocratic rule.

Religion

Religion can be defined as organized collection of belief in superhuman controlling power, especially in God or a system of faith and worship. The beliefs of religion are understood as moral values by the followers. The major religions like Christianity, Islam, Judaism, Confucian, Buddhism, and Hinduism are global in scope.

It has not been possible to find out origin of religion. But it appears people at different times were impressed by some charismatic person in their midst and tried to follow his words. Such a person could be seen by them as a prophet. Whatever he said became religion for his followers. The development of religion has taken different forms in different cultures. While some religions put emphasis on belief, others emphasize practice.

Every religion has certain rituals to be practiced. These rituals vary from religion to religion. Previously these rituals were practiced by the adherents by heart. In the era of globalization, these rituals are no doubt performed with high fanfare, but the same are generally celebrated as a formality without any heart or feelings in them.

The internet is changing the earlier concept of religious practice getting bound by the place where religion exists. One can obtain knowledge of religious practice through internet. Yoga is originated from India. There are quite number of training centers of yoga in USA. There are instances of foreigners learning practice of yoga through internet and then teaching the same to Indians.

Most of the nations have population belonging to different religions. The main function of the state is proper governance and religion is considered as a personal matter with no role in governance. However, it is interesting to note that even where the state is declared as secular, religion plays directly or indirectly a part therein and there is close relationship between the state, politics, culture and religion.

Religion in India

Indian society though on the national scale is predominantly Hindu, it has population belonging to all religions. Table 7.1 shows Distribution of population by religious groups and their sex ratios.

It will be seen from the above Table 7.1 that all religions have a place in the Indian society. In and at the outskirts of towns and villages, there are temples as well as shrines. They are symbols of deep religious faith. People in rural area follow their religion more ardently than their urban counterparts. Even where there are people belonging to more than one religion, in rural area, people have good interpersonal relationship and live in harmony. The functions in a family belonging to a particular religion are also attended by the people of other religions wholeheartedly. That is why even when there is turmoil between two religious groups in towns and cities, the villages are not affected. However, the picture in cities is fast changing and on occasions it is seen that even for some insignificant reasons, fierce communal clashes occur.

Table 7.1: Census 2011: Population by religious communities groups and their sex ratios

Name of religion	*Percentage of total population*	*Sex ratio**
Hindus	79.8	939
Muslims	14.2	951
Christians	2.3	1023
Sikhs	1.7	903
Buddhists	0.7	965
Jains	0.4	954
Other religions (ORP)	0.7	—
Religion not stated	0.2	—
India	100.	943

*Females per one thousand males.

Sebsite: http://pib.nic.in/newsite/PrintRelease.aspx?relid=126326

Fundamentalism

Fundamentalism can be interpreted in different ways. Fundamentalism can be related to strongly advocating "the way of living in the light of a particular religion is only the best." The other interpretation of fundamentalism is to contend that a 'particular religion and its holy books are infallible and the rest are fallible'. In this the follower of a religion has intolerance for all other religions. Fundamentalism is also related to defending his tradition to the hilt.

"Stuart Sim (2004: 29) contends that, "What fundamentalism involves above all else is a desire for certainty and for the power to enforce that certainty over others". Such fundamentalism is usually linked to religion, and religious fundamentalism is a force in various parts of the world." (el-Ojeili and Hayden, 2006: 166).

Though India is a peace loving country, fundamentalism raises its ugly head occasionally, vitiating the whole peaceful atmosphere. Globalization is a process meant for progress and as such fundamentalism and globalization do not go together.

Global Terrorism

The incidence of terrorism is increasing across the world and India is one of the badly affected countries. The Global Terrorism Index is published by the Institute for Economics and PEACE headquartered in Sydney. It publishes the index of 162 countries covering 99.6 per cent of the world's population. The Global Terrorism Index (GTI) is a comprehensive study of the direct and indirect attacks of terrorism, lives lost, and after effects. The definition of terrorism used by the Global Terrorism Index is: "the threatened or actual use of illegal force or violence by a non-state actor to attain a political, economic, religious or social goal through fear, coercion, or intimidation." The following Table 7.2 gives the ranks of the select number of countries.

Table 7.2: Global Terrorism Index 2014

Country	*Rank*	*Country*	*Rank*
Iraq	1	UK	27
Afghanistan	2	United States	30
Pakistan	3	Indonesia	31
Nigeria	4	South Africa	48
Syria	5	France	56
India	6	Brazil	72
Russia	11	Germany	83
China	25	Japan	121

Source: Global Terrorism Index 2014 published by Institute for Economics and PEACE.

Website: http://www.visionofhumanity.org/sites/default/files/Global%20Terrorism%20Index%20Report%202014_0.pdf

It will be seen from the above Table 7.2 that India stands at 6th position out of 162 countries, indicating that India is badly affected by terrorism. The attacks were undertaken by three different terrorist groups who can be categorized into Maoists, Separatists and Islamists. According to the report, terrorism increased substantially from 2012 to 2013. The majority of the attacks were by the Maoists groups. Since majority of the terrorist acts in India were from Maoists groups, socio-economic development of the affected area is of prime importance in the context of India.

The report also mentions that in September 2014, al-Qaida announced a presence in India. The major terrorist groups outside India are Islamic State in Iraq and Syria (ISIS), Boko Haram in Nigeria, Taliban in Afghanistan and Pakistan, and al-Qaeda and its offshoots in other parts of the World. Major terrorist activities have come to be known after 9/11 attack in USA. There appears to be a pattern in the geographical area afflicted by terrorist activities. Terrorism has grown as a response to dissatisfaction of people with the rulers of the countries involved. Absence of healthy political process to address the grievances of the people has been the root of the problem. In particular, ruling dispensations failed to resolve inter-ethnic and inter-religious aspirational differences in time, besides raising overall educational level and economic progress. Involvement of Western countries instead of helping to combat the terrorism has exacerbated the problem because their presence has become an easy tool for the terrorists to garner the sympathy and support of the local population.

Years of civil wars in the countries namely Syria, Afghanistan, Iraq, Nigeria, Libya etc. have resulted in huge tide of refugees (in lakhs) from these countries to European countries. Their journey involve great amount of risk as there is no state help to them in crossing seas. Mortifying images of the lifeless body of three-year old Syrian Aylan Kurdi at Turkish beach resort of Bordum on September 3, 2015 stirred the heart of millions in the world especially Europeans. As stated earlier civil wars are a product of poverty, misgovernance by the state and conflicts generated by the extremists.

Conclusion

Civil is first part of the word civilization and civil means largely polite. Thus, civilization represents socio-economic and cultural development at particular time and place. Generally, there is harmony between different civilizations. But as soon as there is some untoward incident between people belonging to two civilizations, the clash happens to spread like a wildfire and engulf wider area. The peace is ultimately brought about by the concerned governments either by democratic means or by heavy hand with the efforts of civil society. The restored harmony lasts for quite a long time. Then suddenly some other untoward incident happens and there is violence again. Thus, happenings go in circles.

The mass media play a very important role in both escalation of conflicts as well as bringing harmony. The occurrences of conflicts show whatever harmony we see is never lasting. The American and European nations have multicultural societies and they are able to maintain harmony in their countries to some extent due to mature democracies there. But in spite of their best efforts, the occasional conflagrations could not be avoided so far. Interpolating on past clashes and growing differences at different places in the world, Huntington only brought to the fore the possibility of great conflicts between the major civilizations.

Globalization is seen as playing dual role in regard to civilization. It is seen as playing a unifying role as all nations (and as such civilizations) are tied through a common thread of globalization; it is also seen as playing divisive role as there is always lurking fear that any untoward happening anywhere in the world has a potential to turn into a major conflagration between civilizations through the power of technology and media which are part of globalization. For the present, a new world order with acceptance of multiculturism seems to be a distant dream.

CULTURAL CHANGE—AMERICANIZATION?

Prologue

Earlier, different societies were living relatively in isolation and the culture that they developed remained undisturbed. However, under globalization, with close interconnectedness, cultures are getting mingled regardless of geographical location. The changing relationship between the culture and geographical location has now to be understood in the light of mingling of different cultures under globalization.

What are the factors that bring cultural change and how far cultural globalization impact culture at local and national level? What is the final shape that the local culture takes as a result of its coming into contact with the global culture? These are issues which need to be examined in the context of cultural change.

Meanings of Culture

Sociologists attribute different meanings to culture. According to the Oxford Dictionary, culture means refined understanding of the arts and other intellectual achievement; customs and civilization of a particular time or people. According to Webster Dictionary the culture means beliefs, arts, etc., of a particular society, group, place, or time. In broader perspective, some view culture as encompassing everything that concerns life of the group of people. On the other hand, some view culture, on the basic or narrower scale, as referring to literature, music, art, fashion etc. People look to culture as a provider of meaning to their lives. This is different from culture as a provider of material needs.

Process of Cultural Change/Diffusion of Cultures

Dictionary meaning of culture change is modification of a society through innovation, invention, discovery, or contact with other societies. There is a difference between the social change and the cultural change. While social change refers to change in social structure, its institution of stratification, demographic changes, urbanization, industrialization, social relationship etc., cultural change refers to change with regard to language, arts, philosophy, intellectual achievement, meaning to life etc. As an example, losing a grip of caste on choosing only hereditary occupation is a social change. Change from one art form to another such as classical dance and folk music to disco dance and pop music is a cultural change. Broadly it could be said that the cultural change is abstraction as well as extension of the social change.

It has taken time for various facets of globalization to enter into Indian setting and its impact on Indian culture has started becoming more prominently visible during last two to three decades only.

TV has become a major communicator of knowledge about cultures existing at different places. Though watching TV is a matter of choice, many viewers feel inclined to see TV regularly, as they come to know more about life styles which are evolving and new to them.

Under globalization societies and cultures are in greater contact with one another. The globalization with the advancement in information and communication technology has made people to people contact easier and faster, dismantling the barriers between them which existed earlier. This has also brought different societies and cultures in greater contact with each other.

When there is intermingling of different cultures, a process of diffusion takes place. Some societies may retain their culture, may be with certain changes, while some cultures may get merged into another. It depends upon how strong is the bond between the society and its own culture and how strong is the influence of the other culture with which it comes into contact. The outcome also depends upon the nuances of the societies involved and their historical background. The effect can be known from the changes in values, manners, fashion, foods etc.

A term diffusion is often used in the context of different cultures coming into contact with each other. According to Alan Tomlinson (Ritzer, 2012), diffusion is transmission and absorption of social practices and cultural values between societies when they come in contact. While some sociologists contend that the strong cultures try to dominate weak cultures by diffusion, their counterparts contend that when cultures come into contact with each other, no culture remains intact which means all cultures that come in contact change, though, degree of change may vary from one culture to another.

Diffusion of culture takes place in different forms. Similar industrial work and labour practices being adopted by capitalist countries represent the example of the process of diffusion. One of the features of these is the practice of hire and fire of employees. Japan represents another example of diffusion as to how 'tradition dominated country' adapted to industrialization in the second half of nineteenth century. On the other hand there are several countries especially developing countries in which there exist strong barriers leading to slowing the process of diffusion.

Language as a Basis of Culture

During British rule in India, the states were formed on the basis of administrative convenience only. There was no consideration for socio-economic and cultural aspirations of the local or regional people. Therefore, the first and foremost task before the liberated India was to form the states on the basis of language but there were also other considerations such as unity and security of India, economic and administrative viability involved. In order to undertake the work systematically, States Reorganization Commission was formed. Based on its report, states were formed in 1956. Thus, a principle that language is predominantly important feature of the culture was recognized.

Once the states were formed, there was a question of national language. Since Hindi speaking population of the country was more, it was thought that Hindi could be the link language. However, taking into account sentiments of southern states, both Hindi and English were accepted as link languages at the national level. Thus students were required to learn minimum three languages namely regional language, Hindi and English, better known as three language formula.

Subsequently, more states were required to be carved, again taking into consideration language and cultural affinity. The demand for creation of further more states is still there. Meanwhile, the importance of English language has increased tremendously due to the ongoing process of globalization. It offers many career prospects. English is a language of international trade and commerce. Further, anybody wishing to repatriate to US or UK has to learn English. In US, Indians are doing well in Information Technology because Indians know English language better than many other nationals including Chinese. It is evident that early exposure of Indians to English language during British rule has worked to the advantage of India in the modern world.

Knowledge of English coupled with other factors helped Indians to emigrate to West in good numbers for betterment of prospects in their view. Obviously, they have carried the culture of India to the West along with them. Thus, language has become predominantly a culture carrier.

Like Hindi or regional languages, Urdu language has become an identity of Muslim culture for Muslims in India and as such they follow a policy of promotion of Urdu language. There is a move to give more importance to Sanskrit than being given so far. The underlying idea is stated to be that Sanskrit is the language of Hindu heritage. If Sanskrit is to be promoted, it has to be simplified so that it becomes easy for the learners as well as users. Besides cultural aspect, the whole language issue has also to be seen from the perspective of the capacity of the young children to learn number of languages.

Americanization

The term Americanization connotes different meanings, but broadly it refers to the spread of American values, utilitarian attitude, liberal ideas, democracy, freedom of expression, individualism, freedom of adopting lifestyle of one's choice, innovation, capitalism, business practices, economic progress, opportunity, political maturity, modernity, youth culture etc. There has never been in the past so much circulation of the cultural products such as sports goods, popular music, fashionware, books, magazines, TV, Cinema etc. as during the last two decades. For many, American culture is a threat to the local cultures as it is said that they get easily lured by the youth culture of America.

There is a strong feeling that the indigenous cultures which are exposed to American culture are overpowered by the American culture. However, some people contend that there is no hegemony of one single culture and on the other hand, to some degree, American culture too gets influenced by other cultures just as other cultures are influenced by American culture.

It will not be correct to identify globalization with Americanization in entirety, though it can be said that Americanization forms significant part of globalization. Global business is surely dominated by the American corporate culture. In this context, it is generally acknowledged that the American corporate culture brought along with it good work culture like punctuality, efficiency etc. in developing countries.

John Tomlinson brings forth the argument of the skeptics of the cultural aspect of globalization. The critics of globalization argue that the American culture or broadly speaking Western culture, by way of imparting the cultural values and social practices, shapc the form of global culture. Besides, capitalist system operating in West brings in the characteristic of commodification in the global culture. Such a culture dominated by capitalist system of economy, social practices and cultural values of the West, in interacting with local culture, erodes and swamps the local culture and finally what emerges is a monoculture. Critics call this cultural imperialism. But protagonists of globalization contend that this is a exaggerated view which does not represent the ground reality. According to them, the local culture retains its core characteristics while absorbing in its periphery some of the global cultural characteristics. (46 Ritzer, 2012: 365).

Arjun Appadurai on '*Modernity at Large*'

Appadurai's treatise (Appadurai, 2005) has a special significance for India, as the author born and studied initially in Indian culture, migrated to a country of entirely new culture, i.e. American. His works based on his experiences about India, some of which are referred here, are considered as one of the most authentic on the subject of social sciences.

Appadurai explains the transnational phenomena of migration through a narrative of his personal experiences. In order to get the blessings of Goddess for happy marriage of his brother's daughter, coming from America, he visits Meenakshi Temple in Madurai along with his American historian wife, Carol Breckenridge, and son Alok from Philadelphia. His wife on earlier occasions visited the same temple and got well acquainted with a priest Thangam Bhattar there. She therefore was eagerly looking forward to see him there this time too. But to her astonishment, she found that the said priest is in far-away as a priest in Hindu temple devoted to Meenakshi in Houston, which is far away even from faraway Philadelphia (D Appadurai, 2005: 57). Such is the impact of globalization on the lives of the people.

Arjun Appadurai refers globalization as global flows of people, material, money, information and communication, and images that constitute imagination.

Appadurai feels that the theory of rupture better represents the modern culture rather than gradual transformation of culture. He says this because the changes have taken place so fast and so intense. He attributes these changes to three factors namely media, migration and imagination. Electronic media which is a product of modernization and instrument of globalization has introduced added dimension of imagination for interpreting phenomenon happening around. Mass mediated images make a big change in the perception of the people. The events which might earlier been thought of as usual, are now seen as unusual (Appadurai,

2005: 4). For example, mass migration used to take place in the past but no cognizance was taken as much as it is seen now with the display of images of mass migration. The imagination also works as a social force for creating alternatives to the nation-states.

Appadurai (2005: 33) contends that there is certain disconnect between economy, culture and politics and this disconnect can be better explored by way of studying the relationship among five dimensions of global cultural flows namely (a) ethnoscapes, (b) mediascapes, (c) technoscapes, (d) financescapes, and (e) ideoscapes. The scape here denotes the same meaning as the landscape bears the fluid and irregular shape. To Appadurai these landscapes are the building blocks of what can be called as imagined worlds.

Ethnoscape is the landscape of persons: tourists, immigrants, refugees, exiles, guest workers, and other moving groups and individuals. Mediascapes refers both to the electronic capabilities to produce and disseminate information through newspapers, magazines, television stations, and film-production studios. Interestingly, to the viewers, the lines between the realistic and the fictional landscapes they see are blurred. Technoscape refers to the configuration of technology, information and communication technology which now moves at high speeds. Interestingly, the technoscapes are increasingly driven not by rationality but by complex relationships among money flows, political possibilities, and the availability of the level of the skill of labour. Financescape refers to the flow of global capital at blinding speed. Ideoscapes refer to linking together chain of ideas, terms, and images which are often directly political and frequently have to do with the ideologies of states.

The smaller organized society always has a fear that the nearby bigger organized society will absorb their culture. Appadurai believes that when different cultures come in contact with each other, these do not follow the model of center-peripheri, but the cultures assume a complex form.

Conclusion

Earlier societies were bound solidly to their traditions. The globalization with the advancement in information and communication technology has made people to people contact easier and faster, dismantling the barriers between them which existed earlier. Social scientists differ widely about the nature and extent of the impact of globalization on the socio-cultural aspect of the society. While some social scientists contend that there is a wholesale swamping of local cultures, some contend that the core values of the local cultures remain intact, while there is a diffusion of the strong features of the global culture. For example, they contend that in India caste or community is still a dominant feature in shaping the mindset about taking a view of the global culture. Here global culture means more or less Western culture and particularly American culture as Americanization forms significant part of globalization. However some sociologists contend that there is no hegemony of one single culture and American culture is itself undergoing transformation along with increasing contact with far-flung local cultures in this flat world. It is common to see Indian and Chinese restaurants in every city, frequented not only by respective countrymen, but also by Americans. Many academicians of Indian origin are professors teaching social sciences and other subjects in American universities.

While the pre-modern societies had natural feelings toward each other, in modern societies it is rationality that tends to matter. Capitalism is essential part of globalization and along with it commodification. The world is caught up with the characteristic of commodification and it is bringing change in the traditional meaning of life everywhere.

There was a general belief that globalization will lead to greater harmony between different societies. However, religious fundamentalism is not found to be waning. Some people even contend that with more connectivity fundamentalism is growing.

To sum up, in the process of globalization, as an effect of diffusion of cultures, there is neither complete abandonment of one's culture nor there happens to be cultural homogeneity. The result depends upon the nuances of the societies involved and their historical background. We would further discuss the shape that a culture takes as a result of the ever continuing process of globalization.

CULTURAL CHANGE—HOMOGENIZATION

Cultural Convergence/Increasing Sameness

The protagonists of local cultures feel that western culture like say pop music or fashion of wearing short and tight clothes is frivolous though catchy to youngsters. They argue that the giant western cultural industries are propagating Western culture for economic gain and in the process destroying local cultures.

To begin with, the cultures have specificity to times and spatial location. But due to increasing interconnectedness under globalization, when different cultures come in contact with each other, intermixing of cultures takes place. Those who believe in homogenization of cultures contend that this intermixing of cultures is leading to convergence of cultures and thus evolving a monoculture. Another important characteristic is that the dominant culture influences the nature of the emerging culture.

Culture Symbolized by McDonald

The concept of *McDonaldization,* enunciated by George Ritzer (1993), in his book *The McDonaldization of Society* is derived from the name of the brothers Mac and Dick McDonald, who in 1937 opened a hamburger restaurant in Pasadena, California. In 1948 they opened a drive-in hamburger stand in San Bernardino, California, where they ran a Speedee System. The dominance of McDonaldization's speedee system of delivery of standard menu, Disney world as a world of entertainment, coca-cola as a refreshing food drink etc. is so widespread that these have simply overtaken national or local products.

The younger generation is finding these systems catchy and they are spreading to even remote places in countryside like wildfire. This process is leading to standardization of lifestyles and thus culminating in cultural homogenization. The older generation feels very uncomfortable with this development as it sees in this the demise of local culture which they loved so long so much.

Culture Symbolized by Wal-Mart

Wal-Mart is a supermarket shop. In Wal-Mart shop, we find standardized, bigger and cheaper products. Further the consumer gets all retail products under one roof. To attract consumers, they put up entertainment shows such as TV commercials, music and so on. The products in Wal-Mart are sold in bulk, they are cheaper. For example, if we purchase a bunch of 10 pairs of socks for price x, the price per pair works out to one-tenth of x. If we purchase only one pair of the same make and quality of socks from any outlet, the price will be higher than one-tenth of x. Wal-Mart has a global presence. It deals with multi-brand products. India has recently opened its market to foreign companies dealing with multi-brand products. India will soon have Wal-Mart branches in various places.

Since Wal-Mart deals with products in bulk and the products are cheaper, a tendency develops in the consumers to go for products in bulk, try to consume more and more, so that, they are not spoiled by long time storage. George Ritzer therefore refers Wal-Mart as cathedral of consumption. In the same vein, Ritzer refers Las Vegas casino-hotels, which are still more giant and costly to maintain, as dinosaurs of consumption.

Culture Symbolized Disney Theme Parks

Disney theme parks contain many attractions related to entertainment, information about species even other than human beings, thrilling joy rides and so on. There is constancy and coherence running across shows and they are not half-hazard collection of items for show. The showmen also display consistent, coherent and professional behaviour toward the viewers. These are marketing techniques, but very comforting and enjoyable to consumers. Disney theme parks, initially first time creation in USA, have become now extremely popular worldwide and parks on the same lines are now coming up in various parts of the world.

Culture Symbolized by MacWorld

McWorld, like McDonald's fast food chain, symbolizes homogenous and consumerist culture and is a product of economic side of globalization. Benjamin Barber, in an article titled *Jihad* vs. *McWorld* first published in 1992, highlights ever continuing tug of war between cultures emanating from liberalism and ethnic based indigenous cultures.

Summing up

The heart of the homogenization of culture is the increasing sameness in culture found everywhere. Extensive expansion of advanced communication facilities, dissemination of latest fashion and entertainment styles are bringing out wide ranging changes in the local cultural traits. Due to increasing interconnectedness under globalization, the local culture when it comes in contact with the outside culture is giving way to the dominant culture coming from outside. Those who believe in homogenization of cultures contend that the world is moving toward convergence of cultures and thus evolving a monoculture. The concepts of speedee system of delivery of standard menu, standard system of entertainment and increasing sameness in style of living are symbolized as McDonaldization, Disneyfication, Coca-colonization, McWorld. These systems are emanating mainly from West. According to protagonists of local cultures, with domination of American culture, there happens sameness of culture throughout the world and thus local cultures are decimated.

CULTURAL CHANGE—HYBRIDIZATION/GLOCALIZATION

Cultural Hybridization

In this interconnected world, when one culture comes in contact with another, they affect each other. It is generally believed that the Western culture which is catchy and known as dominant culture tries to modify the other cultures. However, there is no consensus about the nature of culture which emerges after different cultures come in contact. Here we are giving the views of authors who subscribe to emergence of hybrid culture as a result of different cultures.

Glocalization

Mixing of cultures has produced a unique hybrid culture wherein it is found that western culture coexists with local culture. This unique combination is being called glocalization. In the theory of sociology, glocalization was first used by Ronald Robertson (1992) to mean blend of the global and the local or the universal and the particular within the globalization processes. Glocalization is a broader concept in the sense that the blend of global and local cultural content is a continuous process. The outcome of this blend will be different at different geographical location depending upon interrelationship and interdependency between local and global cultures.

It is not that in the glocalization process, changes occur only in local culture. It can happen the other way round also ,i.e. global culture is influenced by local cultures. This is evident for example from the TV shows that programmes emanating from West are dovetailed as per the tastes of local where the programme is beamed.

The contention that the cultural homogenization is taking place as a result of dominating western culture is contested on the ground that the perception of western culture is seen as different at different places in the world. It is contended that the concept of glocalization solves this riddle and it can be said that the world is moving toward a concept of glocalization.

In hybrid culture/glocalization, the coexistence of different cultures, different cultural expressions, different types of foods, different types of entertainment, music, and art would be available at a given place, known as cosmopolitan.

Hybridization takes place in the field of language also. Many of the words would be taken straight from the local language because of either popularity or the particular product may be a specialty of the local place. For example dictionaries of English have adopted a word *chapatti* which means a round flat unleavened bread of India that is usually made of whole wheat flour and cooked on a metal surface. Similarly, Hindi or regional language newspapers in India use English words straightaway like the word school or table although their equivalent words are available in Hindi or regional languages in India.

The hybridization in the field of music is widely observed. Mixing of Western pop music with Indian light music is quite common in India now.

The phenomenon of integration of part of the outside culture in the local culture is a continuous process. Interestingly, the result of this integration is tilting more toward heterogenization as compared to homogenization.

Those who hold the view that the world is moving toward cultural-hybridization, do not agree that the local culture is getting eclipsed with the domination of western culture. They contend that whether it is fashion, costume, music or food, a blend of western and local culture is taking place. Kaku (2011) claims that people will be bicultural with local cultural traditions remaining alive. The nature of hybrid culture will vary from one local place to another.

Cosmopolitanism

Cosmopolitanism means culture free from geographic limitations. Therefore, the term cosmopolitanism better explains hybridization. In Indian cosmopolitanism city like Mumbai, Delhi, Kolkata, Chennai, Bangalore, Hyderabad etc. at one place we get different varieties of fashion goods. Music, food etc. some of these might be coming from different countries. These cities showcase muticularalism i.e. acceptance of cultural diversity at a place.

Plurality

Hybridization stems from acceptance of plurality of cultures. Idea of fast food known to have come from western world, can be seen at the age-old *Dhabas* across roads where truck drivers stop for quick food.

Openness of Local Culture

The openness of local culture to absorb good ideas of foreign culture is supposed to be beneficial for the local culture. American and Indian cultures are the examples of this. On the other hand if local culture is closed to recognize leave alone absorb anything good in the foreign culture, such a culture will find difficulty in growing in the present process of globalization.

Summing up

Cultural homogenization and heterogenization lie at two opposite ends of the cultural paradigm. Whereas the former suggests that the process of globalization leads to cultural sameness everywhere, the latter suggests that in spite of the process of global interconnectedness all cultures remain distinct save some peripheral changes in them. Cultural hybridization or glocalization lies just in the middle suggesting that the interplay of global culture and local culture produces the unique blend which may be different at different geographical location depending upon interrelationship and interdependency between local and global cultures.

In hybridization, the characteristics of both global and local, universal and particular are shared in varied measures across the globe. Notwithstanding this, in hybridization, in relative term, there is some, may be slight, tilt toward heterogenization than homogenization, meaning that the identity, in some measure, of both global and local is seen in the hybrid culture.

CULTURAL CHANGE—HETEROGENIZATION

Cultural Differentialism

Cultures vary from region to region. Every culture has some central values and some peripheral values. In the process of globalization, various cultures come into contact with each other. This cultural contact may at most affect peripheral aspect of a culture, but does not affect its Central values. Thus, proponents of multiculturalism contend that heterogeneous characteristic of different cultures exist. Some sociologists such as Samuel Huntington propagate that in a situation of multiculturalism, with growing intolerance for other cultures, there is every possibility of war at least between major cultures such as Muslim, Christian, Confucian and Hindu.

Multiculturalism

Historically, every country has had at different times immigration of people from other countries into their native country as well as emigration of their native people to other countries. Thus, immigration and emigration are historical facts. In spite of geographical dislocation, these people try to keep their cultural identity on the lines of their ethnicity, race, religion, language. Nation-state where they live tries to weave through all these different cultures by a common thread in the spirit of nationalism (Ritzer, 2012: 1450).

America-multiculturalism

America is called a country of immigrants as there are few Native Americans or their descendents alive. Since, immigrants have come from different nationalities, their cultures are also different. For example, Indians have their associations in every place they live. These associations hold regularly cultural functions and thus they keep their separate cultural identity. Further down, there are even associations on linguistic lines such as Gujarati, Marathi, Telugu, Tamil, Malayalam etc. The associations celebrate religious functions according to their faiths. On similar lines, immigrants from other countries such as China, African countries, Japan, South Korea etc. keep their separate cultural identity. At the same time, these different cultures coexist with major cultures, i.e. English and Spanish, without losing their intrinsic characteristics.

Summing up

America is a country of immigrants. By far America and especially United States of America is a unique example wherein different cultures are coexisting. Alongside mainstream English population, there is substantial presence of Hispanic population in USA. The term Hispanic is commonly applied to particularly the countries of Latin America (*especially*: one of Cuban, Mexican, or Puerto Rican origin) which were colonized by Spain. Similarly, Western European countries have growing Muslim populations. The people wherever they go tried to keep their cultural identity on the lines of their ethnicity, race, religion, Thus, different cultures prospered independently. USA can be termed as a nation of Heterogeneous cultures as we find existence of different cultures living side by side. The success for this can perhaps be ascribed to functional democracy in the country.

Pointing toward certain historical background, Samuel Huntington, however, sees in this heterogeneous cultures possibility of clashes at least between major cultures.

CONCEPTUAL DIFFERENCES BETWEEN HOMOGENIZATION, HYBRIDIZATION—GLOCALIZATION AND HETEROGENIZATION

Conceptual Differences

Homogenization in cultural context represents the observation of increasing sameness found everywhere. Intense expansion of advanced communication facilities and fast dissemination of latest fashion and entertainment styles are bringing out far reaching changes in the local cultural traits. It is a sign of cultural convergence and development of global mass culture. Some call this as a phenomena of absorption of weak local culture by dominant culture

Hybridization/Glocalization in cultural context represents the production of new and unique culture as an outcome of mixing of cultures in the process of globalization. Since Hybridization is a combination of global and local, it is also called as Glocalization. In the theory of sociology, glocalization was first used by Ronald Robertson (1992) to mean blend of the global and the local within the globalization processes In hybridization/glocalization, there is existence of cultural expressions different from pure global or pure local culture, it is a blend of both cultures.

The essence of Heterogenization is that the cultural polarity of each culture remains intact. Cultures vary from region to region. Every culture has some central values and some peripheral values. In the process of globalization, various cultures come into contact with each other. This cultural contact may at most affect peripheral aspect of a culture, but does not affect its Central values. Thus, proponents of multiculturalism contend that heterogeneous characteristics of different cultures exist. Some sociologists such as Samuel Huntington propagate that in a situation of multiculturalism, with growing intolerance for other cultures, there is every possibility of war at least between major cultures such as Muslim, Christian, Confucian and Hindu.

Conceptual Differences with Examples

The above conceptual differences can very well be explained by the theory of diffusion. If the culture A is totally absorbed by the interacting culture B, and culture B is only prevailing everywhere, the process can be termed as Homogenization. For example let us assume people with two separate cultures exist, one in which the dress of women is *salwar-kameej* and the other in which the dress is jean-T shirt. On interaction with one another, if the women in the former category dispense with the dress of *salwar-kameej* and adopts the dress of other category, i.e. jean, T-shirt, and the latter dress is the one seen everywhere, it will be termed that Homogenization of wearing a particular dress has taken place. The second example can be cited from the field of music. If the local people who were used to play folk music take to Jazz music played by the people from outside and the latter is the one seen everywhere, such is the case of Homogenization of cultures. Third example can be cited about the language. Let us assume that the local people speak Marathi language and the other interacting people speak Hindi language. If over a period of time the whole lot of people switch over to Hindi language and that language is spoken by all, in this case Homogenization of language is supposed to have taken place. In these cases the diffusion of dress culture of jean-T shirt into *salwar-kameej*, music culture of Jazz into folk and language culture of Hindi into Marathi is total. The other way we can say is that the local culture has been absorbed by the outside culture.

In the second scenario, if on interaction, let us assume that the local women wear *kameez* alright, but adopt jean in place of *salwar*. In regard to music, let us assume that local people continue to use some nodes of folk music and some nodes of jazz music. In regard to language, let us assume, local people belonging to Marathi peak up some words from Hindi language and they bring out the language which is a mixture of both languages. The resultant dress, music and language will be a mixed one which is termed as Hybridization of dress, music and language culture. In these cases the diffusion of one culture into another has been partial.

In the third scenario, let us assume that some women wear traditional dress of *salwar-kameej* and some women wear jean-T shirt. In regard to music, let us assume that some local people play folk music and some local people play jazz music. Similarly, let us assume one section of people speaks purely Marathi and another section of people speaks only Hindi. In all these cases, people with altogether different dress, music and language cultures coexist. This is termed as Heterogenization of cultures with reference to dress, music and language.

The above examples are indicative of the concept and may not be taken in literal sense.

Sociologists' View

While sociologists differ in expressing a common view on whether globalization is leading to cultural Homogenization or Hybridization—Glocalization or Heterogenization, a large body of sociologists holds that globalization is leading more toward Hybridization—Glocalization. Notwithstanding this view, the outcome depends upon the frame of reference adopted such as geographical area and socio-cultural background of the population for judging the impact of globalization. For example, in one country alone, we may find all three categories existing at different locations and only one particular category existing in a small community.

CULTURAL—ETHNICITY

What is Ethnicity?

According to Thomas Hylland Eriksen the term ethnicity refers to the enduring relationship between more or less bounded groups or social categories that perceive themselves as being culturally different from each other. Ethnic identities are, furthermore, based on widely held notions of shared origin and shared culture,

Examples of ethnic groups could be Indians living in any foreign land. While in India, Indians have Indian culture. When they migrate to another country, they carry their culture in that country. Thus, home culture comes in contact with the culture of the host country. In this case over a period of time, while core cultural values may remain intact, peripheral cultural values may undergo some changes.

Though ethnicity denotes distinct cultural identity, the relationship between the two is complex rather than simple. For example, in the eyes of American, *Gujarathis*, *Maharashtrians*, *Telugus, Bengalis* or *Malayalis* living in USA might be regarded as persons of Indian ethnicity. But between different linguists though they may be belonging to one nation, there are many cultural differences. In the light of this, ethnicity denotes distinct cultural identity between two or more ethnic groups.

Relationship within Host Country

In the present network society, whether different ethnic groups help in enhancing the solidarity of the country they adopt or those groups are a threat to that country is a subject of intense debate.

The contention of those who hold that different ethnic groups help in enhancing the solidarity of the host country is that in the process of globalization, the primary bonds that bind ethnic group tightly together gets loosened. For example, the persons in the group will be more concerned about their job and self development than getting bogged down by constrains of their particular ethnicity. For example, in the work place, persons belonging to different ethnicity may be working together. Therefore, this will help in enhancing solidarity of the host country.

On the other hand, the contention of those who hold that different ethnic groups weaken the solidarity of the host country is that the global media which has a long and wide reach keep the ties with the home country so tight that the solidarity of the host country is weakened. Further, many a times global media exacerbates the situation by projecting a feeling that injustice is being done to the ethnic group because the group comes from other homeland. Such propaganda alienates the ethnic group from the mainstream population and increases the possibility of conflicts. The media also strengthens the bonds between members of the ethnic group as the ethnic group in host country remains strongly connected with their dear ones in home country through global media. The situation thus leads to dual loyalty, i.e. loyalty to home country and loyalty to host country.

It is observed that much of the disaffection of ethnic group grows mainly from the feeling that they are not getting a fair share of state resources and that they are not made part of the political process. Such conceptions can be addressed by way of giving them due share of the state resources and encouraging their participation in governance of the nation-state.

In the past, bound by the geographical boundaries, race bearing physiological differences had lot of significance. However, with the advent of the process of globalization, there is so much mobility and interconnectedness that the significance of the term race has started receding. The meanings to the physiological differences like culture rather than the conventional physiological differences have acquired significance. Thus, in social sciences, the term is increasingly getting replaced by the ethnic group.

Eric Kaufmann talks about residential preferences of mainstream population *vis-à-vis* ethnic groups and says that second generation immigrants, once they earn a certain amount of money, tend to leave their existing place of settlement for greener places with better housing, just like whites. The main driving force toward segregation probably now comes from the white population moving away from ethnically diverse areas and choosing to live with other whites. Minorities are less exclusive in their preferences. When the area tips over a certain level of minority, it becomes more and more concentrated with ethnic minorities. But it is to be noted that racial factors are not causing white flight. It seems to be more to do with micro and cultural issues-when looking for a house they are more interested in having cafes near their houses than ethnic food shops.

Summing up

Ethnicity is a geographical and cultural construct. It also represents enduring relationship between the group members as well as between two or more groups. Advancement in Information and Communication Technology with the advent of globalization has a significant impact on ethnicity. The relationship between different ethnic groups with the mainstream population of the host country is constantly impacted by the ICT. In this context, sociologists are differing widely on the view as to whether under globalization, solidarity of ethnic groups with the mainstream population is getting strengthened or weakened. But in overall, it is strengthening the solidarity in the nation-state where there is democratic system of governance, in which case the participation of ethnic groups in the political process is expected to be fairly encouraged.

CULTURAL—IDENTITY

Definition of Identity

According to Ronald Niezen, identity refers to the most important qualities shared by people within a recognized group, the cultural practices that set them apart from others and ultimately their character or personality, sometimes referring to an innermost essence that lacks clear definition but that nevertheless is a foundation for distinctiveness and, at times, sovereignty (Ritzer, 2012: 985).

Multiple Identities

In present times, maintaining identity in the face of globalization is becoming pretty difficult. The factors such as migration, influence of Western culture etc. are contributing to shifting of identities. The process of globalization is changing every aspect of the society. On the economic front, there is a divide between the developed North and developing South. The process of globalization has made differences between rich and the poor more distinct. On labour front, the level of skill is making a great difference. On social front, it has brought more population in the middle class. On cultural front there is a greater interaction between Western and other cultures. The cultural changes at the local level are branded as homogeneous, hybrid, or heterogeneous. The process of globalization has also changed the character of nation-state and in the process the nature of nationalism.

There is now a wave of mobility of people in the form of migration from one place to another, one region to another, one nation to another and one continent to another. Such movements are bringing out new socio-cultural environment. These socio-economic, cultural, political changes are bringing out changes in the identities of the people, degree of change depending on the location where they are situated and their social background. Thus, identities are now fluid, are no more static as they were in societies of remote past or at the time of Marx for whom class was the identity (el-Ojeili and Hayden, 2006: 149-50).

In traditional society the identity was clear as belonging to that society and it was stable. A person was not subjected to frequent changes in work or living environment. However, in the process of globalization, there is so much interconnectedness and physical mobility that for betterment, one is always on the move and he has to constantly cope with new environment. One has therefore to play his role appropriate to the situation in which he is placed. The frequent changes in situations and his role make his identity ever unstable and changeable. It can best be described as multiple (el-Ojeili and Hayden, 2006: 150).

While referring to identity, important question that arises in one's mind is 'who am I?' The answer to this question gives a clue about the identity of the person. There are multiple situations which determine identity. These could be peer groups, lifestyles etc. Identity can also be related to beliefs and values one holds. In modern times there is no particular bounded identity for either individuals or groups. Unlike in the past when individual was more constrained by traditional social ethos, he is now susceptible to ever changing global environment in which he fashions his identity. The same thing applies to group as well (Ritzer, 2012: 985).

Many people are turning away from long working schedule to shorter work schedule and they like to spend time leisurely. We see around more and more people are travelling as tourists. Accordingly, these people are identified as tourists. The movement of people for purposes other than duty is increasing. People are thus tending to be more as consumers than producers in this mobile world (el-Ojeili and Hayden, 2006: 152).

Conservative Identities/Individualism

Some sociologists contend that instead of oneself identifying with particular group or community in the past, in modernity there is no compulsiveness and one can have a choice in maintaining his identity. For instance, Anthony Giddens (2003) regards 'late modernity' as marked by choice, self-identity, and lifestyle (el-Ojeili and Hayden, 2006: 153).

In early stages of mankind, group or community identity was prevalent. This was mainly due to insecure nature of the society as one society could face the threat from other one because there was nothing like secure geographical borders. However, with the French Revolution (1789-1799), idea of nation-state took practical shape. The idea of nation-state gave birth to democracy in West, Europe and then in other countries, giving individual right to vote and choose the government. Further, on account of inherent inefficiency, state entrepreneurship gave way to capitalism. Capitalism inherently means private ownership of the individual. Thus, individual who carried no personal identity before revolutions in the nineteenth century could attain independent personal identity as free individual. In democracy of nation-state and entrepreneurial capitalism one has choices of life. This development led to the cult called individualism.

Individualism can be good for the society in that there is an opportunity for the individual to contribute his best for the good of the society. Individualism can also be bad for the society if one becomes self-centered. Post-French revolution, many sociologists criticized the rise of individualism as they attributed negative backlash of the revolution in the form of chaos to the rise of individualism (Ritzer, 2012: 1019).

Reactive Identities

The process of globalization is supposed to generate liberal, secular, social and political environment and thus identity also is expected to be following positive wider principles. However, instead of this, reactive identities are also getting created around communal lines, instead of becoming secular or liberal, they are becoming conservative (el-Ojeili and Hayden, 2006: 155).

Thus, in the process of globalization, we observe some contrasting situations. Along with rise of progressive political hopes, there are also rise of countercurrents by way of polarization on the lines of ethnicity or civilization (el-Ojeili and Hayden, 2006: 155).

Virtual/Imagined Communities

Technological advancement is changing the characteristic of the society. Many people now a days are interacting with others on social media through internet. Unlike physical community members who physically come into contact, virtual community members communicate with each other through internet on social networking sites such as Facebook, Twitter etc. Except during work, these people do not spend time in physical interaction with others. It is observed that instead of making friendship with known persons, many in the younger generation, make friendship on social media with the persons never seen by them in life earlier. In the process, idea of physical interaction is receding.

This is leading to production of 'virtual communities.' Since these persons are identifying themselves as members of 'virtual communities,' a new identity is getting created. In the process, shared norms, values, beliefs between physical individuals or groups are giving way to sharing of views on internet with physically unknown persons (Ritzer, 2012: 2147).

The advent of printing in 16th century, advancement of technology later and especially advancement of information and communication technology in twentieth century onwards have brought connectivity in a community so much that even though their members are not physically in contact and distantly placed, they facilitated cultural contact that enabled to develop the "imagined communities." The role of TV and Internet in particular for creating "imagined communities" is noteworthy.

Through Skype it is now possible to have eye to eye contact with persons living in different continents. Religion is thus now no more a predominant identity which had been the case in past. Let us take the case of celluloid celebrities. Actors and actresses across the world form a separate group. So also sports persons, painters, musicians and so on. Thus new identities are created in the present world (Ritzer, 2012: 996).

Conclusion

Identity refers to the most important qualities shared by people within a recognized group, the cultural practices that set them apart from others. In remote past civilization and later religion were the principal identity markers. With the advent of printing technology and later advancement of information and communication technology, there has been great connectivity between the people. Individuals have now a choice to choose his work place, hobby and lifestyle. Thus, in the globalized world, multiple identities are created as they move from place to place and choose lifestyle.

However, many sociologists contend that advancement of information and communication technology through social networking is promoting virtual/imagined communities, far from physical contacts, and polarizing the people around conservative principles, i.e. ethnicity and nationalism.

RISE OF SPORTS CULTURE

From time immemorial and specifically Roman Empire, sport formed important part of culture. Gladiator game was part of the Roman martial sport for public entertainment from third century BCE. Presently football and cricket are leading games attracting maximum spectators globally. In Indian context, cricket has become very much part of Indian culture. Apart from watching game in the field, more people are glued to TV in their drawing rooms watching cricket. It is interesting to know how globalization has brought sweeping cultural change in India.

Prior to arrival of TV in India, print media, radio and films were the means of mass communication. That time, the media was engaged with more news about local matters, economic-political developments and film shows, and less about sports except radio broadcasting commentary during sports' competitions at the national level. These competitions pertained to major sports consisting of hockey, football and cricket. It was in mid-twentieth century that TV arrived in India that changed the whole complexion of coverage of the sports by media.

The younger generation is getting more interested in seeing sports than film shows and least in political developments. They are least interested in political developments as if these were subjects that are meant for middle aged and old people.

In Indian villages and towns in earlier times, *kabaddi* and *khokho* were most popular games. Both of these games did not require any equipment or infrastructure except small piece of ground. Hockey and football were more popular in cities. These games required large grounds and hokey sticks and balls. *Kabaddi* and *khokho* somehow carried limited appeal and remained largely as local level games. The reason seems to be that while these games involve physical strength, they involve relatively less manipulation of skill and much less these games are revenue earners.

In December 2014, *Kabaddi* World Cup was held in Punjab in which 12 nations participated. Interestingly, some of the participating teams did not have a single player of Indian origin. The final was played on 20.12.2014 between the teams of India and Pakistan in which India won the hotly contested match. It is unfortunate that this international tournament of the game of Indian origin received practically no attention beyond Punjab in the print as well as TV media.

Hockey and football involve physical strength as well as manipulation of skill. Cricket involves less physical strength compared to hockey and football, but more manipulation of skill. Earlier cricket was played as a test match of five days. Many people looked to this game as slow moving and waste of time for the spectators. Communist countries saw this game as a game of capitalist or elite having long leisure time at their disposal. However, the introduction of one single day play of 50 overs by Kerry Packer as a part of World Series Cricket made a tremendous difference to the game as well as spectators. People are overwhelmingly impressed by the speed and motion in the game.

Even then so long as TV did not appear on the scene in India, the appeal of all three games, i.e. cricket, hockey and football was almost similar. But appearance of TV in India made all the difference. There seems to be number of reasons for this. One is the duration of game. While hockey and football last about two hours, cricket goes on a day long. Thus, while the people have to know and watch live hockey and football at the exact time of the day on TV, cricket can be watched any time of the longer duration when the viewer has a time. The second reason is the winability in the international arena. So far India has not qualified for playing football in international competition. India and Pakistan were excellent at hockey during some years in the past, but both the nations could not keep pace with the Europeans with regard to improvement of skill speed and stamina.

On the other hand, during colonial rule, with the adoption of cricket by the princely families and their encouragement to the skillful players coming from non-princely families, this game continued to make headway. Indian cricket team continued to attain good place in the world teams. The winability of cricket in the international arena gave tremendous boost to the game and popularity of this game far outstripped the popularity of other games. Another important factor is commercial.

Due to abovementioned reasons, revenues from TV commercials

during cricket matches outstripped revenues from other games. This resulted in cricket getting much more attention and encouragement all around. The popularity of game and enormous profit from TV commercials complimented each other. This resulted in sidelining of all other games. The dark side of this game is that high commercial gain gave birth to worst practice like *match fixing*.

To sum up the above narrative, with globalization, we lost our traditional culture of popular games like *kabaddi*, *khokho*, hockey and football and inherited cricket from the colonial power. In a way, this has turned out to be an advantage to India as cricket has become a good revenue earner for the country. However, this game largely continued to remain urban and relatively elite, leaving rural folk with double disadvantage, one—no cricket because of absence of infrastructure, and two—eclipse of traditional games because these games are seen as irrelevant in the face of popularity of cricket. The sunrise of cricket and sunset of all other traditional sports in India is an example of what kind of change, globalization can bring, in an area of culture.

WORK—LIFE—LEISURE

Social Pattern of Leisure

The pattern of leisure seems to have undergone change in line with the social change taking place as a result of globalization. There are variations in the pattern depending upon the situation in which particular community is placed. The pattern of leisure seen in rural society differs from that of the urban society. It varies between elite society and society of commoners.

The pattern of leisure in rural society is seen on the traditional lines. After day's agriculture work is over, being together in the evening, at village *Choupal* is the most popular form of spending leisure time in rural area. Villagers interact there freely on all matters including weather, agriculture, economy, social, cultural, political etc. The other form of leisure is at the time of social or cultural functions like marriages or festivals. Spending leisure time on TV has also started but it is not so popular yet. In urban society, watching TV is the most popular form of spending leisure time, next being social call to friends and relatives.

For elites, clubs, gyms, drive to farm houses, visit to tourist places etc. are popular form of spending leisure time. For commoners, watching TV, interacting with neighbours, spending time with children are popular form of spending leisure time.

The pattern of spending leisure time varies from society in developed country to society in developing country. In developed countries, out of two week days, one is used for cleaning home, laundry of clothes, purchasing of grocery etc. The other day is for outing with the family and eating out in restaurants. In developing countries, outing is still not popular.

Variations are also seen on the lines of religion and so on.

Work—Life—Leisure

It was in 1844 that Marx first coined the term of alienated labour for the labour working in the industry. That time workers were working from twelve to sixteen hours. Marx attributed alienation of labour to the economic system which first adopted exchange of goods by a method of barter and later switched over to money as a medium of exchange. Marx argued that this system led to commodification of labour. Since product no more remained part of the producer-worker, the product became an alien object to the worker. The worker thus did not find satisfaction and fulfillment in his work. Thus, nature of an individual finding work truly as a matter of satisfaction and fulfillment got distorted. This alienation extended to his personal life as he had very little time and money to find better avenues of enjoying life except carrying out functions akin to animals such as eating, sleeping and procreating.

Work—Life—Leisure are intimately connected with working hours of office or factory. The following Table 7.3 shows the working hours being followed by some countries.

Table 7.3: Weekly Working Hours in Different Countries

Country	*Weekly working hours*
US	40
Japan	40
Europe	
UK	Not more than 48 hours
France	35
Germany	40
BRICS Countries	
Brazil	44
Russia	40
India	48
China	44
South Africa	45

Source: Country's Govt. Websites, OECD.

It will be seen from the above table 7.3 that the working hours per week generally are 40-44 hours. In developed countries there is clamour for four working days a week in place of present five. The protagonists of short work week contend that working longer doesn't necessarily mean giving more output. They also contend that short work week will reduce commuting, combat high levels of work-related stress, the employees will be able to spend more time with their families or exercising, and reduce unemployment. It is assumed that with better physical fitness and mental freshness, they will work with vigor. But these are all expectations without testing in reality.

In the present context of globalization, while the working hours are reduced from the Marx era, there is now no line of demarcation between life and work. Although person may be having two days as holidays at the end of the week, the person is more likely to be engaged in office work either by way of answering calls on cell phone or *via* internet. How about time for attending to personal work? It is not uncommon that personal work of a few hours may be done during duty hours by taking a short time off from the workplace. To make up, the worker may work in the office in extended time. The line of demarcation between work and life has become so thin that it is increasingly amounting to merging of work into life.

In earliest days, human being was under stress on account of two counts. One was constant threat from the animals like tigers, lions, bears etc or reptiles. Another was to arrange food and shelter for the livelihood. These were heavily scaled towards physical work by the human being. However, the world has since then undergone a tremendous change and now in the age of information technology, working on computers has become more predominant.

The modern technology of cell phone, computers and internet has changed the lifestyle of people altogether. The merging of work into life is leading to increase of stress level. In earlier times, people used to suffer more from communicable diseases but now there is preponderance of lifestyle diseases, like heart problem main cause being stress. Name any disease and it is found that either it is caused by stress or the condition of the person afflicted by the disease is aggravated by stress. The economic revolution under globalization has benefited the people in terms of creating comforts, but at the same time it has brought new problems to the humanity. The heart problem, which is the foremost killer disease presently, is directly related to stress. Diabetes, cancer and host of other diseases are also linked to stress Coping with stressors has now become major preoccupation of a human being.

Globalization involves market economy and competition. Such a kind of situation makes work stressful. In view of increasing stress level in the process of globalization, there is a growing call for shorter work week and more leisure especially in developed countries.

Flexi-time working and working from home are other ideas to meet the requirement of office as well as family. Though presently limited to few IT multinational companies, the trend is picking up. The pros and cons of this system are dealt in the topic "Globalization and Employment" in detail.

8
Socio-Economic Inequality

GENDER FEMINIZATION IN GLOBALIZATION

Prologue

It is contended that the bias in favour of males and against females stems from the nature of the society that is patriarchal. As girls started acquiring education in a significant way, it was thought that the bias will disappear. Traditionally, women's activities were generally confined to home and agriculture related work. But after industrialization, women started participating in factory and professional work. Under globalization, there is hardly any area which remains untouched by women's presence. However, the question is whether under globalization bias against females has decreased and whether women are given equal opportunities and status in the society.

Discrimination against Girl Child

Preference for Son

History of India as well as scme other countries is replete with bias against females. In India discrimination against girl child has been prevalent right from conception of a child. Preference for son and discrimination against girl child has been a leading cause for female foeticide in India: Female foeticide has been defined as the act of aborting a foetus because it is female.

Sex Ratio as per Census Data

Since phenomena of female foeticide/female infanticide mostly occur in private domain under utmost secrecy, no accurate measure is available and cannot be available about the female foeticide/female infanticide. Therefore, the sex ratio of female to male is taken as an indicator of the relative demographic position of female and male. It is generally assumed that there should be an ideal ratio of unity which means if there is no external variant, there should be equal number of men and women at any given point of time. However, some researchers feel that since longevity of women is more than men, the ratio should reflect more number of female. In order to appreciate the issue in empirical perspective, it is necessary to refer to the data of the Census of India 2011conducted under the auspices of Registrar General of India. The following Table 8.1 gives sex ratio in India (age-wise and rural-urban): 2001 and 2011.

Table 8.1: Sex ratio in India (age-wise and rural-urban): 2001 and 2011

(Females per thousand males)

Year of Census	*Total Population*	*Child Population In age group 0-6*	*Population aged 7 and above*
1991	927	945* (962-1981)	923
2001	933	927*	934
2011	943	914*	944
	Total Population	Rural Population	Urban Population
2001	933	946	900
2011	943	947	926

It will be seen from the above Table 8.1 that firstly there is an improvement in sex ratio from the Census 2001 to 2011. Secondly, the ratio is better in rural area as compared to urban area. Thirdly, and the most striking feature* is that there is a continuous steep fall in the sex ratio in child population in the age group 0-6 from Census 1991 to Census 2001 and then from Census 2001 to Census 2011, *in-spite* of increase in the sex ratio of overall population during the same census years.

The following Table 8.2 gives sex ratio in ten most populous countries.

It will be seen from Table 8.2 that the sex ratio in India is lowest during 2001 and is only next to China during 2011. China is the only country where there is one child policy officially. Like India, China is also generally known for preference for the son and the statistics also indicate the same. Further, Census report notes that the sex ratio in USA, Russian Fed. and Japan has always remained above unity despite minor

Table 8.2: Sex ratio in ten most populous countries in the world during 2001 and 2011

(Females per thousand males)

Sl. No.	*Country*	*2001*	*2011*
	World	986	984
1.	China	944	926
2.	India	933	943
3.	USA	1029	1025
4.	Indonesia	1004	988
5.	Brazil	1025	1042
6.	Pakistan	938	943
7.	Russian Fed.	1140	1167
8.	Bangladesh	958	978
9.	Japan	1041	1055
10.	Nigeria	1016	987

variations meaning thereby females are always outnumbering males in these countries.

Patriarchal Society and Traditions—Historical Perspective

Though female foeticide is a recent phenomenon, its practice in another form, i.e. female infanticide has been prevalent in India from historical times. Against the backdrop of history, the practice has now assumed more prominence because we have entered twenty-first century with this critical social issue still staring at us with almost equal measure, of course in a different form, i.e. from female infanticide to female foeticide.

There is a trend to link the phenomena of female foeticide/female infanticide to the state of the society which is termed as patriarchal. The definition of patriarchal society is given as, "a society recognizing the supremacy of the father in the clan or the family, and the reckoning of descent and inheritance in the male line; *broadly*: men controlling disproportionately larger power." It is inferred from the supposedly characteristics of the patriarchal society that relatively there is less importance given to female member as compared to male. There can be a difference in perception as to whether the society is factually a patriarchal—bearing the characteristics generally assumed to be attached with it, or, every member in the family just enacts the role required to run the family without man wielding disproportionately large power.

Right from the time human beings lived in cave, they had to confront wild animals for survival, fight wars between societies and till the agriculture. For all these, men had to be on the forefront as they are endowed with stronger physique than women. This natural difference of physical power must have led to men assuming the responsibility of heading the family. This seems to be the natural course in which the society took the form of patriarchal character. In this society, woman has to shift after marriage from her ancestral place to husband's place. In the division of work, whereas man has largely to manage the work which requires physical strength and manage the environment external to the family, woman does the work which is internal to the family like cooking food, raising the children and if necessary to work outside the home in the fields.

By the very nature of physical differences, females were facing the general problem of protection from the atrocities of males and therefore it became special responsibility of father to protect the daughter against violence before her marriage and protecting the wife by the husband after marriage. The practice of *Johar* (mass self-immolation by Rajput women after defeat of their men at the hands of enemy) also seems to have taken birth with the idea of protection of honour. Similarly, the practice of *sati* is also borne out of the (naturally wrong) idea that woman has no separate existence from that of her husband.

Earlier agriculture used to be the main occupation. Since, girl goes to her husband's place which is new to her, and division of agriculture was not favoured, boy became the natural inheritor of the property. In earlier times some kinds of superstitions also developed like: the person, after death, will not be able to get the place of heaven unless his funeral pyre is lit by his son.

The centuries—old practice of dowry is also cited as a potential reason behind son preference. There are several reports of ill treatment of women in their in-laws house on the pretext that adequate dowry was not given by their parents at the time of marriage. They are also coerced to bring material benefits even after marriage and bride burning on the issue of dowry.

The notion that in patriarchal system, a girl after marriage goes to her husband's place whereas boy stays at ancestral home and in course of time bears the responsibility of family, carries a kind of gender disparity even in a matter like education.

In the present competitive world, people are not prepared to devote more time for the child care. They, therefore, generally do not wish to have more than two children. So, if parents have already one male child out of two, parents generally go for the abortion of the third child irrespective of its sex. But if parents have two daughters, many of the parents go for the third child, and if it is male, they are comfortable. But if third child also happens to be female, parents tend to go for the abortion. This practice follows the theory of preference.

It appears the above factors led to the process of giving undue importance to male child, which reflected in providing to boy nutritious food, better education and other comforts, compared to girl, and sometimes even at the cost of girl. In the chain of events, the female foeticide/female infanticide is seen as culmination of the extreme form of manifestation of the aforesaid beliefs.

Influence of Factors other than Historical Background

There is no direct evidence about the direct relationship between education and social equality as far as preference for son is concerned. Method of production seems to have an influence on the sex ratio. While among unpropertied groups, utility of female for labour supports the survival of females, among the propertied groups there is less use of female labour with resulting sex ratios favouring males, Looking from rural-urban perspective, it is observed that the ratio of females to male is better in rural area as compared to urban area. Besides, usefulness of female for supporting families in rural area, this could also be on account of the reason that the migration of male members is more than the females from rural to urban area.

The son preference is more prevalent in relatively rich and educated families. The rich and educated both men and women becoming more career minded, tend to prefer fewer children and with preference for the son, though unreasonable, the axe falls on the female child. While there is no consensus about the basis, there is a general realization that the bias in any form against the females is unjust. It was thought with the progress on education and economic front, the bias will disappear, but this has not happened as seen from the low female-male ratio that is still prevailing in countries like India and China.

Practice of Female Foeticide Prevalent in Other Countries

Among developing countries, in China, there is a one child norm and a strong preference for the male child. Mo Yan of China who has been awarded Nobel Prize for literature on 11.10.2012 highlighted, among other issues, sensitive issue of forced abortions in the case of female foetus.

Among developed countries, in USA, there is no preference for the male child. Similar seems to be the case of Russian Fed. and Japan. As per report of Registrar General of India, the sex ratio in USA, Russian Fed. and Japan has always remained above unity despite minor variations. In Europe, many of the people are turning away from producing the children, because they feel bringing up of children is a burden. But there is no perceptible preference for the male child.

Summing up Discrimination Against Girl Child

Socio-cultural factors greatly influence son preference and discrimination against girl child. Those who commit female foeticide somehow carry the notion that girl child will be a liability for the reasons which are totally unfounded. On the other hand female has certain qualities which surpass male. Dowry is a major demeaning factor for both man and woman and disturbs harmony throughout life.

Dual Work/Division of Work

According to the latest 68th Round (July 2011-June 2012) of National Sample Survey Organization (NSSO) report, around 64 per cent of women in urban area and 60 per cent of the women in rural area are engaged in domestic work. Higher percentage of women in urban area doing domestic work is attributed to—no other member in the family being available for doing domestic work due to growing number of nuclear families. Lower percentage of women in rural area doing domestic work is attributed to poverty which compels women to work in agriculture for money.

Earlier, women were taking care of home work including childcare, care of sick and old members of the family at home. However, gradually more and more women are taking up work outside. In such cases, women are facing added problems both at home and at the work place. They are expected to do full work at home beside job outside. The difficulty is more pronounced in the families who are poor. This is loosening the strong bond which existed earlier between the members of the family. Thus the work for women becomes very demanding.

The traditional roles carried on by men and women have been productive and reproductive respectively. Men as earners worked outside home and women as care givers looked after home based work. This division of work prevailed till men were able to earn enough to meet the family expenses. However, with the rising cost of living, as men were not able to meet the expenditure of the family fully, in rural area, women started working in the farms. With education and acquiring skills, women started getting employed in different professions.

The employment of women in the workforce is to be welcomed as it gives a choice of lifestyle for women to work at home or outside. Besides, the idea entails utilization of ability and skill of the women who constitute half of the population.

However, in spite of working outside, women are seen not disconnected with home based work. In this context, just to manage home based work also, many women prefer less formal working arrangements, accepting even lesser wages for the same, instead of taking up formal employment offering higher wages.

No-monetization of Work/Differential Payment

It is ironical that while men's work is monetized, women's work is not monetized. Robert Went (2000) claims that though globally more than 65 per cent of work is done by women (including work at home), income earned by women is about 10 per cent. Thus, it appears our monetary remuneration system *vis-à-vis* work is men oriented. The household work that the women do is not only not monetized but unfortunately this aspect of dual work is also not given due recognition by the society or by world bodies.

Hitherto women were confined to home and childcare was seen as their natural duty without any consideration of its monetary value. However, with globalization, as women started getting into workforce working outside home, there has been increasing demand of women for childcare. This development made the value of childcare in monetary terms evident. The same applies to other home-work also.

The practice of paying less to women as compared to men for the same or similar work is seen as gender biased. Some people contend that the difference in payment will reduce as the competition in the market under globalization will compel the employers to recognize the performance as more important factor than any other.

Marginalization of Rural Women

It would be difficult to say that in the age of globalization, women's conditions have improved in rural India. The elementary facility of toilet is not available in most of the homes and the women have to go in the open for attending to nature's call. For bath too, curtains are used as a temporary measure to cover the bath area. These conditions prevailing in rural India are very embarrassing to women and shameful to society as a whole.

The rural population is quite hard put in the face of impact of globalization on agriculture. With passage of time, viability of agriculture is becoming more and more difficult. Earlier women used to work in the land owned by them, though this land may be small. Since cultivation of small land has become unviable, women have to work as labourers on the land of somebody else. Here too, they are paid less than the men for the same work.

There is a shift in the socio-cultural values on account of economic aspect under globalization. Material production and profits are valued highly compared to upbringing of family and care giving services which are mainly provided by women. Rural women are especially heavily discounted firstly on account of non-valuation of home based work and secondly due to poverty which is generally experienced in rural area. This is resulting in low self-esteem of rural women.

It is contended that men are the main recipients of the technology which is a product of modernization. The modern agriculture is associated with technological inputs. Since, opportunities of developing entrepreneurial skill are not available to rural women, rural women in developing countries could not benefit from capital and technology intensive agriculture Thus, it is claimed that modernization and its economy have marginalized rural women.

Feminization/Flexibilization of Labour

Feminization of Labour

According to Zach Richer (Ritzer, 2012) the feminization of labour is a term used to describe the generally observed phenomena of women's increased participation in labour markets worldwide since the 1980s. In Indian context, the participation of women in workforce has started increasing since 1990s, close to liberalization of economy in India, the time when the process of globalization started picking up the momentum. Depressed wages following slowdown of economy started exerting pressure on women to work for paid employment to meet the household budget. Since then they have taken up not only softer white collar jobs in office and business establishments, but also harder jobs in industries. Now, there is no field where women are not working.

As mentioned, women were looking after home work and men were working outside home. Gradually women started working in agricultural land which was owned by their own families. Later, due to economic pressure, women started working not only in others' farms as labour, but in all fields of work. The number of working women worldwide increased by leaps and bounds.

The process of globalization is marked by increasing engagement of women in work force. The special qualities that women possess in relation to men arc that they are more amenable, have greater endurance to hardship, and they are good at handling things more neatly in performing standardized and repetitive work. They bear even poorer working conditions with patience. These are some of the unique qualities which weigh in their favour for paid employment and they are competing with men in any of the fields which were earlier traditionally thought to be exclusive domain of men.

Flexibilization of Labour

Flexibilization (Ritzer, 2010) refers to (i) engagement of labour when required and dispensing when not required, (ii) part time employment. Flexibilization is referred more in the context of engagement of female labour. It suits them to work for part time jobs as they have to look after household work also. Flexibilization has emerged from the process of globalization as MNCs started establishing manufacturing activity in developing countries to take advantage of cheap labour there. Women found entry into the workforce due to their qualities as well as their preparedness of working at lower wages compared to men.

Many women started doing work like stitching clothes at their homes for others. Gradually they started doing work outside their homes for others. Since, they are also required to look after cooking, childcare and other home work, many women prefer to work outside home on part time basis. This also suit many employers as they have to pay less remuneration and employers can terminate the arrangement if required. Such arrangement offers flexibility of employment to women workers as well as employers.

Increasing Participation of Women in Work Force is Seen as Empowerment of Women

In earlier times, women were confined to home work. Under globalization there is increasing participation of women in work force. The participation could be achieved as women developed the skill for doing the particular job. This has increased a feeling of self confidence and self-esteem of women. Thus, increasing participation of women in work force is seen as empowerment of women. However, liberalization process under globalization has resulted in subcontracting the work which led to integration of formal and informal labour. Deregulation resulted in labour especially women working in unsafe conditions and getting less than the prevailing market wages.

Women as Reserve Labour

In global context, some economists see women's formal and informal employment, full time and part time employment, less payment compared to prevailing market rate and last come and first retrenchment, as women being considered as reserve labour in the work force, getting in and out of job market in a very uncertain job market conditions. The proponents of women empowerment hold the view that treating women as reserve force as underestimation of women's participation in job market. According to them, women should have equal standing with men in the job market.

Feminization of Poverty

In 1978, Diana Pearce, a visiting researcher at the University of Wisconsin, published a paper noting that poverty was becoming "feminized" in the United States. This was based on the analysis of incomes between 1950 and 1970 which showed increased concentration of income poverty among women. The contention of Diana Pearce is that women are relatively poor and that the gap between the income of men and women is increasing with time. However, this contention is widely contested in the present context. The critics argue that the gains in women's employment and earnings are closing the poverty gap between men and women. It is difficult to reach a conclusion about the poverty gap between men and women in developing countries where the poor plight of women is more pronounced. The difficulty is arising as there is no segregated data available about earnings between men and women in developing countries. If we take it that the basic idea of Diana Pearce's feminization of poverty is to draw attention to the problems that females face, then it is worthwhile to include the privations that females face and not just the problem of income (Ritzer, 2012: 646-48).

Impact of Capitalism/Modernism/Postmodernism/Globalization

In pre-globalization period, women's activities were generally confined to home and agriculture related work. Women's home-related work which consisted childcare and raising family, though important, was not given due recognition.

In the chain of change in the world order, globalization is termed as an extension of the capitalism, modernism, postmodernism. These processes had indelible impact on women's position. In view of large-scale poverty and the labour being cheap in developing countries, globalization enhanced the opportunity for labour in these countries. Due to their agreeable nature and readiness for doing flexible (part) time jobs, employment of women has been on the increase. Women are doing jobs side-by-side of men in indigenous industry as well as multinational companies. There is, however, differentiation between the remuneration paid to men and women even for doing same or similar jobs.

As mentioned, there has been increase in opportunities for employment for women outside home and agriculture related work. Women are now seen employed in industry, services sector, education, health etc. There is now no field that remains untouched by women. Their presence in all fields is now visible. Many people attribute this to the process of liberalization. Since women, besides employment outside, have varying degree of connect with home related work, many women prefer part-time work. Employers also find advantage in providing part-time and contracting work because they can employ or reduce work force as per their time to time fluctuating requirement.

There are, however, physical limitations for females. In the context of global business, the employees are required to travel within as well as outside the nation. Since women do some part of home related work as well as due to physical constraint, they find movement outside their regular place of work difficult. This works as a constraint in respect of remuneration as well as career development. Notwithstanding these constraints, many Indian women have reached the level of CEOs of leading MNCs abroad.

Working as Maids/Migration/Tourism/HIV

Raising family, looking after children and cooking are traditionally considered as the responsibility of women. Besides, many women in rural area are working in the fields. Men usually do not contribute in the home related work. Poor women in urban area have to work as maids in number of houses on daily basis to meet the family expenses.

Economic aspect of globalization has made living at local level more difficult due to limitation of opportunities. Therefore, men and women are on the move in search of better avenues. This process is more burdensome to women as they have to cope up with new physical and social environment. Globalization has led to migration of women not only from their local to another place in the home country but even to other countries.

The process of globalization has enabled Western culture to spread to non-Western world. Globalization is seen as providing opportunities not only in home countries but also in foreign countries. There is steep increase in migration of women to other countries to work as maids. There is also steep increase in transnational travel of men and women. However, while conceding that globalization is offering opportunities for women to work outside home, there is also negative side of this. There are cases of abuse of women going to foreign countries as maids. Also there are reports of use of women for sex tourism as transnational tourism is growing. There is a global concern about increasing trend of HIV/AIDS cases which many people attribute to globalization. These are some of the examples which illustrate the downside of globalization for women.

Global Gender Gap Index

Gender inequality is very much pervasive inequality existing in the society. However, some societies are doing better than others. The World Economic Forum introduced the Global Gender Gap Report in 2006. Recently, it has come out with the Report 2014. The report provides the status about the magnitude and scope of gender based disparities in 142 countries around the world. The index benchmarks national gender gaps on economic, political, education and health based criteria. The following Table 8.3 gives the Global Gender Gap Index 2014 of select 13 countries.

It will be seen from Table 8.3 that India ranked 114 out of 142 countries (higher the rank, more the gender gap), indicating large gender disparity. Thus India has a long way to go for bridging the gap even comparing with the countries having similar economies that of BRICS bloc namely Brazil, Russia, China, and South Africa. The main factor for large disparity in India is socio-economic. With second largest populated country in the world, the per capita income is quite low. Quarter of the total population is still below poverty line. With limited resources at hand,

Table 8.3: Global Gender Gap Index 2014

Iceland	1	Russian Fed.	75
Germany	12	China	87
France	16	Indonesia	97
South Africa	18	Japan	104
United States	20	Malaysia	107
U.K.	26	India	114
Brazil	71		

Source: World Economic Forum: Global Gender Gap Report 2014
Website: http://reports.weforum.org/global-gender-gap-report-2014/rankings

families prefer to spend first on the son and then on the daughter. This is happening due to preference for the son as explained above. The parameters of index become poorer in respect of education, health and participation in labour. The Global Gender Gap Index thus follows just the Human Development Index.

However, there is a silver lining that as far as political empowerment of females is concerned, India's position is impressive. Women are as per law well represented on local government bodies. Women are thus empowered to take decisions in local governments.

Representation of Women in Legislatures/Self-Help Groups (SHGs)

Though there is a large participation of women in political activities, women constitute only 11 per cent representation in the Lok Sabha and 10.6 per cent in the Rajya Sabha. Thus, it is a long way for women to have respectable representation in the Indian Parliament. Notwithstanding poor representation in Parliament, women have equal representation with men in Panchayati Raj Institutions like Gram Panchayats etc. The reservation of 50 per cent seats in these institutions has helped women to have equal representation with men.

In order to provide engagement of women in rural area and supplement the income of the family, Self-Helf Groups (SHGs) and Credit and Thrift Societies have been formed with the financial assistance and guidance of the government. These institutions not only led to empowerment of women but also helped to reduce caste barrier. This has also increased a feeling of cooperation among women.

Social Change Necessary for Equality

Some people contend that the benefits of advancement of technology in the wake of globalization are more appropriated by men in their favour and globalization is leading to increasing inequality between men and women. For example, there are many operations in the factories which run in night shifts and there are certain works for which hard physical labour is required. Many employees have to do extensive travelling in connection with the business. These type of assignments do not suit women in general and thus their career development chances are not as bright as those of men.

The economic aspect of globalization is widely discussed. But the social implications arising from globalization does not get due attention. The manner of giving lesser priority to girls in a matter of education can be seen from the fact that if the education in private school is costlier and in government school cheaper, parents admit son in private school and daughter in government school. Thus, girls in general possess lesser skill level as compared to boys. This aspect affects their prospects for future development. There is discrimination between boy and girl in matters related to health as well. This is observed in providing to a boy better nutritional diet compared to girl.

It was thought that the literacy and economic development will bring in its wake equal social status between men and women. However, this does not seem to have happened as seen from the female-male ratio, which is unfavourable to female. Overall, the ratio is favourable in rural area as compared to urban area irrespective of the fact that rural area is synonymous with poverty and less education, and urban area with better economic condition and education. It appears, though presence of women is now seen in all fields, progress in the estimation of women will happen only if there is a change in the attitude of society toward female.

Conclusion

As mentioned above, there is no doubt that gender inequality is very much there in the society. Its manifestation can be seen in different forms. It is contended that the bias in favour of male and against female stems from the nature of the society that is patriarchal. While there is no consensus about the basis, there is a general realization that the bias in any form against the female is unjust. It was thought that with the progress on education and economic fronts, the bias will disappear but this has not happened as seen from the low female-male ratio that is still prevailing in countries like India and China.

In pre-globalization period, women's activities were generally confined to home and agriculture related work. Women's home-related work which included childcare and raising family, though important, was not monetized. But under globalization, women are participating side by side men.

There is growth in opportunities for women for employment outside home and agriculture related work. Women are now seen employed in industry, services sector, education, health etc. There is no field that remains untouched by women. The increasing participation of women in employment all round is termed as feminization of labour. The critics of globalization, however, highlight the point that there is a bias against women as they are paid less as compared to men for the same work.

Since women, though working outside, have still to do home related work, many women prefer part-time work. Employers also find this advantageous as they can employ or reduce work force as per their time to time requirement. This process has now been termed as flexibilization of labour.

The process of globalization has enabled Western culture to spread to non-Western world. The form of liberalization seen in pop music, new fashion etc. seems very alluring to new generation of men and women. It is unfortunate that media tends to project female as sex symbol rather than projecting their role as nation builder.

There is steep increase in migration of women to other countries to work as maids. There is also steep increase in transnational travel of men and women. It is held that the aforesaid factors are leading to females' exploitation and sex-tourism, and as a consequence, the cases of HIV/AIDS are increasing. This, aspect is seen as downside of globalization.

It is contended that the benefits of advancement of technology in the wake of globalization are more appropriated by men in their favour and thus globalization is leading to increasing inequality between men and women.

Taking into account pros and cons of globalization, there is no doubt that the position of women has vastly improved in the sense that they are now having many options in leading their life instead of being relegated to leading a life as a housewife only. As far as removal of social bias is concerned, it can be achieved only through a social change. Needless to say, removing gender inequality is very important from the point of view that the goal of full development would always remain unrealized if full potential of half the humanity remains unrealized.

GLOBALIZATION AND MARGINALIZED COMMUNITIES—*DALITS*/TRIBALS

Prologue

In India, historically certain sections of people are unfortunately relegated to the lower level of hierarchy and deprived of normal status in the society because of the caste system. Among them are the *dalits* who are most deprived. However, gradually there has been a change in the occupational structure of *dalits* in the village. Some of them have become land owners. *Dalit* youths prefer to migrate to urban area as job opportunities have increased. Nevertheless, there is a question mark as to whether the aforesaid change under globalization has led to improvement in the quality of life of *dalits* or not.

Major Handicap of *Dalits*

Dalits in India face discrimination on various counts. They have been made to live in village in settlements which are separate from the mainstream population. The separate location of their settlement excludes them from many common basic facilities. Earlier they were assigned to do the work like lifting or skinning dead animals, the work which is considered as below dignity by the other castes. They were suffering from a stigma of untouchability. Gandhiji held that the caste system, if at all, could be social construct, but without labelling anybody high or low in social status on the basis of caste, and that the system of labelling anybody high or low in social status on the basis of caste is repugnant to the common sense. He held that untouchability is an evil, it is not part of the original Hinduism and its practice is the greatest blot on Hinduism. He fought for eradicating untouchability and upliftment of *dalits* throughout his life.

Dr. Babasaheb Ambedkar who was one of the leaders in the forefront of the movement for improving the lot of *dalits*, put more emphasis on education, achieving economic progress and gaining political power. According to him other things will follow in natural course once progress is achieved in these areas. Addressing a meeting at Worli, in Bombay, on September 28, 1932, Ambedkar said: "The object of temple entry movement is good. But you should care more for your material good than for spiritual food. You do not get food to eat, clothes to wear, opportunities of educating your children, and medical help for want of money. You should, therefore, be watchful of the political gains, and you must develop your strength and struggle for gaining material advancement in life." (Keer, 1971: 217-18).

Mahatma Jyotirao Phule is another great reformer who contributed immensely toward removal of untouchability and upliftment of *dalits.*

Dalits are having number of handicaps; few are internal and many are external. The habit of drinking liquor has been quite prevalent in *dalit* men just next to tribals. Their women counterparts dislike this habit and because of their resistance, there has been improvement in this area.

Occupationally, *dalits* were working as agricultural labour on the farms of landowners. With the decrease in bullock population and increase in labour cost, their retention as labour by the landowner became unviable. There has been increasing trend of the use of machineries in agriculture. Introduction of machineries has increased the cost of tilling the agriculture. This coupled with increasing cost of other inputs such as seeds, fertilizers, pesticides etc., the agriculture has become almost unviable. Therefore, the owners started adopting *dalits* working in their farms as partners or sharecroppers and traditional landowners started withdrawing from doing agriculture. Thus, gradually land is getting into the hands of peasant labour who are predominantly *dalits*. This has changed the age-old social dynamics in the rural area.

With increasing mechanization in agriculture the requirement of peasant labour is considerably reduced. Even otherwise because of tediousness of working in agriculture and the social stigma attached to caste in villages, the younger generation of *dalits* is no more interested in doing the agriculture. Therefore, *dalit* youth are shifting to urban area and getting into jobs there. Thus, the change of earlier status of untouchables to that of becoming land owners and younger generation having the benefit of getting educated and getting into jobs, are important shifts. Nevertheless, there does not seem to be significant improvement in their quality of life especially landless labour as they are still mostly dependent on the state food subsidy.

As regards *dalit* women, most farm work was being done by them. They were earlier going for farm work in others' farms. However, as *dalit* families have become landowners, they have stopped going to others' farms and instead are doing work in farms owned by them. Further, as awareness about the importance of education has increased, most of the parents started sending their girls to schools instead of using them in the farm work.

The major handicap of *dalits* is their abject poverty which reflects in low level of education, less skill development and less exposure to outside world resulting in less access to opportunities (D 29 Palanithurai and Ramesh, 2011: 250). The main emphasis of *dalit* youth is, therefore, now on shifting to towns and cities for education or employment as they find this as a way out to avoid centuries old injustice and social stigma of being relegated to the low position in the social ladder.

It is not incumbent for capitalist system of business to employ even a few *dalits* in their organizations in acknowledgement of the historical injustice. Similarly, in private educational institutions also there is no special consideration for admission to *Dalit* children. Globalization stands for competitive market conditions in which only people with knowledge, skill and capital can benefit. For those who are historically marginalized sections of people not having these qualities, there is no special consideration to accommodate them in the business organizations. This disconnect (a feeling of left out) of marginalized sections of people from the process of globalization is often expressed by the organizations which espouse the cause of *dalits*.

The social status of *dalit* family precludes *dalit* person getting competitive edge in education which generally becomes a handicap for him to get into private or public service except through statutory quota in public service. The process of globalization is an extension of capitalism, i.e. promoting privatization of industries and reducing the role of government or public sector in business. The result is that the ownership of public sector by the government is reducing and government is restricting itself to act as regulator of the business practices. This has resulted in reduction of employment in government and public sector. It is thus noteworthy that while reservation policy on the basis of caste offers equality of opportunities to *dalits*, opportunities in public employment in the era of globalization have so shrunk that employment-wise *dalits* are now hardly benefited. As regards employment in private sector, the big problem for *dalits* is how to stand in competition with their disadvantaged background.

Interconnectedness of globalization notwithstanding, caste based discrimination world over is continuing unabated. More than 260 million people across the world are still victims of human rights abuses due to caste-based discrimination, a group of independent experts appointed by the United Nations warned and asked South Asian countries to strengthen legislation to protect them. People considered low caste in South Asia are also known as *dalits*. In many countries, they face marginalization, social and economic exclusion, segregation in housing, limited access to basic services, including water and sanitation and employment, and work. Recently, the British government decided the equality act would cover caste discrimination to protect *dalits* in diaspora communities.

Progress in Socio-Economic Status of *Dalits*

As per Tendulkar poverty line (which is close to the UN and World Bank's poverty line), the economists have calculated that in the seven years between 2004-05 and 2011-12, the all-India poverty ratio fell by 15.7 per cent. The decline was much higher at 21.5 per cent for *dalits* and 17.0 per cent for tribals. The decline in the poverty ratio of the upper castes was much lower, at 10.5 per cent.

In the earlier decade, between 1993-94 and 2004-05, the decline was only 9.6 per cent for *dalits* and 3.7 per cent for tribals. The overall poverty ratio declined by 8.0 per cent. This represents significant progress in poverty reduction in *dalits*.

The process of globalization has opened newer opportunities in urban area for *dalits* to get engaged. However, the opportunities for *dalits* seem to be more in unorganized sector as compared to organized sector as organized sector requires skilled workers. Thus, though globalization may not have offered quality opportunities to *dalits*, it has offered variety of opportunities from which *dalits* can choose. This is in a way a better situation compared to hanging on to seasonal employment in agriculture.

On political front, though they have statutory representation in the local governing bodies, on occasions their voices are subdued before elite/higher in hierarchical class. However, there has been a slow, but steady change in the socio-economic status of dalits due to constitutional provisions, the efforts from *dalits* themselves, change of mindset of right thinking people of other classes and opening of employment and business opportunities under globalization.

Globalization and Tribals

It is said that tribals are the original humans living on earth. That is why they are described as indigenous or natives. The habitat of tribals has been in remote areas in deep forests and hilly areas. To start with, our first ancestors were also supposed to be living in such areas. India has the second largest concentration of tribal population after Africa. They have much less contact with the culture of mainstream population.

Tribals face somewhat different problem from what *dalits* face. There is no untouchability factor in case of tribals. But the biggest problem is that their livelihood is lost when any project such as hydro project comes in their area. The tribals in Odisha, Madhya Pradesh, Jharkhand, Chhattisgarh and in other states of India faced serious problems on this account. Since, there is increased development activity under globalization, tribals are facing all the more problems.

In a way, the condition of tribals is worse than *dalits* for two reasons. One is that the *dalits* live in villages where there is some security of life and a kind of governance through Panchayati Raj. On the other hand, Tribals live in remote areas in deep forests or hilly area where there is always danger from wild animals and no state administrative support. Second is, *dalits* are organized and they can fight for their just rights, whereas due to living in inaccessible areas, it is just not possible for tribals to get organized to fight for their just rights.

In order to ameliorate the poor conditions of tribals, Forest Rights Act was passed in 2006. The Act seeks to recognize and vest the forest rights and occupation in forest land in forest dwelling Scheduled Tribes and other traditional forest dwellers who have been residing in such forests for generations but whose rights could not be recorded. As per the provisions of the Act, the onus of implementation of the Act lies with the state governments.

Culturally tribals follow their own traditional culture and there is practically no impact of globalization on tribal society. There is a need to provide them special support to bring their living in line with the mainstream population.

Conclusion

Historically *dalits* were placed at the bottom rung of the caste system. The practice of untouchability toward *dalits* has been a blot on the Indian society. Social injustice toward *dalits* resulted in their marginalization in the society. *Dalits* were mostly engaged as peasant labour in agriculture. Gradually, there has been a slow but steady change in the socio-economic status of *dalits* after independence. Since, traditional landowners found agriculture unviable due to rising labour and other input costs, land started slipping into the hands of *dalits*. The younger generation of *dalits* however prefer to migrate to urban area to get away from the social discrimination and avail the opportunities thrown up by industrial development and process of globalization.

Globalization stands for competitive market conditions in which only people with knowledge, skill and capital can benefit. Since *dalits* have been marginalized for centuries, they are far behind in education as well as skill development. With dwindling of the role of government and public sector in business, where they had some assurance of employment through job quota, the opportunities in government and public sector have reduced. Further, they find employment in private organized sector extremely difficult because they had much less opportunities to get quality education and skill. However, they are readily engaged in unorganized sector which is any way some improvement over previous state in which they were only serving as seasonal agricultural labour in rural area. Nevertheless, there is no significant improvement in their quality of life especially of those who are working as landless labour.

The condition of tribals is still more precarious as they live in isolated areas in forests and hilly areas where there is namesake state support, though state claims that it is doing all that it can do for them. They are practically out of the reach of globalization.

ECONOMIC INEQUALITY

Prologue

Inequality is part of human race. No two humans leave alone two groups of humans are equal in all respects. Every human being is unique in physique, mind or nature. The analogy can be extended to socio-economic matters also. Having agreed that inequality is part of life, the point is, whether the process of globalization is increasing or decreasing socio-economic inequality? There are divergent views about the impact of globalization on socio-cultural aspect of the society. Regarding the economic aspect, while some people contend that the process of globalization has benefited the economies of nation-states across the globe, some people contend that it has benefited developed nations only. There are also divergent views about the aspect as to whether it has benefited the poor especially the rural poor.

Again there are divergent views on whether rich-poor and rural-urban economic inequality has reduced or increased. Generally inequality is seen in the context of economic perspective. This may perhaps be based on the view that other aspects such as socio-cultural aspects are influenced by the economic situation. But this may tantamount taking a simplistic view of the situation, as it is observed that poor especially rural poor are not only economically marginalized but they do not have access to even basic facilities such as education and health.

Statistics about Increasing Trend of Inequality

According to IMF, the trend of increasing inequality is not specific to India and the same is increasing globally. The statistics show that it is prevailing all over the world. Delivering the Richard Dimbleby Lecture in London, International Monetary Fund (IMF) Managing Director Christen Lagarde has said (PTI 04.02.2014) that income inequality is increasing dangerously globally. The richest 85 people in the world own the same amount of wealth as the bottom half of the world's population. Referring to India, she says the net worth of the billionaire community increased twelve-fold in 15 years, enough to eliminate absolute poverty in this country twice over. According to development organization Oxfam, 1 per cent of the world's families own almost half (46%) of the world's wealth.

UN Report on Inequality

Inequality is gauged from the fact that the world consists of some super rich and large population extremely poor. According to the *United Nations Development Report*, the richest 20 per cent of the world's population accounts for 86 per cent of total consumption while the poorest 20 per cent accounts a mere 1.3 per cent.

Hans-Peter Martin and Harald Schumann also in their book, *The Global Trap*, portray the inequality as the creation of a "20:80 society" wherein the rich account for top 20 per cent and the poor account for 80 per cent of the globe's population.

It is estimated that in India, the inequality has doubled in the last two decades, a period that starts from the time India embraced globalization. During the period of 7 years, i.e. between 2004-05 and 2011-12, the Gini coefficient has increased by 0.1 and 0.2 percentage points in rural and urban areas. A Gini coefficient is commonly used as a measure of inequality of income or wealth. A Gini coefficient of zero expresses perfect equality, where everyone has as exactly equal income. A Gini coefficient of one (i.e. 100%) expresses maximal inequality where one person has all the income. The increase in Gini coefficient shows that inequality has increased. It is however seen that the numbers of Gini coefficient are not always consistent. Too much economic inequality in society also leads to increase in social tension.

Causes of Inequality

As mentioned, there can be no complete equality in any field. The basic differences between species, between humans, between men and women, and between men, and between women, answer the point that there can be no complete equality. Complete equality is neither practical nor desirable. This principle is applicable to economic aspect too. The economic inequality is implicit in the principle of division of labour which is prevailing in global society.

Thus, there should be no argument about existence or desirability of inequality. However, the important point is that if inequality increases beyond the point of sustainability, it is bound to create turmoil in the society. Unsustainable inequality has given birth to many revolutions in the past and it has become a potent factor for a regime change.

Two-tier Education System

There is no other factor that matters so strongly for inequality as education. Presently inequality is a manifestation of two-tier education system in which boys and girls belonging to higher income group of families, with higher education, are enabled to become rich within a short span of time, and those belonging to poor families even after acquiring skill do not take them beyond subsistence level throughout their lifetime. In this context the fate of rural students is the worse. Save exceptions, they are destined to become second class citizens as the quality of education that they get just do not help them to compete with the urban students.

Capital and Technology

Among many factors, two factors are more causative for increasing inequality. One is that while rich are becoming richer by earning more and more profit out of businesses, the wages of the employees are not rising proportionately and not even enough to overcome price rise inflation. The second factor is the influence of technology on inequality. As it is, the spread of technology is not uniform in the country and so also benefits thereof. With advancement in technology, owners of businesses are earning much more and faster than the employees working for the owner. Also a peasant is earning much less compared to a person working on computer although both may be devoting the same number of hours of work.

Global Competition

The economy of a country has two parts. One is doing business globally which involves competition in the international market. Another is purely catering to domestic market. For export, high skill and capital are the prime requirements, as quality and competitiveness in cost matter. Thus, those who possess skill and capital are the benefactors of globalization. Others have perforce to depend only on domestic economy.

There are number of examples of those who participated in globalization, but for some or the other reasons failed. This happens partly because there are wide fluctuations in the demand and supply in the international markets. Further, international market requires high quality of products. Thus, participating in export business involves more uncertainty and only those players who have sufficient capital and skill can benefit from it.

Digital Divide

Besides economic inequality, there is inequality in sharing of information. Poor especially those who live in rural area suffer from taking advantage of the advancement of information and communication technology because they have little access to it. Thus inequality in access to internet is causing 'digital divide.' Many people do not know English language. The absence of knowledge of English language is an area which is contributing to digital divide as internet language is mostly English. Further, non-availability of electricity in rural area, which is a basic infrastructure for internet operation, is also a contributor to inequality.

Is Economic Growth Jobless Growth?

International Monetary Fund (IMF) Managing Director Christen Lagarde says that, in the past, economists have underestimated the importance of inequality. They have focused on economic growth, on the size of the pie rather than its distribution.

In the Indian context, there is a debate as to whether globalization has benefited the society and if it has, whether it has benefited poor? Seen purely from economic aspect, the growth rate in terms of GDP just a decade prior to 1991, the economy was growing at the rate of about 4 per cent. This rate was characteristically termed by economists as Hindu rate of growth. The name of Hindu has been given as the Hindu religion and for that matter even most of the other major religions per se give more importance to values than material progress. A decade after 1991, the year liberalization policy was given effect to, economy grew at the rate of 6 per cent, which has been termed as Bharat rate of growth and a decade later saw the growth rate of about 8 per cent, which is termed as India rate of growth. The names of Hindu, Bharat and India are symbolic representation of shift of emphasis purely from values to graded value plus economy.

The increase in GDP growth undoubtedly indicates economic prosperity after embracing globalization. By a trickledown effect, the overall economic growth has benefited the poor also and resulted in poverty reduction. However, it is observed that the globalization has benefited rich more than the poor resulting in increase in inequality. Another resultant factor is that the share of agriculture in the GDP has gradually reduced and the share of services increased. In India, since agriculture is the livelihood of about 60 per cent of total population, and manufacturing sector not growing, the period of globalization is being increasingly viewed by some people as a period of 'jobless growth'.

Democratic India is not the only country where income disparity is increasing. Communist country China too is facing the same problem and there is growing popular anger due to mounting income disparity. Thus, increasing disparity of income seems to be one of the several fall outs of globalization.

Rural-Urban Inequality

National Sample Survey Organization (NSSO) collected the data on household spending patterns for 1999-2000 and 2011-12. The results are given in Table 8.4. Household spending is closest measure of income of the people.

Table 8.4: Increase in spend/income: 1999-2000 and 2011-12

		Rural (%)	*Urban (%)*
Poorest	5%	31	34
	5-10%	32	36
	10-90% (avg)	37	46
	90-95%	46	54
	>95%	60	63

Source: NSSO data on household spending patterns for 1999-2000 and 2011-12; TOI/ET 28.07.2013.

It will be seen from Table 8.4 that in rural area, while the spending by the richest 5 per cent increased by over 60 per cent, it increased only by just over 30 per cent by the poorest 5 per cent. In urban area, the figures are 63 per cent and 34 per cent. Thus, spending by rich is about double that of the poor during the period. The effect of inflation was not taken into account while making these comparisons.

Similar high growth rate in spending by the richest 10 per cent and low growth rate by the poorest 10 per cent can be seen. The remaining 80 per cent of the people have seen the growth rate of 37 per cent in rural and 46 per cent in urban area in 12 years. This means growth in income of 80 per cent of the people was just over 3 per cent in rural India and just about 4 per cent per year in urban India. This shows that rich are getting richer faster than poor are getting better off and that economic disparity is increasing.

It is an established fact that all over the world, rural people are poor. Not only economically they are poor but they lack even basic facilities like education and health. There is a huge gap between rural and urban area as regards availability of these facilities and the gap continues to increase.

The benefit of globalization is best reaped by those who have knowledge, skill, technology and capital. In rural area, there is land and labour. But they lack technology and capital. Therefore resources in rural area are not fully utilized and hence rural poor are not benefited well enough.

Karl Marx espoused the cause of proletariats because he held the view that they are exploited by the capitalists. In the Marx's espousal, the proletariats are the underprivileged and capitalists are the privileged. The same analogy is applicable to rural poor and urban elites. Through hard work in agriculture, rural people produce life giving food. But rural area remains always undeveloped. It lacks even most basic facilities such as roads, education and health. Thus rural people are underprivileged. On the other hand urban people are more vocal and organized. They manage lion's share of financial and other resources to be utilized for development of urban area. That is why we find good roads, education and health facilities in urban area. This has resulted in huge rural-urban inequality.

Social justice is the corner stone of democracy. It calls for equitable distribution of economic progress. Thus, in democracy there should not be large gap between the rich and the poor. Otherwise, democracy will be seen as promoting hierarchies.

Further, in democracy every person expects if not equal, but fair living standard. If people who are rich display their wealth in public, the poor feel too anguished about their poverty. For example, if a rich man throws a big party entailing wastage of food and side by side there are people who are not in a position to satisfy their hunger, the feelings of poor toward inequality are bound to get exacerbated.

Inequality: Cause of Naxalite Movement

There is a general view that the globalization has provided opportunities not only to the rich but also to the poor. By a trickledown effect, there has been a reduction in poverty. But there are large areas particularly hilly and forest areas where tribals are living, and development could not reach there. In these areas, not only economic development has not taken place, but even basic facilities such as roads, education and health are not available. Society is thus divided in two parts. In one part, globalization has made rich people richer. In the other part, there is utter poverty. This glaring inequality has given birth to Naxalite movement particularly in the area bordering Andhra Pradesh, Chhattisgarh, Jharkhand, Orissa and Maharashtra. The movement is often taking violent turn and is now posing a formidable challenge to the government.

Positive side of Globalization

Economic growth during 7 years, i.e. between 2004-05 and 2011-12 led to 15.7 per cent fall in all-India poverty rate (TOI 3.11.2013) (Poverty rate down from 37.2% in 2004-05 to 21.5% in 2011-12). There is a debate over the relationship between globalization and inequality. Some people believe that globalization has benefited developing countries and the poor also, thus reducing the inequality. They contend that in the process of globalization, not only in economic but in social aspect like health also, inequality has declined especially during last two decades. However, a large body of people contests this contention and maintains that inequality is rising constantly across the world including India.

There are a few ways to reduce inequality. These are by way of providing to low income group of people: increasing their wages; increasing their domestic consumption; providing them subsidies; the last one, i.e. providing subsidies to poor is vehemently opposed by the better off class. The other way of reducing inequality is by taxing more ultra rich people.

Conclusion

Inequality is part of human race. No two humans or two groups of humans are equal in any respect. Having agreed that inequality is part of life, the point arises: whether the process of globalization is increasing or decreasing that inequality.

Globalization involves *per se* capitalism. Capitalism involves characteristics of competition and profit on the one hand and demand and supply on the other. Therefore, globalization and in particular economic globalization is bound to create inequality.

Regarding the economic aspect, while there are some dissenting voices, large number of people contend that the process of globalization has benefited the economy of nation-states across the globe. But there are divergent views as to whether it has benefited the poor especially the rural poor. There is a large body of people who contend that rich-poor and rural-urban economic inequality has increased, though some hold the view that the inequality has reduced. In the debate on inequality, generally inequality is seen in the context of economic perspective. This may perhaps be based on the view that other aspects such as socio-cultural aspects are influenced by the economic aspect. But this amounts to taking a simplistic view of the situation. Practically, it is observed that poor especially rural poor are not only economically marginalized but they do not have access to even basic facilities such as education and health. Thus, while the lot of poor has improved a bit, inequality as such is increasing in all spheres of life.

Inequality in a developed country, where people at even lower rung are earning enough for living or people have a social security from the state side, does not pinch the common man. However, in a developing country like India where quarter of the total population is below poverty line, inequality is a serious matter. In society, when rich people show off ostentatious lifestyle and side-by-side there are people who do not have money enough to sustain minimum family expenditure, there is bound to be deep resentment. Inequality beyond certain level generates social tensions. Such inequality is a breeding ground for the violent movements like Naxalite movement.

It is generally accepted that globalization has benefited India economically in absolute term. It is also generally accepted that inequality is increasing under globalization. It, therefore, rests on the state to adopt suitable policies to provide social justice to deprived section of people. This can be achieved through adopting prudent taxation policies and supporting social sector adequately, which includes education, health etc.

9
Mahatma Gandhi and Globalization of 21st Century

Introduction

Historically, nobody in India has inspired Indian masses as Mahatma Gandhi. Alongside his contribution as a tallest leader during independence movement, his ideas on various socio-economic matters evoked universal appeal.

Studying law in UK, his contacts with many English theosophists, influenced by the writings of Tolstoy, Thoreau and Ruskin, and spearheading movement against apartheid in South Africa gave him enough background of being a man of globalist thoughts. Swadeshi movement that Gandhiji started during independence struggle gives an impression that he was against the globalization, which is erroneous. In order to find out how Gandhiji's ideas would coincide or disagree with globalization, it is necessary to relate these with the concept of globalization.

Adam Smith and David Recardo

In 1776, Adam Smith who is considered as father of modern economics in his classic work *The Wealth of Nations* stated that markets worked most efficiently when there was equality between buyers and sellers. Later, the theory of 'comparative advantage' was propounded by the British economist David Recardo which became the basis for propagation of globalization. The theory was developed in 1817 by Ricardo in his *Principles of Political Economy and Taxation*. Ricardo held that nations should specialize in producing goods in which they have a natural advantage. He believed this would benefit both buyer and seller but only if certain conditions were maintained. Recardo did not envisage movement of capital in exchange. However, this concept of non-movement of capital never worked in the capitalist system and now huge capital flows are witnessed all the time.

Gandhiji's ideas seem to be quite nearer to the original concept of globalization propounded by Adam Smith (1776) and David Recardo (1817) in as much as both Smith and Recardo propounded equality between buyers and sellers and did not favour movement of capital. However, in actual practice, both these conditions are violated in the process of globalization. Thus, having attained independence, Gandhiji would agree with the original basic concept of globalization governed by equality between buyers and sellers. As far as movement of capital is concerned, no country invests capital in another country without expectations. The expectations could be economic, i.e. earning profit, favourable foreign/military policy or some other. Since strings are always attached with the capital, Gandhiji would not agree with movement of capital that is attached with strings.

Gandhiji and Karl Marx

The similarity and dissimilarity between the ideas of Gandhiji and Karl Marx is a subject of importance. Both Gandhiji (1869-1948) and Karl Marx (1818-1880) championed the cause of poor and downtrodden. Gandhiji advocated that "everybody should be able to get sufficient work to enable him to make the two ends meet. And this ideal can be universally realized only if the means of production of the elementary necessities of life remain in the control of the masses" (p. 90). The monopolization of the means of production by any country, nation or group of persons would be unjust. These views were similar to that of Marx.

Both advocated new socio-economic-political order in which the common people would enjoy full human rights without exploitation by the privileged class. Both opposed monopolistic nature of economy. There were, however, basic differences of approach for achieving the objectives. Gandhiji as such was not against wealthy but he expected them to use only that portion of wealth which is sufficient to fulfill their need and for the rest they should act as trustee. While Gandhiji believed in persuasive approach in bringing about a new social order, Karl Marx believed that the privileged class would never like to part with their wealth willingly and therefore justified the use of coercion and force against the rich if necessary. This philosophy of Marx encouraged class war in the pursuit of achieving the objective. For Marx, cause was more important than the means to achieve the cause. For Gandhiji, means were as important as the cause.

Village-self-sufficient

Gandhiji envisioned a village to be a self-sufficient entity. The idea was that the village should not be dependent too much on outside support so that, it retains its independence and importance. His idea of industrialization was that the industrial production should be based on locally available materials and should in no way come in conflict with environment. In this context, internet and renewable energy through solar and wind power stand perfectly in line with his thinking.

Swadeshi

On *swadeshi* Gandhiji said, "the broad definition of *swadeshi* is the use of all home-made things to the exclusion of foreign things in so far as such use is necessary for the protection of home-industry more especially those industries without which India will become pauperized" (p. 333). He opposed the idea of British buying raw material from India cheaply and then selling end products to India at a price which entailed good amount of profit by the colonial power. This is how he started *charkha* movement and wished every Indian to spin the cloth rather than importing cloth from Britain.

Gandhiji's Economics

Gandhiji's concept of economic equality was unique. He said, "Economic equality of my conception does not mean that everyone would literally have the same amount. It simply means that everybody should have enough for his or her needs. True economics never militates against the highest ethical standard. That economics is untrue which ignores or disregards moral values" (pp. 90, 91).

Gandhiji was not against wealth creation but he opposed creation of wealth for selfish purposes. In this context, he propounded the concept of trusteeship. Trusteeship: "No matter how much money one earns, one should regard himself as trustee holding the money for the welfare of all his neighbours. One must regard himself not as owner but as a trustee of his wealth, and use it for the service of society, taking for himself no more than a fair return for service rendered" (p. 349).

Gandhiji could not envisage economics to be separated from ethical standards. "True economics never militates against the highest ethical standard just as all true ethics to be worth its name must at the same time be also good economics. That economics is untrue which ignores or disregards moral values. True economics stands for social justice, it promotes the good of all equally including the weakest" (pp. 90/91).

Environment

Globalization and capitalism go hand in hand. For maximizing profit, capitalists tend to utilize natural resources to the maximum extent without regard to exhaustion of natural resources as well as damage to environment. Gandhiji said, "Earth provides enough to satisfy every man's need, but not every man's greed."

Cultural

On cultural front, Gandhiji said, "I do not want my house to be walled in on all sides and my windows to be stuffed. I want the cultures of all lands to be blown about my house as freely as possible. But I refuse to be blown off my feet by any." By this he meant that while he was open to learning and assimilating good ideas of cultures other than his, he loves his own culture in which he is deeply rooted. Gandhiji deeply studied texts of various religions, respected them and expounded good things in them to the world.

He did not perceive any problem due to mingling of different cultures but he did perceive a danger of Western consumerism getting foothold in our country.

Conclusion

Are Gandhian ideas contradictory to globalization? The answer is yes and no. He envisaged in his times critical issues facing globalization such as social injustice, poverty, environmental concerns rise in fundamentalism and evils of violence. To each of these he gave answers which are relevant in the present times of globalization. With his progressive ideas, Gandhiji would not have opposed globalization per se as he was not opposed to industrialization and private property so long as these are utilized for the welfare of the society.

What Gandhiji propagated during his lifetime was that we should use products which are made locally. Conversely, we should make products locally which are of our use. USA which has been in the forefront of free flow of goods and services and outsourced manufacturing activity largely to China and IT services to India is now taking steps to revive both activities in its own country. So also India is striving to give fillip to manufacturing activity in India. Thus, what Gandhiji propagated in his times, we are trying to pursue the same very philosophy now. Similarly, all other countries are also trying to follow the same.

Whatever there is good universally for the common man in globalization is found in the Gandhian ideas. The disagreement centers around exploitation in the name of competition and domination of one culture over another under globalization.

(*Reference*: Hingorani, A.T., *The Encyclopedia of Gandhian Thoughts,* AICC Publications Department, New Delhi, 1985).

10
Future Prospects/Alternatives of Globalization

Prologue

There is perhaps no aspect of socio-economic process as contested as globalization. Some people see it as helping the mankind to fulfil their aspirations. Some people see it as a stumbling block in the pursuit of their way of life which they feel is best for them. Some people feel that with certain checks and balances, the globalization can work better. Some people feel that they seem to be getting uprooted from their traditional warmth by the incessant speed of the winds of change brought by the process of globalization. Notwithstanding differing perceptions about globalization, large body of people contend that globalization is here to stay and we should make best use of it, and the future will be shaped as we make use of it.

Economic Progress with Shortcomings

Global Institutions

The process of globalization operates through institutions, which themselves are creations of the process of globalization. At the global level, these are IMF, World Bank, WTO, MNCs etc. These institutions are having certain objectives. Many a times it is found that these objectives are not met. For example, Structural Adjustment Programme (SAP) which was drafted after WWII as a precondition for advancing a loan by IMF did not help in improving the conditions in many countries, because the programme laid undue emphasis on economic progress at the expense of social sector.

Due to more financial contribution of developed countries to financial institutions like IMF, WB, WTO etc., they have more say in the decision making process. Thus, whatever decisions are taken by these institutions, they are perceived to be in favour of developed countries. In this context, developing countries feel that for better outcomes from these institutions, the structure of these institutions should be changed so as to give them greater say in decision making process.

Third World countries are under tremendous debt from international financial institutions and their economy is unable to pay even the interest part of it. Therefore, many economists are of the opinion that there is no way for them to get out of the debt trap except by writing off/foreclosing the debt.

Multinational Companies/Outsourcing-Jobless Growth

Globalization enabled Multinational Companies to establish their manufacturing works in whichever countries they found cheap and skilled labour. There is increasing tendency of outsourcing the work to economically cheaper destinations, resulting in increasing the employment opportunities in host countries and decreasing the same in home countries. Of late, trend is to give the work on contract, and engaging the labour on casual basis instead of on permanent basis. The increased developmental activities increased the labour requirement. However, with the mechanization in agriculture, extensive use of technology especially computerization and more emphasis on productivity and efficiency, there has also been reduction in the employment. In this context, the perceptions differ about the overall impact of these factors on the employment. Critics of globalization call the present economic growth as a 'jobless growth'.

Uncertainty of Growth

If we look at the uninterrupted process of globalization from the past to this date, it can be safely and surely predicted that globalization is here to stay. There has been growth in the global economy from the end of WWII except for some years of slowdown. As regards its growth trajectory in future, it is not certain whether it will grow at the same rate as it grew in the past. The uncertainty about the growth stems from the policy changes that may be adopted by the developed countries. So long, developed countries especially USA and Western European countries were at the forefront of liberalization of market economy.

The process of globalization enabled India to expand its services sector especially Information and Communication Technology as well as

China to expand its manufacturing capacity to high levels. Ironically USA which has been frontrunner in the process of globalization has started now feeling concerned about depletion of jobs in that country. It believes that due to outsourcing, jobs in their countries are being taken away by India and China. USA has, therefore, started implementing policies favouring redevelopment of manufacturing base in USA and reducing outsourcing of IT services. These policies will lead to reducing its dependence on China for manufacturing and India for IT services. The trend indicates just reversal of the liberalization process that USA was strongly advocating so far. Such reversal of policies may come from other developed countries also on the same ground.

Similarly on agriculture front, every country whether it is developed or developing wants to protect its own agriculture sector making it difficult to move forward in respect of agreements on agriculture or other fronts. Due to such disagreements, it is possible that in future there may be more stress on entering into bilateral agreements.

Crony Capitalism

Capitalism is the basis of globalization. Crony capitalism is a term used for the economy wherein there is collusion between the businessmen and the politicians and officials in the government who are friendly to businessmen. In crony capitalism the politicians and officials in the government dovetail the policies in favour of certain businessmen in return for the financial or other help extended by businessmen to the former. Normally, the process of help starts from the time of election when politicians are in need of funds for fighting elections. Business lobbies are active even in country like USA which is known for its democracy. Crony capitalism is going to stay so long as there is no solution for better way of funding required for fighting the elections which have become quite expensive now. Rather it will grow as the cost of election is continuously growing. In India, there is some improvement in the position from the time Right to Information Act was promulgated and some steps were also taken by the government in right direction.

Crony capitalism is one of the misuses of the globalization process. The economic depression of 1930s, economic crisis in South-East Asia in late 1990s or melt-down of US economy in 2008 are the examples. These happenings underscore the uncertainty in predicting the prospects of globalization with any degree of accuracy.

Globalization too Fast

Any social change if it takes place slowly, the society gets time to evaluate and adapt it peacefully, instead of reacting to it adversely. Regarding globalization, it is contended that changes accompanying it are happening too fast. The traditional mode of life which was continuing for centuries is undergoing radical change from the time of end of WWII, the time globalization process got institutionalized. The changes have taken place even at the micro level, i.e. family. Earlier only family head used to be bread earner and rest used to help him in his occupation. Now, his wife, children are all independently working in different assignments and at different and faraway places some even working in different countries.

There is emergence of competitive market. Social and cultural changes are also taking place faster for example joint family system is giving way to nuclear family system. It appears as though the traditional institutions and ethos are getting transformed by the process of globalization, with no adequate time for evaluation or adaption. The situation is as if all are just cog in the wheel.

Advantage of Natural Resources

Presently, globalization is benefiting especially those countries which are rich in natural resources. Under globalization, non-renewable resources are being used with so much speed that they are likely to get exhausted much earlier. Therefore, these countries in their own interest will try to erect walls of protection against the onslaught of globalization. USA is already restricting production of North oil in order to conserve it for the future.

Summing up Economic Progress

While progress is expected in alleviation of poverty, the issue of increasing inequality between the rich and the poor is unlikely to be resolved.

The competitiveness on the economic front is likely to become fiercer with many developing countries coming forward in taking the lead in economic progress. Howsoever, with no effort to restrict the use of natural resources, the ever increasing competition will aid rapid exhaustion of the non-renewable resources. In view of this for quite some time, Indian economy is expected to stabilize at the rate at which upper middle Income Group countries are finding now.

Integration of global economy has advantages as well as disadvantages. In August and September 2015, there has been crash in the stock market of China and China is experiencing deep crisis in the economy. The external factors like expectation of rise in interest rates in USA, general slowdown in growth rate of world economy and now abrupt slow down of economy in China together with internal factor like low export volume of India, have affected Indian economy adversely. The value of rupee per dollar has come down to 66.5. Repetition of economic crisis situations happened in past as well as now cannot be ruled out in the future.

Agrarian Position

Agriculture Needs Second Green Revolution

Uncertainty of rains is a permanent problem for agriculture. In India where only 40 per cent of arable area is irrigated, agriculture continues to depend on good monsoon rains. Unless varieties which are resistant to various type of stress particularly due to delayed monsoon or drought conditions are developed, Indian agriculture will always face difficulty in case of deficient monsoon. Scientists have started working in this direction like creating seeds which can sustain drought but there seems to be a long way to go to succeed.

Agribusiness

Globally, there is a shift from the traditional diet of staple food to what is called Atkinson's diet which includes low carbohydrate items like fruits, salad, and vegetables. Accordingly agriculture is undergoing change in the crop pattern. Under globalization this trend is going to be increasingly pronounced. Traditionally India has been producing staple food products. However, there is a growing trend of producing these products in developed nations and on the other hand, global market demand for Indian agriculture now is in the area of horticulture, floriculture, oilseeds, fruits and vegetables, area called agribusiness.

Organic Food

Presently farmers are using chemical fertilizers and pesticides. Due to increasing health awareness, people world over are looking forward to chemical free food. The study by experts led by New-castle University in UK published in the British Journal on 12.07.2014 shows significantly lower levels of toxic heavy metals in organic crops. Cadmium, which is one of only metal contaminants along with lead and mercury for which the European Commission has set maximum permitted contamination levels in food was found to be almost 50 per cent lower in organic crops than conventionally grown crops. The study funded jointly by the European Framework 6 programme and the Sheep-drove Trust, further found that concentrations of anti-oxidants were between 18-69 per cent higher in organically-grown crops. Numerous studies have linked anti-oxidants to a reduced risk of chronic diseases and certain cancers. (13.07.2014)

People are becoming very conscious of health. With adverse effect of use of chemicals in agriculture, people in developed countries are trying to switch over to organic food and more and more people in South are also expected to do the same. Thus, organic food is going to be very popular in future and poised for large expansion. However, the farming of organic food is a tedious process as well as costly and it will be quite some time before this becomes commercialized on a big scale.

Agriculture as an occupation has become unviable due to high input costs and low price of the produce. Small land holders who constitute 80 per cent of the total land holders are unable to take advantage of technology as they do not have the necessary capital. The prices of the produce are governed by global market hence fluctuating all the time. Farmers are thus compelled to take loan from whatever source they get. Private lenders charge exorbitant interest charges on the loan. The result is that there are increasing cases of suicides in as many as four major states. This is the case when government claims it is providing subsidies to agriculture. There is vociferous demand from other sectors for removal of subsidies. Some economists claim that the subsidies to agriculture are counterproductive. But even developed countries are providing them in one form or the other.

Summing up Agrarian Position

Agricultural production is likely to increase with intensive as well as extensive mode of agriculture. However, with the mounting internal pressure by the aggressive and vocal middle and upper class and external pressure by WTO to reduce subsidies in agriculture, position of farmers and farm labour is bound to become increasingly precarious.

Technology and Well being of Humanity

With the advancement of technology, the comfort level of physical body of human being has increased. In view of many facilities available, he will do less and less physical work. Robots will take over many jobs being done by human beings now. The life of human being is expected to become faster ever. The jet planes will replace ordinary planes and afterwards rocket speed driven planes will replace jet planes. Increasing competition for success will increase stress to new levels. Less of physical work and ever faster lifestyle will make man a machine and there will be little of emotional or feeling man. Though research in medicine will help in enhancing life span, it is doubtful if the quality of life in terms of inner happiness will increase.

Mass Media

After introduction of TV in late twentieth century in India, the role of mass media has become extremely important as the images of the events are more impressionable to the audience. Media can play purposeful and educative role. However, like any other technology, media can be used for positive as well as for wrong purpose. In general it is observed that it is used more for commercial purpose than for educative purpose. Much of the time is given to advertising the products. It is difficult to say if advertisements are believable about the quality of products that they advertise.

The role of media in politics has become very important. However, rather than disseminating the opinion of the public on issues objectively, many a times TV is used to propagate channel's own judgment on the issues. Since, there is extreme competition within media itself to increase TRP, media tends to add its own flavour to the content. There are instances of ethnic violence getting exacerbated due to images shown on TV or Internet.

It is said that the information and communication technology has turned the world into a 'global village,' meaning thereby both time and space got compressed to a great extent and anybody can connect from anywhere to anywhere and that too in split seconds.

Social networking is becoming increasingly popular and gradually face to face contact is likely to be seen as superfluous. Some sociologists contend that the use of social networking is not undermining the relationship in the communities, but on the other hand there is more integration in the community as increased interaction through internet is strengthening the community feeling. However, it cannot be denied that face to face contact can never be equated with interaction through internet. Face reading, expression and body language through face to face contact reveal much about the relationship as against mere interaction through internet.

Globalization and information and communication technology are highly interwoven and both will keep advancing the cause of each other. In future, the gadgets of ICT are likely to be more and more miniaturized and their speed further increased.

Development vis-à-vis Social Sector

There are two approaches to development. One is that which is advanced by the process of globalization. Globalization involves capitalism and capitalism is mostly concerned with economic activism. Thus, globalization means state should frame policies to help economic activity regardless of slowing down other activities. It expects the state to develop infrastructure in order to establish industries, and that the state should not burden business with taxation. If state follows these policies, all of its finances will be used up for promoting the business activity and there will be little left for supporting the social sector. The argument of the protagonists of globalization is that the benefits of globalization will automatically percolate down the level by a 'trickledown effect.'

The second approach is to have a balanced approach to development. In this approach, priority to economic progress will not be at the cost of social sector. In this case the requirements of education, health services, poverty alleviation programme, and rural development will not be ignored while pursuing progressive economic policies.

The way globalization is proceeding, the state will come under increasing pressure to follow the first approach in which case interest of social sector is likely to get ignored, which is detrimental to the overall interest of the country in the long run.

Ecology/Environment/Sustainability

> *"Earth provides enough to satisfy every man's need, but not every man's greed."*
>
> —Mahatma Gandhi

Globalization involves utilizing natural resources. Many of these resources are not renewable. Therefore, humanity has two choices. One is to utilize the resources taking into account its long term availability that is with consideration even for future generations. The second is to maximize the use thus enjoying in present times without thinking about future generation. The future will thus be shaped by the choice we make. In capitalism or globalization, there is more preponderance of exhausting natural resources rather than adopting the policy of sustainable development.

The ever increasing concentration of greenhouse gases is leading to depletion of ozone layer, warming of the climate system, oceans getting warmer, melting of glaciers and rising of sea level. This has serious implications for the present as well as future generations. The developed countries where the industrialization started earlier have a large share of bringing the above situation. Ironically, they expert developing countries to restrict the emission of greenhouse gases. The developing countries argue that they are in the developing stage and their development agenda will suffer if they are to reduce the emission which is the creation of developed countries. In the competitive world, the countries will become more and more stubborn to adhere to norms even though the norms may be logical. All species on earth will thus be subjected to more adverse outcome because of the undesirable actions of human beings.

Though there is more awareness about the importance of ecology now more than ever, primacy of economic progress under globalization is likely to overshadow imperative need of sustainable development.

Nation-State

There are two schools of thoughts. According to critics, globalization has compromised the autonomy of the nation-state as interconnectedness under globalization has impacted all aspects of the nation-state including economy as well as governance. With the advancement of information and communication technology, funds to the time of millions of dollars can be transferred from one nation to the other in milliseconds. Economies have thus become fragile due to the factors which are external to the nation. Nation-state has also to compromise its position with respect to global treaties. The proponents of globalization, however, contend that under globalization the nation-state does not wither away or lose its significance but it undergoes transformation with respect to its functions.

Notwithstanding the contention of the proponents of globalization, since, liberalization and speed are the major characteristics of globalization, with increasing interconnectedness, nations will witness reduction in their autonomy. It is a common knowledge that economic links with the nations try to influence even foreign policy decisions. For example, special economic tie with a super power is bound to inhibit India to adopt foreign policy stance against that super power even if India's stance may be logical. Due to increasing influence of media, even political outcomes are expected to be affected by the process of globalization.

Visualizing Positive aspect of Globalization

Economic Status is Improving under Globalization

With the very nature of multitude of problems being faced by the world population, it is difficult to visualize a system which can be termed as ideal that will provide solutions to all problems. With this background, protagonists of globalization insist on seeing the positive side of globalization.

Traditional approach is synonymous with *status quo*. With ever increasing population compounding the problems of poverty and the gap between the demand and supply of products and services, closed economy would not work. The protagonists of globalization feel that globalization alone can provide economic growth and as such it should be supported. The message is that we ought to be optimistic about positive outcome from globalization in future.

There are some positive aspects of globalization. If there is anything good beyond one's tradition, there is nothing wrong in imbibing the same in one's traditions. One need not feel inferiority in reaping the benefit coming out of the process of globalization. Even if somebody has traditional background, he can always make use of what is best in globalization for him.

With efficient use of natural resources, the economic position of all nations across the world is improving. While abject poverty is still prevalent in developing countries, the economic status all round is steadily improving. After fast economic growth witnessed in East Asia, according to recent World Bank report, sub-Saharan Africa is now the second fastest growing region in the developing world. Bill Gates predicts that extrapolating the present trends, there should hardly be any poor country in the world by 2035. With India's better performance in economic field, the eradication of poverty is expected to be achieved much earlier.

The protagonists of globalization contend that it has helped to spend more on social sector including education and health resulting in improvement in skill level and reducing poverty. The advancement of technology especially information and communication technology has contributed to this economic progress. According to them, the generations to come are likely to be better off than present generation.

The old picture of village in a rural area is fast changing. Many of the things which were exclusively to be found in urban area like mobile sets, motor cyçle, TV etc. are abundantly found in rural area. People in rural area are taking up small enterprises too. Thus, transformation is taking place in the character of village, though process is slow.

Energy Business by NTPC can also be Best Energy Diplomacy

Both India and China are in a race for establishing their presence globally. As an example, NTPC—a leading central power utility in India is making strategic investment for installing 500 MW coal based power plants in Sri Lanka and 1320 MW in Bangladesh *via* Joint Venture with respective electricity boards. Apart from utilization of investment opportunities created by globalization, the engagement with Sri Lanka and Bangladesh will also serve to strengthen India's relations with neighbouring countries.

India's Growth Story in the Field of IT and Space Technology

Globally, India has already attained a niche in the area of Information Technology. India's IT sector has grown by leaps and bounds. Further to India's own IT work force, some of the world's largest IT companies have more employees in India now than in their home countries. Moreover, these companies are increasingly shifting their consulting base to India. Around one third of the workforce employed in top IT companies is based in India. This is an acknowledgement of India's prowess in software services globally.

In space technology too India is quite advanced. People on earth are fascinated by moon from ancient times. India's moon mission Chandrayan-1 was launched by the Indian Space Research Organization in October 2008 and operated until August 2009. It has detected evidence of water across the lunar surface.

On November 5, 2013 India embarked on Mars odyssey with its polar rocket carrying Mars Orbiter Mission (MOM) successfully lifting off from the Satish Dhawan Space Centre at Sriharikota in its first-ever inter-planetary expedition in a bid to join a select elite club comprising United States, the erstwhile Soviet Union and the European Space Agency. The Mangalayan is majestically orbiting the Mars since 24.09.2014 making India the first in the world to achieve the feat in the first attempt. Mars Orbiter Mission is a watershed in the history of India.

The feat of above achievements is an ample proof that India stands one among the technologically few highly advanced countries. On economic front, the sustained average GDP growth during the last decade also shows that among developing countries, India and China are likely to do well in future though China is expected to be frontrunner in the size of economy till about 2050 beyond which India's economy is expected to be larger than that of China.

China is Embracing Globalization more Vigorously

China is embracing globalization more vigorously. Chinese economy which is world's second-largest economy is half way to reaching the World Bank's yardstick of a high income country with a per capita annual income of $12,616. In order to escape the middle income trap, on 15.11.2013, China pledged further reforms like allowing private capital to take equity stakes in state-funded projects, In the financial sphere, China will push forward liberalization of its interest rates and free convertibility of its Yuan currency, loosen control on capital flows, allow more overseas investment by companies and individuals, encourage companies to make foreign acquisitions to find supplies of raw materials and secure market access, set up more free trade zones etc.

Rising Inequality

Inequality is by nature. No two human beings are equal in all respects. But inequality matters when problems are created by its size in the society. Economic aspect of globalization is based on capitalism. Capitalism is based on market economy and earning profit. Earning profit is achieved through increase in productivity and through methods of mass production. Obviously, by efficient use of natural resources, globalization leads to economic progress. While in globalization, economy grows as a whole, it is observed that the progress is not shared across all sections of society.

Rich get richer faster than poor getting better off. This is a natural corollary of globalization.

In such a situation, the role of state becomes crucial. They are supposed to evolve policies such that fair part of the increased wealth generated in the economy should be utilized for taking care of social sector that includes education, health and rural development. But here lies the rub.

Globalization favours government intervention least. Capitalists would not like taxation policy that takes away their profit margin. They, therefore, lobby with the government for framing policies which are in their favour. Since capitalists are more resourceful, social sector does not get its due share. The result is that the inequality goes on increasing unstoppably. This is evident from the rich-poor and urban-rural gap in every aspect of life whether it is income, education or healthcare. Social tension is the natural fall out of this huge gap.

Inequality is the natural corollary of globalization and since globalization is not only going to stay but grow in future, inequality is also going to grow. Thus, apart from natural inequality, human beings will be subjected to ever increasing inequality produced by globalization, i.e. added unnatural differentiation between human beings. This is the price to be paid on the social front for the overall economic progress under globalization. Whether the price to be paid on social front is less or more than the advantage gained through overall economic progress is a subject of wider debate and research.

Socio-Cultural Change

Social Change

As mentioned earlier, caste system existing in India has distinction of being unique in India. As societies evolved, their social structure was also evolved in response to the requirements of their times. Since survival and development are intimately connected with the occupations, the social structure has intimate relationship with the occupations. It is in response to this relationship that social structure of Hindu society has been based on caste system as a lineage of the four *varnas.*

Globalization has not made much difference in rural society as far as caste system is concerned. While untouchability is no more practiced, they follow old traditions with few changes. But high degree of interconnectedness between people and mass media have influenced youth in rural area to migrate to urban area to seek better employment opportunities and lifestyle. The joint family system that existed earlier is thus undergoing fast change, undermining tradition based rural society.

Some sociologists say that caste system did not allow high degree of socio-cultural change to happen, that globalization has done in urban area where influence of caste system has now little significance. However, some sociologists contend that caste system came in the way of socio-economic progress. Though it will take time to end caste system, it is going to be increasingly diluted under globalization.

Gender Preference

In India, though there is steady improvement in overall sex (female-male) ratio, there is a continuous steep fall in the sex ratio in child population in the age group 0-6 from Census 1991 to Census 2001 and then from Census 2001 to Census 2011. It is noteworthy that the ratio is better in rural area as compared to urban area. This is a clear indication that progress in the field of education and economy has not improved sex ratio which means son preference has still a strong pull in the society. The era of globalization is generally perceived as an era of progressive ideas, but its failure in such an important area has made futuristic prediction about globalization most difficult. Thus, if there is a need to have a social change in any of the aspects of society, correcting its attitude toward girl child is the foremost. Otherwise, this would be termed as the greatest downfall of the Indian society. Son preference prevalent in some other countries is no consolation to India as one wrong doing cannot justify the other wrong doing.

Cultural Change

In this highly interconnected world, changes are bound to happen in every field. Globalization has brought changes globally not only in the field of economy but also in the field of culture. There is general perception that Western culture has influenced non-Western cultures in a big way. However, opinions differ what kind of changes have taken place across the world.

In India, caste plays dominant role, especially in rural area. While rural landscape has been changed by local, regional or national politics, culturally rural people are still holding on to their traditional core culture with slight changes occurring on the periphery. In urban population, however, cultural change is quite discernible.

Sociologists have put forward three concepts in the cultural context under globalization namely homogenization, hybridization-glocalization and heterogenization. Homogenization represents the observation of increasing sameness found everywhere. Hybridization/Glocalization represents the production of new and unique culture as an outcome of mixing of cultures. The essence of Heterogenization is that the cultural polarity of each culture remains intact.

It appears globalization is leading the world more toward hybridization-Glocalization, which represents the production of new and unique culture as an outcome of mixing of cultures. Therefore, although there is more and more preponderance of the influence of Western culture, while absorbing likable traits of Western culture, people in the non-Western world are still holding on to very many strong traits of the local cultures. The result is production of hybrid culture. As the time passes, cultural hybridity is expected to spread and encompass untouched newer areas.

In respect of ethical values, there is a general perception that under globalization the ethical values are becoming less important compared to material progress. In the competitive spirit of market oriented globalization, ethical values are generally considered as less important because the trend is to somehow achieve material progress.

Alternatives of Globalization

Globalization stands for liberalization of national economies allowing freer transfer of capital, goods and services across the nations. Globalization does not, however, envisage unhindered movement of labour. If we mean alternative to globalization as rollback of liberalization process, it will amount to going back to static state of economy which will neither be possible nor desirable. Globalization is, however, found to be hurtful to smaller, least developed and fragile economies.

The inequality between the rich and the poor is widening. In spite of overall the economic progress, quarter of the India's population is still below poverty linc. Especially rural population is experiencing maximum brunt of the poverty. Therefore, there has to be a way for redistribution of income so that the inequality is reduced.

Many people feel that the present shape of globalization is fraught with several shortcomings and that it will be more popular if there is some course correction. It is seen from the past experience that the economic crises have happened in those countries where the financial regulation was not in place. Therefore, financial regulation is required to be in place at least in developing countries as their economies are relatively fragile and they are not in a position to bear big financial shocks.

There is no subject that is not encompassed in globalization. Economy though important is only one of them. It also involves movement of socio-cultural ideas and effects across the nations. Advancement of information and communication technology under globalization has only spurred the interconnectedness between the people globally. Having come so far, it would be impossible to snap this interconnectedness by any imagination.

Conclusion

The impact of globalization on the society is the most contested subject as the perceptions of the people about the impact vary so widely. Some people see it as helping the mankind to fulfill their aspirations. Some people see it as a stumbling block in the pursuit of their way of life which they feel is best for them. Some people feel that with certain improvements, the globalization can work better. Some people feel that they seem to be getting uprooted by the incessant speed of the winds of change brought by the process of globalization.

There is, however, a consensus that globalization has brought overall economic progress. But it has created uncertainty about the future as anything happening in one part of the world has immediate effect on other parts of the world like economic meltdown, oil shocks or upheavals in the nations. It has also contributed to increasing inequality which is a factor for creation of social tension.

It is to the credit of globalization that it has offered several lifestyle options to choose from. There has been phenomenal advancement in medicine which brought succour to ailing. But it has also increased the competition to a level which has made life more stressful and thus exacerbated the incidence of lifestyle diseases like heart disease.

As it is, no alternative could be visualized to take the place of globalization. There is overwhelming consensus that globalization is an irreversible process, it is here to stay and we should make best use of it and the future will be shaped as we make use of it.

Finally

The author of this book will like to quote from the article of Manfred B Steger on 'The Future of Globalization' (Dasgupta and Ray, 2006: 119-21).

I identified what I considered to be the three most-likely future trajectories of the ongoing ideological trajectories… I called the first possible future scenario "globalism with human face," perhaps best characterized by the slogan "rhetoric of reform, but business as usual.' Referring to the second future scenario as the "global new deal," I argued that there existed the slim possibility for the rise of political forces that might create a "global civil society" committed to "globalization-from-below." Finally, I held out the possibility of a "severe backlash against globalization" caused by the geopolitical and cultural dynamics associated with the neoliberal economic dimension of globalization.

Author of the book in your hand believes that human being is extremely genius and that is how in spite of many challenges he has conquered the world, though unfortunately, there have been instances of his occasional indulgence in destruction through strife and wars. Therefore, in his own interest, he is expected to move the world toward globalization that promotes social justice, democratic form of governance and globalization that excludes exploitation of poor by rich and dominance of one culture over another.

References

Ahluwalia, M., '*Statelevel Performance under Economic Reform in India*', in Krueger, A. (ed.), *Economic Policy Reforms and the Indian Economy,* University of Chicago Press, Chicago, 2002.

Akram-lodhi, A. Haroon and Kay, Cristobal. Editors, '*Peasants and Globalization: Political Economy, rural transformation and the agrarian question,*' Routledge, London, 2009.

Appadurai, Arjun. '*Modernity at Large: Cultural Dimensions of Globalization,*' University of Minnesota Press, Minneapolis, 2005.

Aravamudan, Gita. '*Disappearing Daughters: The Tragedy of Female Foeticide,*' Foreword by A.P.J. Abdul Kalam, Penguin Books, New Delhi, 2007.

Arrighi, Giovanni. '*The Long Twentieth Century: Money, Power, and the Origins of Our Times,*' Verso, London, 2010.

Asian Development Outlook, Asian Development Bank, Manila, 2002.

Atkinson, A.B., *The Economic Consequences of Rolling Back the Welfare State,* MIT Press, Cambridge, MA., 1999.

Barro, R., *Determinants of Economic Growth: A Crosscountry Empirical Study,* National Bureau of Economic Research, Cambridge, 1996.

Bhagwati, J., *Writings on International Economics,* Oxford University Press, New Delhi, (1997).

Bhagwati, Jagdish. '*In Defense of Globalization,*' Oxford University Press, New York, 2004.

Bhatnagar, Rashmi Dube; Dube, Renu; Dube, Reena. '*Female Infanticide in India: A Feminist Cultural History,*' State University of New York Press, 2005.

Bhattacharya, R.N. (ed.), *Environmental Economics; An Indian Perspective,* Oxford University Press, New Delhi, 2001.

Burbach, Roger. '*Globalization and Postmodern Politics: From Zapatistas to High-Tech Robber Barons,*' Pluto Press, London, 2001.

Cabral, L., *Introduction to Industrial Organisation,* MIT Press, Cambridge, MA., 2000.

Chamsy el-Ojeili and Patrick Hayden. '*Critical Theories of Globalization,*' Palgrave Macmillan, New York, 2006.

Chandra Bipin, "*India's Struggle for Independence*"; Penguin Books India Pvt. Ltd., New Delhi, 1989.

Cheshire, Lynda; Higgins Vaughan and Lawrence Geoffrey. Editors, '*Rural Governance: International Perspectives,*' Routledge, London, 2007.

Dasgupta, Samir and Kiely Ray. "*Globalization and After*"; Sage Publications, New Delhi, 2006.

Desai, A.R., "*Rural Sociology in India*"; Popular Prakashan, Mumbai, 1978.

Desmarais, Annette Aurelie. '*La Via Campensina: Globalization and the Power of Peasants,*' Pluto Press, London, 2007.

Doshi, S.L., "*Rural Sociology*"; Rawat Publications, Jaipur; 2002.

Dossani, Rafiq. '*India Arriving: How This Economic Powerhouse Is Redefining Global Business,*' AMACOM, New York, 2008.

Dreze, Jean and Sen, Amartya. '*India: Development and Participation,*' Oxford University Press, New York, 2002.

Dunning, J., *Multinational Enterprises and The Global Economy,* Addison Wesley, London, 1993.

Edited by Schafft, Kai A. and Jackson, Alecia Youngblood. '*Rural Education for the Twenty-First Century: Identity, Place, and Community in a Globalizing World,*' The Pennsylvania State University Press, 2010.

Edited by Solbrig, Otto T.; Paarlberg, Robert; and Castri Fransisco di. '*Globalization and the Rural Environment,*' Harvard University, Cambridge, 2001.

Ellwood, Wayne. '*The No-Nonsense Guide to Globalization*' Rawat Publications, Jaipur, 2005.

Engardio, Pete. Editor, '*CHINDIA: How China and India Are Revolutionizing Global Business,*' McGraw-Hill, New York, 2007.

Ethier, W., *Modern International Economics,* 3rd edn, Norton and Company, New York, 1995.

Falk, R., *Predatory Globalisation,* Policy Press, London, 1999.

Feenstra, R. and Hanson, G., '*Global Production and Rising Inequality: A Survey of Trade and Wages*', NBER Working Paper, Cambridge, 2001.

Ferguson, P. and Ferguson, G., *Industrial Economics,* 2nd edn, Macmillan, London, 1994.

Friedman, Thomas L. '*The World is Flat: A Brief History of the Twenty-first Century,*' Thorndike Press, Waterville, 2005.

Goldsmith, E. and Mander, J. (eds), *The Case Against the Global Economy,* Earthscan, London and New York, 2001.

Griffiths, A. and Wall, S., *Applied Economics,* 6th edn, Longman, London, 1995.

Gupta, Akhil. '*Postcolonial Developments: Agriculture in the Making of Modern India*,' Duke University Press, Durham, 1998.

Harold, James. '*The End of Globalization: Lessons from the Great Depression*,' Harvard University Press, Cambridge, 2001.

Haugen, David and Mach, Rachael. '*Globalization: Opposing Viewpoints*,' Greenhaven Press, Farmington Hills, 2010.

Heine, Jorge and Thakur, Ramesh. Editors, '*The Dark Side of Globalization*,' United Nations University Press, Tokyo, 2011.

Hingorani, A.T., "*The Encyclopedia of Gandhian Thoughts*"; AICC Publications Department, New Delhi; 1985.

Hoekman, B. and Kostecki, M., Th*e Political Economy of the Global Trading System,* Oxford University Press, Oxford, UK, 1995.

International Fund for Agricultural Development (IFAD). '*Rural Poverty Report 2001: The Challenge of Ending Rural Poverty*,' Oxford University Press, Oxford, New York, 2001.

Kaku, Michio. '*Physics of the Future: How Science Will Shape Human Destiny and Our Daily Lives by the Year 2100*,' Doubleday, New York, 2011.

Karan, Kavita. Editor, '*Cyber Communities in Rural Asia: A Study of Seven Asian Countries*,' Marshall Cavendish, Singapore, 2004.

Kenen, P., *The International Economy,* 4th edn, Cambridge University Press, Cambridge, UK, 2000.

Krugman, P. and Obstfeld, M., *International Economics,* Addison-Wesley, 2000.

Kumar, N., *Multinational Enterprises and Industrial Organisation: The Case of India,* Sage Publications, New Delhi, 1994.

Kuppuswamy, B., "*Social Change in India*"; Konark Publishers, New Delhi; 2010.

Lekoko, Rebeca N. and Semali, Ladislaus, M. '*Cases on Developing Countries and ICT Integration: Rural Community Development*,' Information Service Reference, Hershey PA (USA), 2012.

Marjit, S. and Mitra, S., '*Convergence in Regional Growth Rates: Indian Research Agenda*', Economic and Political Weekly, 17 August, 1996.

Marsden, T. and Murdoch, J. '*Between the Local and the Global-Confronting Complexity in the Contemporary Agrifood Sector-Research in Rural Sociology and Development,*' Vol. 12, Emerald Group Publishing Ltd., Oxford, 2006, p. 12.

Martin, Hans-Peter and Schumann, Harald. '*The Global Trap: Globalization and the Assault on Prosperity and Democracy,*' translated by Camiller, P., Zed Books, London, 1997.

Miller, Barbara D. '*The Endangered Sex: Neglect of Female Children in Rural North India*,' Oxford University Press, Delhi, 1997.

Nissanke, Machiko and Thorbecke, Eric. '*Globalization and Poor in Asia: Can Shared Growth be Sustained*?' Palgrave Macmillan, New York, 2008.

O'Rourke, K., '*Global Inequality: Historical Trends*', in Pleskovic, B. and Stern, N. (eds), Annual World Bank Conference on Development Economics, 2001-2002, World Bank, Washington, DC. 2002.

Oxfam, *Rigged Rules and Double Standards—Trade, Globalization and the Fight Against Poverty,* Oxfam International, 2002.

Palanithurai, G. and Ramesh, R. '*Globalization and Rural Development*,' Concept Publishing Company, New Delhi, 2011.

Pandey, R. '*Modernization and Social Change*,' Criterion Pub, New Delhi, 1988.

Piketty Thomas, "*Capital in the Twenty-First Century*"; The Belknap Press, Cambridge; 2014.

Reddy, A. Vinayak and Bhaskar, G. '*Rural Transformation in India: The Impact of Globalization*,' New Century Publication, New Delhi, 2005.

Reddy, K. Venkat, "*Agriculture and Rural Development*"; Himalaya Publishing House, Mumbai; 2001.

Rifkin, J. '*The Biotech Century: Harnessing the Gene and Remaking the World*,' Tarcher/Putnam, New York; 1998.

Ritzer, G. (ed.) '*The Blackwell Companion to Globalization*,' Blackwell Publishing, Malden, 2007.

Ritzer, George and Atalay, Zeynep. Editors, '*Readings in Globalization: Key Concepts and Major Debates*,' Wiley–Blackwell, Chichester, 2010.

Ritzer, George. '*Globalization: A Basic Text*,' Willey-Blackwell, Chichester, 2010.

Ritzer, George. '*Globalization: The Essentials*,' Wiley-Blackwell, West Sussex, UK, 2011.

Ritzer, George. Edited, '*The Wiley-Blackwell Encyclopedia of Globalization*,' Wiley-Blackwell, Chichester, 2012.

Rodriguez, P. and Rodrik, D., *Trade Policy and Economic Growth: A Sceptic's Guide to the Cross-National Evidence, NBER Macroeconomics Annual, 2001,* MIT Press, Massachusetts, 2002.

Rodrik, D., *Feasible Globalizations*, Harvard University, manuscript, 2002.

Rodrik, Dani. '*The Globalization Paradox: Democracy and the Future of the World Economy*,' W.W. Norton & Company, New York, 2011.

Roy, Pashupati Kumar and Sharma. Shiw Pershan. "*Globalization and Agricultural Diversification of India*"; Regal Publications, New Delhi, 2010.

Sachs, J.D., Varshney, A. and Bajpai, N., *India in the Era of Economic Reforms,* Oxford University Press, New Delhi, 1999.

Sassen, Saskia. '*A Sociology of Globalization,*' W.W. Norton & Company, New York, 2007.

Sharma Shalendra D. '*China and India in the Age of Globalization,*' Cambridge University Press, New York, 2009.

Sikdar, Soumen. '*Contemporary Issues in Globalization: An Introduction to Theory and Policy in India,*' Oxford University Press, New Delhi, 2010.

Singh, Kartar, "*Rural Development: Principles, Policies and Management*; Sage Publications, New Delhi; 1999.

Singh, Yogendra, "*Indian Sociology*"; Sage Publications, New Delhi; 1985.

Singh, Yogendra. '*Culture Change in India: Identity and Globalization,*' Rawat Publications, Jaipur, 2008.

Srinivas, M.N., "*Social Structure*"; Hindustan Publishing Corporation, Delhi; 1982.

Srinivasan, T.N., *Developing Countries and the Multilateral Trading System,* Oxford University Press, New Delhi, 1998.

Stiglitz, Joseph E. '*Globalization and its Discontents,*' W.W. Norton & Company, New York, 2002.

Sumner, Jennifer. '*Sustainability and the Civil Commons: Rural Communities in the Age of Globalization,*' University of Toronto Press, Toronto, 2007.

Sunstein, C., *Free Markets and Social J*ustice, Oxford University Press, Oxford, UK, 1997.

Trebilcock, M. and Howse, R., *The Regulation of International Trade,* Routledge, London and New York, 1999.

Vickers, J. and Yarrow, G., *Privatization: An Economic Analysis,* MIT Press, Cambridge, MA., 1998.

Went, Robert. '*Globalization: Neoliberal Challenge, Radical Responses,*' Pluto Press, London, 2000.

Wood, A., *North-South Trade, Employment and Inequality: Changing Fortunes in a Skill-Driven World,* Clarendon Press, Oxford, 1994.

Zakaria, Fareed. '*The Post-American World,*' W.W. Norton & Company, New York, 2008.

Journals/Reviews

I

American Economic Review, Pittsburgh.

American Journal of Sociology, Chicago.

American Sociological Review, Washington D.C.

British Journal of Sociology, London.

Contribution to Indian Sociology, SAGE, New Delhi.

Currncy Sociology, SAGE, New Delhi

Economic and Political Weekly, Mumbai.

Economic Development and Cultural Change, Chicago.
Economic Journal, London.
European Economic Review, Amsterdam.
IMF Staff Papers, Washington D.C.
Indian Journal of Agricultural Economics, Mumbai.
Indian Journal of Labour Economics, Delhi.
Journal of Development Economics, Amsterdam.
Journal of Economic Growth, Heidelberg.
Journal of Economic Literature, Pittsburgh.
Journal of Social Change, Walden University.
Journal of Social and Economic Development, Bangalore.
Journal of Economic Perspectives, Pittsburgh.
Review of Economic Studies, Stockholm.
Sociological Bulletin: *Journal of the Indian Sociological Society*, New Delhi.
Social Forces, Oxford Journals, Oxford.
The Economist, New York.
The Sociological Review, Staffordshire
World Bank Economic Review, Washington D.C.
World Development, Amsterdam
World Economy, U.K.

II

Reports

Agriculture in Maharashtra, *Yesterday, Today and Tomorrow*; Krishi Saptak Programme, Government of Maharashtra, Pune.

Business Standard, Mumbai.

Census of India 2011; Registrar General and Census Commissioner, India; New Delhi.

Economic Times, Mumbai.

Hitavada Newspaper, Nagpur.

Inequality in Asia by Asian Development Bank; 2007.

Proceedings of Seminar on Impact of Foreign Direct Investment in Retail Sector (Article by Prof. Jadhav, S.K., 2012, p. 39); BMV Amravati.

Rural Development Statistics; National Institute of Rural Development; Hyderabad.

Statistical Abstract, India; NSO, Ministry of Statistics and Programme Implementation, GoI, New Delhi; 2003.

Times of India, Mumbai/Nagpur editions.

UNDP Human Development Report, Oxford University Press, New Delhi; 2004.

World Investment Report, UNCTAD, New York.

Index